JOURNEY TO THE *Heart* OF GOD

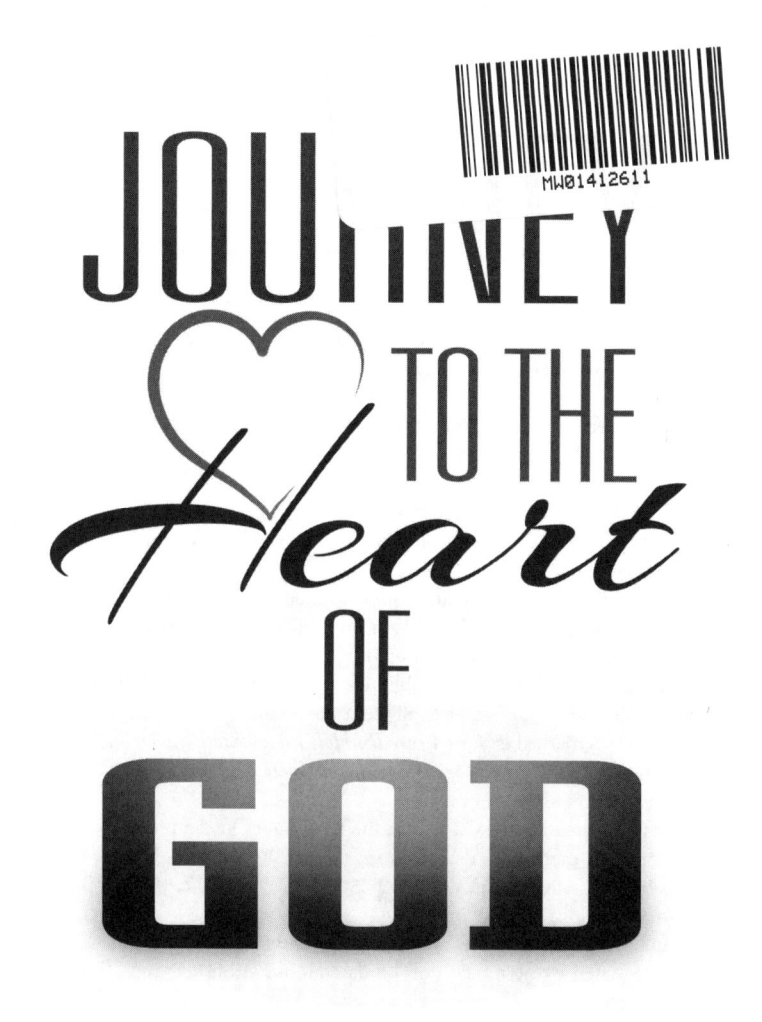

S. JOSEPH KIDDER

Pacific Press®
Publishing Association

Nampa, Idaho | Oshawa, Ontario, Canada
www.pacificpress.com

Cover design by Steve Lanto
Cover design resources from iStockphoto.com

Copyright © 2019 by Pacific Press® Publishing Association
Printed in the United States of America
All rights reserved

The author assumes full responsibility for the accuracy of all facts and quotations as cited in this book.

To order additional copies of this book or other books by S. Joseph Kidder, call toll-free 1-800-765-6955, or visit AdventistBookCenter.com.

Unless otherwise noted, Scripture quotations are from THE HOLY BIBLE, NEW INTERNATIONAL VERSION®. Copyright © 1973, 1978, 1984, 2011 by Biblica, Inc.® Used by permission. All rights reserved worldwide.

Scripture quotations marked ESV are from The Holy Bible, English Standard Version® (ESV®), copyright © 2001 by Crossway, a publishing ministry of Good News Publishers. Used by permission. All rights reserved.

Scripture quotations marked GNT are from the Good News Translation® (Today's English Version, Second Edition), copyright © 1992 American Bible Society. All rights reserved.

Scripture quotations marked HCSB are from the Holman Christian Standard Bible®, copyright © 1999, 2000, 2002, 2003 by Holman Bible Publishers. Used by permission. Holman Christian Standard Bible®, Holman CSB®, and HCSB® are federally registered trademarks of Holman Bible Publishers.

Scripture quotations marked ISV are from *The Holy Bible: International Standard Version*. Copyright © 1995–2014 by ISV Foundation. All rights reserved internationally. Used by permission of Davidson Press, LLC.

Scripture quotations marked KJV are from the King James Version.

Scripture quotations marked NASB are from the NEW AMERICAN STANDARD BIBLE®, copyright © 1960, 1962, 1963, 1968, 1971, 1972, 1973, 1975, 1977, 1995 by the Lockman Foundation. Used by permission. www.lockman.org.

Scripture quotations marked TLB are from *The Living Bible*, copyright © 1971 by Tyndale House Foundation. Used by permission of Tyndale House Publishers Inc., Carol Stream, Illinois 60188. All rights reserved.

Scripture quotations marked REB are from the Revised English Bible, copyright © Cambridge University Press and Oxford University Press, 1989. All rights reserved.

Library of Congress Cataloging-in-Publication Data

Names: Kidder, S. Joseph, 1953- author.
Title: Journey to the heart of God / S. Joseph Kidder.
Description: Nampa : Pacific Press Publishing Association, 2018.
Identifiers: LCCN 2018044788 | ISBN 9780816364626 (pbk. : alk. paper)
Subjects: LCSH: Spiritual life—Christianity. | Christian life—Seventh-day Adventist authors.
 | Spirituality—Christianity.
Classification: LCC BV4501.3 .K525 2018 | DDC 248.4—dc23 LC record available at
 https://lccn.loc.gov/2018044788

March 2022

CONTENTS

5	**CHAPTER 1**	Journey to the Heart of God: Spiritual Practices That Will Transform Your Life

PART 1 — **Journey to the Heart of God Through Seeking and Experiencing His Presence**

8	**CHAPTER 2**	Experiencing God's Presence: Immanuel, "God With Us"
15	**CHAPTER 3**	Seeking God's Presence: He Is Closer Than You Think

PART 2 — **Journey to the Heart of God Through Worship**

24	**CHAPTER 4**	Personal Worship: Meeting God Face-to-Face
32	**CHAPTER 5**	Corporate Worship: Praise Him Joyfully Whose Love Endures Forever
40	**CHAPTER 6**	Family Worship: Praising God Together

PART 3 — **Journey to the Heart of God Through Prayer**

52	**CHAPTER 7**	The Privilege of Prayer: Knowing God
58	**CHAPTER 8**	Prayer: Releasing the Power of the God of the Impossible
68	**CHAPTER 9**	Prayer: Connecting With God

PART 4 — **Journey to the Heart of God Through Feeding on His Word**

78	**CHAPTER 10**	Feeding on God's Word: Knowing God Through His Word
85	**CHAPTER 11**	Feeding on God's Word: How to Read the Bible for Transformation

PART 5 — **Journey to the Heart of God Through Outrageous Forgiveness**

92	**CHAPTER 12**	Outrageous Forgiveness: Unpayable Debt
101	**CHAPTER 13**	Outrageous Forgiveness: The Miracle of Starting Over

108	**CHAPTER 14**	Outrageous Forgiveness: Loving and Praying for Our Enemies

PART 6 — Journey to the Heart of God Through Christian Fellowship

118	**CHAPTER 15**	Christian Fellowship: God's Venue for Transformation
125	**CHAPTER 16**	Christian Fellowship: God's Design for Growth
131	**CHAPTER 17**	Christian Fellowship: Finding God in Community

PART 7 — Journey to the Heart of God Through Fasting

140	**CHAPTER 18**	Fasting: Gaining by Denying
147	**CHAPTER 19**	Fasting: Working Up an Appetite for God

PART 8 — Journey to the Heart of God Through Giving

156	**CHAPTER 20**	Giving: Blessed to Be a Blessing
161	**CHAPTER 21**	Giving: Let Go and Trust God

PART 9 — Journey to the Heart of God Through Touching Lives

168	**CHAPTER 22**	Divine Appointments: Making Yourself Available to Be Used by God
177	**CHAPTER 23**	Serving: Surrender Everything to Jesus

APPENDIXES

186	**APPENDIX 1**	Bible Study Journal
190	**APPENDIX 2**	Reasons for Unanswered Prayer

CHAPTER 1

JOURNEY TO THE HEART OF GOD
Spiritual Practices That Will Transform Your Life

For I resolved to know nothing while I was with you except Jesus Christ and him crucified.

—1 Corinthians 2:2

When it came time for the apostle Paul to summarize what was really important, he wrote, "For I resolved to know nothing while I was with you except Jesus Christ and him crucified" (1 Corinthians 2:2). Paul took great joy in knowing, walking with, and loving Jesus Christ, and his overarching mission was to spread the good news of Jesus' life, death, and resurrection.

What makes this so amazing is that Paul did not always hold this position. He had once been opposed to Christ and His message. . . . He sought to destroy anyone who believed the message of the cross. However, all this changed one day as he journeyed to Damascus. The Bible tells us that on that journey he came into direct contact with the crucified and resurrected Jesus (see Acts 9:1-18 for the full story). This encounter forever changed Paul's life and thinking. He was converted. The one who had sought to destroy the message of the cross and all associated with it, now sought to proclaim its message![1]

What did all this mean for Paul? For him, it was the beginning of a lifetime journey to know the heart of God.

What does it mean for us to know the heart of God? It means spending our lives intimately pursuing Him. This book focuses on enjoying God through an intimate relationship with Him—a relationship that can take place anytime, anywhere.

Although Paul was a prominent teacher of theology, he said that the focal point of his life was simply "Jesus Christ and him crucified." Clearly, he was not just talking about the day when Christ was crucified but about everything in relation to Jesus: His will, life, grace, work, teaching, and salvation. Paul wanted to teach the Corinthians about the deep things of God and how to connect with Him intimately. He gave many instructions about prayer, worship, offering, and ministry, which can facilitate a deep connection with Him. We truly get to know God through a personal relationship with Him, cultivated through spiritual disciplines such as the ones we will discuss in this book.

In order to deeply connect with His heavenly Father, Jesus intentionally practiced many spiritual disciplines. He prayed, fasted, worshiped, studied the Scriptures, and gave His life for others. He found joy and comfort in doing these spiritual practices.[2] Men and women of God, such as Abraham, Moses, David, Esther, Paul, Peter, and Mary the mother of Jesus practiced these things in order to be closer to God. Faithful followers continue these timeless spiritual disciplines today.

As a pastor, I receive a lot of questions about spiritual life:

- How do I grow in my love, commitment, and service to Jesus Christ?
- What are the hallmarks of a spiritually mature person?
- Why does it take so long and seem so hard to achieve a higher level of spirituality?
- Will I ever really be any different?
- Will I ever be like Jesus?

If you have ever been frustrated with your spiritual life, wondered if real change were possible, or felt confused or stuck, I wrote this book for you and for me.

The Christian gospel insists that the transformation of a human's character and conduct through knowing Jesus and the power of the Holy Spirit really is possible: "Therefore, if anyone is in Christ, the new creation has come: The old has gone, the new is here" (2 Corinthians 5:17; see also Psalm 51:10; Ezekiel 36:26; Romans 12:1, 2). Change is never easy and rarely quick, but it does happen. I see it happening in people all around me and can personally testify that the power of God has transformed me many times.

In this book, I will explore this intimate journey to the heart of God by dealing with several Christian spiritual practices, such as worship, prayer, Bible study, fellowship, fasting, giving, forgiveness, and touching lives. We do not do these practices out of fear, obligation, or drudgery. They are done out of joy to facilitate a relationship with God. As the love of God compels us to live out these spiritual practices, the Holy Spirit will transform our lives and make us more like Jesus (verse 14).

I can personally testify that the spiritual practices we are about to explore have brought me closer to God, changed my life, and filled me with joy. My prayer is that you will experience the same.

---

1. Scott Savell, "To Know Jesus Christ, and Him Crucified," SermonCentral, November 14, 2006, https://www.sermoncentral.com/sermons/to-know-jesus-christ-and-him-crucified-scott-savell-sermon-on-discipleship-98019.

2. Ellen G. White, *Steps to Christ* (Nampa, ID: Pacific Press®, 1999), 93.

PART 1

Journey to the Heart of God Through Seeking and Experiencing His Presence

CHAPTER 2

EXPERIENCING GOD'S PRESENCE
Immanuel, "God With Us"

*"Do not fear, for I have redeemed you;
I have summoned you by name; you are mine."*
—Isaiah 43:1

When a president comes to town, the streets are blocked off and buildings secured. Access to the president is severely limited. When he leaves home, he often flies out on *Air Force One* and is surrounded by armed Secret Service agents. Every minute of his schedule has been mapped out and practiced.

Recently, when former president Barak Obama came to Chicago for a fundraiser, tickets for the dinner were more than $50,000 each. This price got you a plate of chicken and asparagus and a piece of cake while sitting in the same room as the former president. If you wanted to be in his sight line, you had to shell out closer to $100,000. (Think how much chicken and asparagus you could buy with $100,000!) If you wanted to have a picture taken with the former president as evidence of your proximity to him, it would set you back $250,000. Most likely he would not remember your name or that you were even there in the first place.

Thankfully, I don't have that problem when I want to spend time with God. He invites me to come into His presence for free. I don't have to meet any security requirements or have a certain amount of money in the bank. I don't have to be famous or dressed in a tuxedo. He won't make me wait in line for His attention.

Being in God's presence provides me with a banquet of blessings. He remembers our time together, and He not only knows my name but also the number of hairs on my head (Matthew 10:30). Every detail of my life is important to Him.

GOD'S MOST FREQUENT PROMISE
Throughout both the Old and New Testaments, God repeatedly says, "I am *with you*." This is His most frequent promise in the Bible.[1] In the beginning, God was with Adam and Eve in the Garden (Genesis 2:4–3:24). God continued to be with His people. He promised to be with Noah, Abraham and Sarah, Isaac, Jacob,

Joseph, Moses, David, Jeremiah, Isaiah, Daniel, Mary, the disciples, Paul, and the list goes on. God initiated contact and made Himself known and available to humankind.

When God asked Moses to go back to Egypt and free His people, Moses was hesitant, but the Lord said, "I will be with you" (Exodus 3:12). Later, when Joshua took over the leadership of Israel, he was anxious and fearful about leading the Israelites, but the Lord said, "No one will be able to stand against you all the days of your life. As I was with Moses, so I will be with you; I will never leave you nor forsake you" (Joshua 1:5). God's presence gives us the strength and courage to do whatever He asks of us.

When the Israelites entered the desert, God was with them. "By day the LORD went ahead of them in a pillar of cloud to guide them on their way and by night in a pillar of fire to give them light, so that they could travel by day or night. Neither the pillar of cloud by day nor the pillar of fire by night left its place in front of the people" (Exodus 13:21, 22). Once the sanctuary was built, the tabernacle, mercy seat, and Shekinah glory were symbols of God dwelling with His people (Exodus 25:8). God's presence in the camp gave them protection and hope.

Jesus, the Messiah, was prophesied to be called *Immanuel*, meaning "God with us" (Isaiah 7:14). This was His purpose—to be God with us. " 'The virgin will conceive and give birth to a son, and they will call him Immanuel' (which means 'God with us')" (Matthew 1:23; see also Isaiah 8:10). When Jesus called the disciples, it was first and foremost "that they might be with him" (Mark 3:14).

Jesus' desire to be with those He loved transcended His life on Earth. Jesus' last words to His disciples, after giving them the Great Commission, were, "Surely I am with you always, to the very end of the age" (Matthew 28:20). In addition, Jesus promised us the Holy Spirit, who now dwells in our hearts (John 14:16).

Wherever you are, He is there. God is with you all the time. You may not feel His presence, but that does not make it any less true. God will *never* abandon you. "The LORD himself goes before you and will be with you; he will never leave you nor forsake you. Do not be afraid; do not be discouraged" (Deuteronomy 31:8). This is God's promise to us today—Immanuel, God with us.

WHAT DOES IT MEAN TO HAVE GOD WITH US?

There are several reasons why pursuing and maintaining an intimate relationship with God offers hope, joy, and peace. Let's look at each one in the sections that follow.

1. Living in the awareness of God's presence means we can face every situation in our lives with courage and assurance. We live in a scary world. The threats of disease and terrorism are hitting closer to home. It can be tempting to stay locked in our homes, safe from the outside world. But because God goes with us, we have nothing to fear:

> Even though I walk
>   through the darkest valley,
> I will fear no evil,
>   for you are with me;
> your rod and your staff,
>   they comfort me. (Psalm 23:4)

A few years ago I had my own "darkest valley" experience when I was involved in a severe car accident that took the life of my best friend, left me in a coma for several hours, and fractured my knee. Eventually, I had to have surgery on my knee. Just before the surgery, the doctor told me I had the option of two forms of anesthesia—general or local. I asked him about the risks involved with each one. He said with the general anesthesia, the probability of never waking up was one in one hundred thousand; with the local, the chance of being paralyzed was one in sixty thousand.

I replied, "Are you telling me that I might be studied in medical books because I will never wake up or become paralyzed? I am scared to death." He advised me to pray about it. I mentioned I was a pastor and that was what I said to other people when they were in the hospital. He said, "This is your chance to practice what you preach." He prayed for me and read from Isaiah 41:10:

> Do not fear, for I am with you;
>   do not be dismayed, for I am your God.
> I will strengthen you and help you;
>   I will uphold you with my righteous right hand.

These verses gave me the courage to trust in God and His ability to take care of me. There was nothing I could do on my own; it was up to God to keep me safe. He honored His promises. " 'For I am with you to rescue and save you,' declares the LORD" (Jeremiah 15:20).

2. Living in the awareness of God's presence means God has a purpose and plan for our lives. I came to the United States from Nineveh (Mosul), Iraq, to study engineering. As the semesters passed, I strongly felt the call to be a pastor. I decided to study both theology and engineering. I was set to graduate in the spring of 1980, but I didn't have a job lined up. In December 1979, there was a banquet for the graduating students and conference employers to help them get to know us and see if we would be a good fit for any of their churches. The calls started to come to the theology majors in January 1980.

No call came to me. In fact, one of the conference presidents told me I would never get a job in ministry. I did not know the language well enough and did not understand the culture or the people. He reminded me that I came from a place ten thousand miles away. His last words to me were, "Just forget about it. You will never make it."

I thought that maybe he was right. I interviewed for an engineering job. After half an hour, I told them, "I am wasting your time. I really want to be a pastor." Then a friend of mine called his father who worked in Kuwait. They offered me a high-paying engineering job in their company. I declined it.

Another friend encouraged me and kept telling me that God had a wonderful plan for my life. He claimed the promise of Jeremiah 29:11–13 for me: " 'For I know the plans I have for you,' declares the LORD, 'plans to prosper you and not to harm you, plans to give you hope and a future. Then you will call on me and come and pray to me, and I will listen to you. You will seek me and find me when you seek me with all your heart.' " My friend told me that God had a purpose in mind for me. It did not matter what the conference president said. The call would ultimately come from God.

The day before graduation in June, six months after everyone else had gotten their calls, I got a call from the Upper Columbia Conference. I could move forward knowing that God was leading me. What I once thought of as a hopeless situation affirmed for me that God would fulfill His plans and purposes for my life.

God has a plan and purpose for each one of us. It is through living in His presence that we can become confident that He is preparing the way.

3. Living in the awareness of God's presence means we don't have to worry about being overcome by failure. When God is with us, there is no need to worry about failure. Jeremiah, called as a youth, felt inexperienced and unqualified. But the Lord said, "Do not say, 'I am too young.' You must go to everyone I send you to and say whatever I command you. Do not be afraid of them, for I am with you and will rescue you" (Jeremiah 1:7, 8). Much like Jeremiah, I was young and inexperienced when I went to my first church as a pastor in July 1980. That first Sabbath, when I showed up to meet the members, they asked me to read the scripture. It was 1 Timothy 1:17: "Now to the King eternal, immortal, invisible, the only God, be honor and glory for ever and ever. Amen." I tried to speak with confidence, hoping to impress the church. Unknowingly, I said the *immoral*, not *immortal*, God. Everyone laughed.

I was confused. I asked the senior pastor what happened. He laughed and avoided me. Later on, when I discovered what I did, I became very discouraged. I had blown it on my first day. I felt that I would never make it as a pastor. The words of the conference president came back to haunt me: "You are not equipped to pastor here."

Thankfully, someone came to me and said, "Joshua was inexperienced and felt inadequate to lead the people of Israel, but God had these words for him, which also apply to you: 'Have I not commanded you? Be strong and courageous. Do not be afraid; do not be discouraged, for the LORD your God will be with you wherever you go' " (Joshua 1:9). I realized that because God was with me, He would make up for my failure. He has continued to be with me and bless me with success during my more than thirty-five years of ministry.

God's presence makes up for our weaknesses, imperfections, fears, and inadequacies. God's presence is our ultimate resource in the battle against life's difficulties.

4. *Living in the awareness of God's presence means we have the assurance that we are loved.* On a recent flight from Houston to Chicago, I was upgraded to first class and sat next to an executive from Hewlett-Packard. He flew all over the world and was away from home more often than not. He missed his family very much when traveling. Not only did he fill his cell phone with pictures of his family, but he also had a special cell phone number exclusively for their use. Normally, his calls were screened through four levels of administration before he could be reached. But his family could call him anytime, and they knew he would answer. "No voices sound sweeter to me than those of my wife and children. I will stop everything to answer the phone and connect with them," he explained. Nothing brought him more joy than being with his family. He told me that while he was in China, his son became sick. While he was able to talk to him on the phone, it was still heartbreaking to be so far away, unable to physically comfort his son.

My conversation with this executive reminded me that I have a direct line to my heavenly Father. He never feels that I am interrupting Him when I reach out in prayer. When I am sick or discouraged, despite the distance between Earth and heaven, He is able to reach down to comfort me or direct others to comfort me on His behalf. When I am excited, I can call out to Him. I am no longer just one out of seven billion people on Earth; I have a one-to-one connection with God. God is waiting for our call, waiting for us to reach out to Him.

Zephaniah 3:17 reiterates the personal desire God has for each of us:

> The LORD your God is with you,
>   the Mighty Warrior who saves.
> He will take great delight in you;
>   in his love he will no longer rebuke you,
>   but will rejoice over you with singing.

God wants to be with each of us individually. When we are out of fellowship with God, not only do we miss Him but He misses us. If I drop out of my relationship with God, there is a Joseph Kidder–shaped hole in His heart. If you drop out of your relationship with Him, there is a *you*-shaped hole in His heart that cannot be filled by any other person. Each one of us is special to and loved by Him. God delights in you; you are precious in His sight.

Ellen White beautifully captures the essence of God with us: "Since Jesus came to dwell with us, we know that God is acquainted with our trials, and sympathizes with our griefs. Every son and daughter of Adam may understand that our Creator is the friend of sinners. For in every doctrine of grace, every promise of joy, every deed of love, every divine attraction presented in the Saviour's life on earth, we see 'God with us.' "[2]

NEVER ALONE

You don't have to face anything alone. "The LORD Almighty is with us; the God of Jacob is our fortress" (Psalm 46:7). But God will only go where He is invited. Invite Him into your situation every moment of every day.

When you lose your job or face financial difficulties, when you feel like you are drowning, the Lord is still there with you. David says in Psalm 9:9, 10:

> The LORD is a refuge for the oppressed,
>   a stronghold in times of trouble.
> Those who know your name trust in you,
>   for you, LORD, have never forsaken those who seek you.

God's presence manifests in our lives in whatever manner we need. For the orphan, He is the everlasting Father (John 14:18). For the newborn baby, He is the compassionate Mother (Isaiah 49:15). For the lonely, He is the omnipotent Companion who is with us wherever we go and whatever we do (Psalms 68:6; 69:33). For those in unsupportive relationships, He is a Friend (John 15:15). For the sick, for the deserted, and for those going through the valley of death, "he upholds the cause of the oppressed and gives food to the hungry. The LORD sets prisoners free" (Psalm 146:7). This promise was fulfilled in a powerful way in the life of Jesus:

> The Spirit of the Lord is on me,
>   because he has anointed me
>   to proclaim good news to the poor.
> He has sent me to proclaim freedom for the prisoners
>   and recovery of sight for the blind,
> to set the oppressed free. (Luke 4:18, 19)

Immanuel: God with us. He *is* with us! He took on Himself our nature. He took on Himself our form, feelings, and emotions so that He would know what we go through. So that He could not just sympathize but empathize, He was with us, He was for us—but He was God. And "if God is for us, who can be against us?" (Romans 8:31).

God's presence can overcome all the forces and challenges that work against us. Isaiah 43:1–3 gives us a list of these challenges and how God's presence is our ultimate source of protection and victory:

- Verse 1: "Do not fear, for I have redeemed you; I have summoned you by name; you are mine." God's presence dissipates our fears by reminding us that we are His.
- Verse 2: "When you pass through the waters, I will be with you; and when you pass through the rivers, they will not sweep over you. When you walk through the fire, you will not be burned; the flames will not set you ablaze." God's presence will take care of any problems we have. God's presence faithfully sustains us in the midst of trials.
- Verse 3: "For I am the LORD your God, the Holy One of Israel, your Savior; I give Egypt for your ransom, Cush and Seba in your stead." God works our salvation out of who He is.

The preceding verses remind us of God's past deliverance (verse 1), His current presence (verse 2), and His eternal, loving, and saving character (verse 3).

He is Immanuel, God with us. You never have to be alone. God is with you all the time. He is determined to stay with you and be your Companion in life. The big question is, Are you willing to let Him?

---

1. John Ortberg, *God Is Closer Than You Think* (Grand Rapids, MI: Zondervan, 2005), 16.
2. Ellen G. White, *The Desire of Ages* (Mountain View, CA: Pacific Press®, 1940), 24.

CHAPTER 3

SEEKING GOD'S PRESENCE
He Is Closer Than You Think

Seek the LORD *while he may be found;*
call on him while he is near.

—Isaiah 55:6

So many people are chasing after fame, power, security, and material things in an effort to find perfect happiness, peace, and fulfillment. But God purposely created us with a void in our hearts. The only thing able to fill that void is the Lord Himself. Only God the Father, Jesus Christ, and the Holy Spirit can completely fill this hole in us.

Jesus is the Fountain of living water who gives perfect peace and happiness to all those willing to seek Him and drink from Him. The source of a fulfilling life is Jesus, and He wants us to establish a close, intimate, and personal relationship with Him.

If we are willing to seek after the face of God like Moses, Ruth, David, Josiah, Paul, and even Jesus did in order to establish a personal connection with Him, we will experience His presence. Then we will find happiness, peace, joy, and fulfillment that can never be found in the worldly pursuits of this life.

GOD SEEKERS

As we read Scripture, we find many examples of passionate God seekers who sought after His glorious presence and thus experienced renewal and fulfillment.

Moses craved more of the presence of God. He said to Him, "Show me your glory" (Exodus 33:18). Moses was seeking to know more about God, His character, and His love. The Lord responded by revealing Himself to Moses.

Ruth left everything to seek God in order to fill the vacuum in her life. When the time came for Naomi to leave, she urged Ruth to stay in her homeland, but Ruth replied, "Don't urge me to leave you or to turn back from you. Where you go I will go, and where you stay I will stay. Your people will be my people and your God my God" (Ruth 1:16). It would have been easier for Ruth to stay in her homeland—a familiar place that would have offered her the protection of family and relatives—but she desired to seek after God. The Lord rewarded her for that, and she became an ancestor of Jesus.

David's priority was to seek after God and have an intimate, personal relationship with Him. Psalm 63:1 reads,

> You, God, are my God,
>   earnestly I seek you;
> I thirst for you,
>   my whole being longs for you,
> in a dry and parched land
>   where there is no water.

King David wrote this song when he was forced to leave the throne. He left his kingdom, his possessions, and his wives behind him. His son Absalom, whom he loved, was attempting to kill him. Yet in spite of these difficult circumstances, David didn't seek after material things or other human relationships to fill the vacuum in his heart. He did not pray, "O God, give me my kingdom back. Give me my possessions back. Give me my wives back." Rather, he prayed earnestly to know God intimately. He said, "I seek *you*; I thirst for *you*, my whole being longs for *you*." What an amazing prayer!

David admonished Solomon to seek after God with all of his heart and mind: "And you, my son Solomon, acknowledge the God of your father, and serve him with wholehearted devotion and with a willing mind, for the Lord searches every heart and understands every desire and every thought. If you seek him, he will be found by you; but if you forsake him, he will reject you forever" (1 Chronicles 28:9). When Solomon sought pleasure, possessions, and other gods, he ran into serious problems. None of those things filled the hole in his heart. But when he sought after God, he was blessed.

King Josiah sought after the ways of God and cleansed himself and the nation accordingly. "In the eighth year of his reign, while he was still young, he began to seek the God of his father David. In his twelfth year he began to purge Judah and Jerusalem of high places, Asherah poles and idols" (2 Chronicles 34:3). As Israel pursued sinful pleasures and the worship of idols, the sixteen-year-old Josiah began seeking the Lord and, at twenty, became the instrument to destroy the idols of Israel.

Paul sought after God by desiring to know more of Him. He wrote,

> But whatever were gains to me I now consider loss for the sake of Christ. What is more, I consider everything a loss because of the surpassing worth of knowing Christ Jesus my Lord, for whose sake I have lost all things. I consider them garbage, that I may gain Christ and be found in him, not

having a righteousness of my own that comes from the law, but that which is through faith in Christ—the righteousness that comes from God on the basis of faith. I want to know Christ—yes, to know the power of his resurrection and participation in his sufferings, becoming like him in his death, and so, somehow, attaining to the resurrection from the dead. (Philippians 3:7–11)

Seeking after God was Paul's most important priority. For him, everything else was not even secondary but rubbish. For Paul, nothing else compared to seeking after God. Paul reoriented his life, putting the past behind him, pressing on toward the future, and earnestly seeking after the Lord.

Jesus knew the Father by intimate fellowship with Him. He knew Him so well that He frequently had conversations with Him through prayer. "Righteous Father, though the world does not know you, I know you, and they know that you have sent me" (John 17:25). Jesus found so much joy and fulfillment in His relationship with the Father that He admonished His disciples to do the same: "But seek first his kingdom and his righteousness, and all these things will be given to you as well" (Matthew 6:33). Although Jesus was extremely busy, teaching and healing the people and going about the Father's business with the weight of the universe resting on His shoulders, He always carved out time to be with His Father. He would wake up early and go out into nature to spend time with Him.

As we look at those giants of faith, we see that the ultimate desire of their hearts was to know God, to be close to Him, and to fulfill His will in their lives. A. W. Tozer, in his devotional classic *The Pursuit of God*, wrote:

> Come near to the holy men and women of the past and you will soon feel the heat of their desire after God. They mourned for Him, they prayed and wrestled and sought for Him day and night, in season and out, and when they had found Him the finding was all the sweeter for the long seeking. . . .
> . . . Complacency is a deadly foe of all spiritual growth.[1]

You seek God by putting love, desire, and passion for Him at the center of your relationship with Him. You also seek Him by spending consistent quality time alone with Him. As you seek God, you integrate Him into every aspect of your life.

SEEKING GOD'S PRESENCE IN YOUR LIFE

God is all around you. He wants to talk to you and make a difference in your life. God desires to show Himself to you in your day-to-day routine. The only way that you can see Him, the only way that you can realize His presence, is to set your mind and your heart to seek Him. The only way to find something is to look for it.

Ellen White urges us:

In sincerity, in soul hunger, cry after God. Wrestle with the heavenly agencies until you have the victory. Put your whole being into the Lord's hands, soul, body, and spirit, and resolve to be His loving, consecrated agency, moved by His will, controlled by His mind, infused by His Spirit.

Tell Jesus your wants in the sincerity of your soul. You are not required to hold a long controversy with, or preach a sermon to, God, but with a heart of sorrow for your sins, say, "Save me, Lord, or I perish." There is hope for such souls. They will seek, they will ask, they will knock, and they will find. When Jesus has taken away the burden of sin that is crushing the soul, you will experience the blessedness of the peace of Christ.[2]

God outlines the method for seeking Him in Jeremiah 29:12–14: "Then you will call on me and come and pray to me, and I will listen to you. You will seek me and find me when you seek me with all your heart. I will be found by you." When we desire God more than we desire food, water, and air, that is when we will find Him. To seek after God means to go after Him with an intense desire or passion. The ultimate result of seeking the Lord is experiencing and enjoying God's presence.

The promise in Jeremiah 29 was originally given to the Jews in captivity. They were being encouraged to return to God and to have their faith restored in Him and His promises of blessing. Through spiritual renewal, they would learn again how to call out to God and seek Him. The same is true for us today. God is calling us to do two relationship-building things.

1. "Call on Me": Seek His presence and talk to Him about all the issues in your life. The Israelites often worshiped the gods of their neighbors and captors. Sometimes they turned completely away from God; at other times, they worshiped both God and idols simultaneously. For example, in Exodus 32:1–7, many of the people used the golden calf as a representation of the one true God. God waited for them to give all of themselves to Him. He did not want partial loyalty.

We distance ourselves from God because we are distracted by many things, such as our work commitments and busy lifestyles. The problem is not on His end—it's on ours. We can profess the nearness of God but not really live in the assurance of it. Remember not to leave Him out of your life. Seek Him. Talk to Him every day. Share your life with Him. Let Him guide you and bless you. He is reaching out to you today—wherever you are.

Philip Yancey says in his book *Prayer*, "When I am tempted to complain about God's lack of presence, I remind myself that God has much more reason to complain about my lack of presence."[3] In other words, I am the one who leaves God. He is always there for me. We humans are the ones that have gone away instead of seeking Him.

A few weeks ago I was having a hard time sleeping. I was replaying in my mind a frustrating situation. Negative thoughts were circling in my head. Restless, I got up. I tried watching television, surfing the internet, and reading to quiet myself. I kept hearing a voice softly saying, *"Call on Me. Call on Me."* I decided to stop ignoring it and opened my Bible. I turned to Acts 2:25–28:

David said about him [God]:

"I saw the Lord always before me.
  Because he is at my right hand,
  I will not be shaken.
Therefore my heart is glad and my tongue rejoices;
  my body also will rest in hope,
because you will not abandon me to the realm of the dead,
  you will not let your holy one see decay.
You have made known to me the paths of life;
  you will fill me with joy in your presence."

A sense of peace and calm came over me. I took my situation and negative feelings to God in prayer. His presence was with me, and I soon fell asleep. I had the same experience as David: when I sought God's presence, He brought me stability, joy, and hope.

2. *"Come to Me": Determine to seek God in earnest prayer and don't allow anything to distract you.* We are to diligently come to God every day, placing a desire for Him in our hearts. If I saw my wife or wanted to spend time with her only once every few weeks, we would not have much of a marriage. I want my wife to know that I am thinking of her. I intentionally schedule time for us to be together. Even though we have been married for more than thirty-five years, I am still excited to be with her and learn more about her. Likewise, we are to be intentional about coming to God. God is always waiting to meet with you, but do you want to meet with Him? When we set aside our distractions and take the time to search Him out, we are showing our desire for God. He has already sought us out; now we need to let God know that we want to be with Him.

During a recent devotional time, I was reading in Mark 5 about the story of the woman who had been bleeding for twelve years. She knew that if she could only touch Jesus, she would be healed. She inched her way through the crowd, seeking to touch His cloak. Jesus knew right away what she had done; He wanted to know who had reached out to Him. The disciples, knowing that the large crowd was pressing in on all sides, thought Jesus was being ridiculous. Everyone was touching Him! But this woman reached out, coming to Jesus with all she had. I pictured myself in the crowd, reaching out toward this Divine Presence. I wanted nothing more than to touch Jesus. At that moment, as I was seeking, God answered my prayer and helped me really feel His presence.

One day "Jesus stood and said in a loud voice, 'Let anyone who is thirsty come to me and drink. Whoever believes in me, as Scripture has said, rivers of living water will flow from within them' " (John 7:37, 38). This is God's desire. He wants you to draw near to Him. Will you? God is closer than we think. He is never farther than a prayer away. He is right here even now.

GOD IS ALWAYS WITH US

In January 2014, Mohamed El-Erian, the CEO of the Pacific Investment Management Company, which manages more than one trillion dollars in assets, made news when he quit his job. He didn't leave because of a shady business deal or corporate conflicts. He left for his family. His daughter, ten years old at the time, was starting to become rebellious. When questioned about why she wasn't listening, she came back with a list of more than twenty milestone events in the previous few months when her father had chosen work over her. El-Erian had valid reasons for missing his daughter's first day of school, the many soccer matches, and parent-teacher conferences. Travel, important meetings, and emergency situations were to be expected because he ran an international company. Making work a priority was helping the business grow, but at what cost? He realized that he no longer had a relationship with his daughter—someone he loved very much, someone who was counting on him to be there. When he realized the true cost of his job, El-Erian quit so he could focus on being a dad.[4]

Just like El-Erian, God is a father. But even though He is the Father to every person on Earth, He is the Daddy that will never miss anything in our lives. God is always there. God is there when you are born, when you learn to walk, and when you learn to tie your shoes. He is there for your first day of school, first date, and first breakup. He is there when you are baptized and when your parents pass away. He rejoices when you rejoice and cries with you in your sorrows. He sits with you in the hospital room when you have your first child and when you are diagnosed with cancer. He is there to lead you to your job and introduce you to your friends. He is with you when you get married and when you celebrate your twenty-fifth anniversary. He delights in being by your side in good times and bad, in trials and victories. God is always with you. And like El-Erian's daughter, God is always waiting expectantly for us to seek and meet with Him.

FINAL THOUGHTS

Every one of us should seek to establish a close, intimate, and personal relationship with the Lord. The Bible tells us that we are to approach God anytime, anywhere through prayer and intimate communication, with complete confidence and boldness. God is looking for seekers. God is looking for those unafraid to establish a one-on-one, personal, passionate, intense, willing, and loving relationship with Him.

"God does not expect this kind of passionate intensity to be built up overnight. For many, this will be a slow and gradual process, with the Holy Spirit being the One to slowly guide you further and deeper into this realm with God."[5] This is all part of the sanctification process that God would like to accomplish with each of us. If we seek after God, we will experience His presence and have inner satisfaction, joy, stability, strength, perspective, and balance.

SELECTED BIBLE VERSES ABOUT SEEKING AFTER GOD
The following Bible verses center on pursuing God:

- "Now devote your heart and soul to seeking the LORD your God" (1 Chronicles 22:19).
- "One thing I ask from the LORD, this only do I seek: that I may dwell in the house of the LORD all the days of my life, to gaze on the beauty of the LORD and to seek him in his temple" (Psalm 27:4).
- "And without faith it is impossible to please God, because anyone who comes to him must believe that he exists and that he rewards those who earnestly seek him" (Hebrews 11:6).
- "God did this so that they would seek him and perhaps reach out for him and find him, though he is not far from any one of us" (Acts 17:27).
- "I have not spoken in secret, from somewhere in a land of darkness; I have not said to Jacob's descendants, 'Seek me in vain.' I, the LORD, speak the truth; I declare what is right" (Isaiah 45:19).
- "Ask and it will be given to you; seek and you will find; knock and the door will be opened to you. For everyone who asks receives; the one who seeks finds; and to the one who knocks, the door will be opened" (Matthew 7:7, 8).
- "Seek the LORD, all you humble of the land, you who do what he commands. Seek righteousness, seek humility; perhaps you will be sheltered on the day of the LORD's anger" (Zephaniah 2:3).
- "I love those who love me, and those who seek me find me" (Proverbs 8:17).
- "You will seek me and find me when you seek me with all your heart" (Jeremiah 29:13).
- "Look to the LORD and his strength; seek his face always" (1 Chronicles 16:11).
- "The LORD is with you when you are with him. If you seek him, he will be found by you, but if you forsake him, he will forsake you" (2 Chronicles 15:2).
- "I sought the LORD, and he answered me; he delivered me from all my fears" (Psalm 34:4).
- "Those who know your name trust in you, for you, LORD, have never

forsaken those who seek you" (Psalm 9:10).
- "Blessed are those who keep his statutes and seek him with all their heart" (Psalm 119:2).
- "The lions may grow weak and hungry, but those who seek the Lord lack no good thing" (Psalm 34:10).
- "This is what the Lord says to Israel: 'Seek me and live' " (Amos 5:4).
- "I revealed myself to those who did not ask for me; I was found by those who did not seek me. To a nation that did not call on my name, I said, 'Here am I, here am I' " (Isaiah 65:1).

---

1. A. W. Tozer, *The Pursuit of God* (Abbotsford, WI: Aneko, 2015), 15, 17.

2. Ellen G. White, *Our Father Cares* (Hagerstown, MD: Review and Herald®, 2013), 99.

3. Philip Yancey, *Prayer: Does It Make Any Difference?* (Grand Rapids, MI: Zondervan, 2006), 208.

4. Mohamed El-Erian, "Father and Daughter Reunion," *Worth*, June 7, 2014, https://www.worth.com/father-and-daughter-reunion/.

5. Michael Bradley, "Seek the Lord," Bible Knowledge, accessed January 23, 2019, https://www.bible-knowledge.com/seek-the-lord/.

PART 2

Journey to the Heart of God Through Worship

CHAPTER 4

PERSONAL WORSHIP
Meeting God Face-to-Face

With it he touched my mouth and said, "See, this has touched your lips;
your guilt is taken away and your sin atoned for."
Then I heard the voice of the Lord saying,
"Whom shall I send? And who will go for us?"
And I said, "Here am I. Send me!"

—Isaiah 6:7, 8

In the Bible, a handful of people were given a glimpse of God. They all struggled to describe what happened. Perhaps the clearest record of such an encounter was set down by the prophet Isaiah.

King Uzziah, the greatest king since David, had died. Israel, while politically and economically strong, was spiritually bankrupt. With the death of King Uzziah, there was a vacuum of power that left the nation vulnerable to the Assyrians and Egyptians. Brokenhearted, Isaiah made his way to the temple to worship and seek to renew his faith.

When Isaiah went to the temple, he learned that though his earthly king was dead, the heavenly King was alive. God was still on His throne. Isaiah had lost a king whom he had loved, but he had a life-changing experience with the King of kings.

Isaiah's encounter with God is one model of personal, life-changing worship. When he saw the Lord in the temple, he felt his own sinfulness, felt God's cleansing power, and accepted the call to service. It became a turning point in his life and ministry. This chapter details Isaiah's life-changing experience and applies it to personal worship.[1]

UPWARD VISION: ISAIAH SAW THE LORD

The greatest vision that anyone can have is seeing the Lord. Isaiah had the privilege of seeing the Lord in His throne room. Let's examine some details found in Isaiah 6:1–4.

God's power. Isaiah saw the train of God's robe, and it filled the temple. A monarch's train signals the presence of royalty. Notice how royal God is. Just the train of His robe filled the temple. God is showing Isaiah that He is not only sitting at the seat of power but He is also all powerful, all royal, and almighty.

Isaiah's entire encounter took place in front of God's throne—the place of power. But this honor is not just reserved for prophets. We are all welcome to approach the throne of God in worship: "Let us therefore come boldly unto the throne of grace, that we may obtain mercy, and find grace to help in time of need" (Hebrews 4:16, KJV).

God's holiness. Isaiah saw a heavenly worship service. God, surrounded by angelic beings, was the center of all praise. The seraphim were singing responsively, filling the court with adoration. "Holy, holy, holy, is the LORD of hosts: the whole earth is full of his glory" (Isaiah 6:3, KJV). By their adoration, "the seraphs claim that God is completely, totally, absolutely, the holiest of the holy. Holiness is the essence of God's nature and God himself is the supreme revelation of holiness."[2]

As they come before God, the angels give Him adoration and praise, worship and love. Adoration flows from within our innermost being. It is not thankfulness but praise to God for *who* He is, not what He has done. The holiness of God makes Him worthy of adoration. When we adore God, we are like the angels, awed by His glory.

These angels hover by the throne of God, ready and available to do His will. They come and go based on God's command. Therefore, the heart of worship is being available to God on a daily basis. It is not a weekly act on Sabbath morning. It is a day-to-day experience. Worship is a lifestyle.

For Christians, there is no such thing as sacred and secular. Everything belongs to God. Whether we eat, drink, play, or work, we do it all in the presence of God and for His glory. We are to be a people who are constantly available to Him. If we have not worshiped on Sunday, Monday, Tuesday, Wednesday, Thursday, and Friday, how can we expect to worship on Sabbath? All we have done is attend church.

It is possible for one person to be moved to tears during a church service while the person beside her remains untouched. One repents while another trusts in his own self-righteousness. One responds willingly to the claims of Christ while another desperately resists the persuasion of the Holy Spirit. Are you going through the motions of a cold, formal religion, trying to satisfy your conscience? Or are you meeting with God? Are you open to the Lord as He knocks at the door of your heart?

If you and I leave church in the same condition in which we came, we have not had worship. We have just been to a service.

In true worship, we experience the presence of God, and it changes us. It shakes us to our core—the foundation of our being. In the same way, the songs of the seraphim shook the room and ushered in the presence of God (Isaiah 6:4).[3] Isaiah was dramatically affected by this wonderful worship experience. That is what will happen to us as we encounter God face-to-face.

Once we have made ourselves available to God and have adored Him, we will then experience God's presence in our lives. We cannot help but be changed when we worship.

INWARD VISION: ISAIAH FELT HIS SINFULNESS

When Isaiah saw the Lord and the worship scene taking place in the throne room, he was overwhelmed by a sense of his own sinfulness. Let's examine how Isaiah felt as described in Isaiah 6:5.

Overwhelmed by holiness. Isaiah saw himself as he had never seen himself before—in relation to the holiness of God. "Thus when the servant of God is permitted to behold the glory of the God of heaven, as he is unveiled to humanity, and realizes to a slight degree the purity of the Holy One of Israel, he will make startling confessions of the pollution of his soul, rather than proud boasts of his holiness."[4]

This is always true. The closer we get to God, the more clearly we see our sins. The contrast between His holiness and our unrighteousness gives us a vivid awareness of how we continually fall short of God's glory (Romans 3:23). "The reason for Isaiah's recognition of guilt is simple: he has seen the King, the Lord Almighty. . . . The necessary first step before any true confession of sin is having an understanding of the glory and holiness of the Almighty God who rules the heavens and the earth."[5] It was this face-to-face encounter with God that brought out the reality of Isaiah's sinful state.

Overwhelmed by sinfulness. Once we've seen the King, we confess our sin. "Woe is me! for I am undone" (Isaiah 6:5, KJV). As we truly see God, we must humble ourselves before Him. The closer we walk with God, the faster we recognize our sin and realize how much we need Him. Returning to the presence of God is not enough. We must confess our sinfulness and acknowledge the greatness of God in order to truly restore a relationship with Him.[6]

Walking with God is like facing a huge mirror with a big light over it. When you stand away from the mirror, things look pretty good. Your shirt looks tidy and your hair is combed. As you move closer to the mirror, things begin to show up. Your shirt has a spot on it. Some of your hair is out of place. The closer we get to the mirror, the more we realize our defects. It's the same when we get close to God. We're convicted of our sin, and we realize how much we need Him and how far we are from Him.

In Isaiah 6:5, Isaiah confessed to having "unclean lips" because what was spoken from them was a reflection of his heart. "For out of the abundance of the heart the mouth speaketh" (Matthew 12:34, KJV; see also Luke 6:45). Once he had seen how heaven worships, Isaiah looked at himself and probably thought,

My worship? That's been very ritualistic. I come to the temple every Sabbath. I have a quiet time every day. But is it just routine? Something has to be done. Seeing the holiness of God and heavenly worship, Isaiah felt that he was undone. He was ruined. "I dwell in the midst of a people of unclean lips: for mine eyes have seen the King, the Lord of hosts" (Isaiah 6:5, KJV).

Just before Thanksgiving, my brother and his family came to stay with us for a few days. Preoccupied with spending time with my family and friends, I forgot to take out the trash. Soon, the garbage started to pile up. I confess that this is not an uncommon occurrence. But with the extra people and food, the smell started to waft into other parts of the house. I finally moved the garbage outside so we wouldn't have to smell it. But every time we walked outside, we were greeted by the odor of rotting leftovers. Just moving the garbage wasn't enough. I needed to put it in the dumpster so it could be taken away by professionals. When I finally did, we could go about our daily tasks unhindered by the stench.

If you don't take out the garbage on a daily basis, it piles up. It begins to stink. It can pollute your relationship with God and others. If we want to be cleansed by God, we must confess to God daily and give Him our garbage to take away. This is another part of worship—understanding and voicing our need for cleansing because we are undone. Once He removes our garbage, we will have room for His holiness and righteousness.

INWARD MISSION: ISAIAH EXPERIENCED GOD'S CLEANSING POWER

Once we are convicted of our sin and we confess it, God's cleansing power takes over. Let's look at this power as experienced by the prophet in Isaiah 6:6, 7.

Touch of grace. Notice where the coal was placed. Isaiah had a particular need—the cleansing of his lips. The seraphim applied it directly to his lips, directly on his need. Some of you are thinking, *My sins are too great. Surely God cannot forgive me.* God's grace is so abundant that it not only takes care of that sin but it also covers all the others you forgot about. God's grace can take care of every facet of your sin. But we cannot enjoy God's cleansing without confession.

If all we ever see is the weakness of our sin—the depravity of our hearts—without discovering the cleansing power of God, what miserable people we would be. But God *does* have power to cleanse! Isaiah could do nothing to save himself; it was only through of the grace of God that he could be given atonement. God desires to provide the cleansing that brings restoration. When Isaiah confessed his sin, God was "faithful and just to forgive" his "sins, and to cleanse" him "from all unrighteousness" (1 John 1:9, KJV).

Power of transformation. The cure for our sinfulness can only come from God. Once we seek to understand the gospel, the sacrifices Christ has made for us, and the grace of His enduring love, then we will realize that renewal and cleansing come from above. Only God can purify. Only God can save. Only His love brings life.⁷ He calls us righteous because of the blood of His Son. Then He makes us righteous through the working of His Holy Spirit.

Through worship, we invite God to revolutionize us and make us new creations. "The Christian's life is not a modification or improvement of the old, but a transformation of nature. There is a death to self and sin, and a new life altogether. This change can be brought about only by the effectual working of the Holy Spirit."⁸ A life of worship makes us available to the Holy Spirit and eager to see His work done in us.

Isaiah's experience shows us a God who takes a personal interest in each one of us. He longs to show Himself to us, so that we can feel our sin and brokenness and be cleansed. He desires to give restoration to all those who believe in Jesus—today, tomorrow, and until the end of time.

OUTWARD MISSION: ISAIAH ACCEPTED THE CALL TO SERVICE

Isaiah saw the Lord, felt his sinfulness, experienced God's cleansing power, and then responded, as recorded in Isaiah 6:8, 9.

Purified for a purpose. The cleansing power of God, as demonstrated by the live coal that touched the prophet's lips, was not manifested for the purpose of making Isaiah a better speaker or a more joyful person. It was a cleansing that would prepare him to reach out to a sinful world and share the grace and mercy that only comes by knowing God.⁹

An experience with God affects how we see the world. Isaiah heard God's heartbeat for a lost and dying people. He heard God's summons for a messenger to reach out to them, and he immediately accepted the call.

God calls sinners to go into the world for Him but *only* after they've been cleansed of their sins. Our pasts will not exclude us from being used by God, but how we're living today might. God desires to use us for His glory, if only we'll live cleansed, purified lives for Him.

Inspired for service. Unlike the prophets Moses and Jeremiah, Isaiah did not hesitate. He did not say, "What's in it for me? What is the salary? What are the retirement benefits?" Isaiah signed a blank check for his whole life. He volunteered for God's mission with no regard for the details or duration of the task at hand,¹⁰ because he had seen God's nature and character—"glorious in holiness, fearful in praises," and awesome in glory (Exodus 15:11, KJV). "The experience of having a glimpse of the majesty of God's glory dramatically impacted his theology and caused him to understand God's purpose for his life in a new way."¹¹

God called and Isaiah answered. This unconditional response comes only from the heart of one who has seen the vision—one who has met with God. Once we've seen the King, we go where He sends us. Notice the progression of the passage. Before we can be available to God,

- we must see God;
- we must feel our sinfulness and be ministered to by God;
- we must listen to God's voice telling us what He wants us to do; and
- we must respond with an attitude of gratitude, not obligation, because He has cleansed us through the blood of Jesus.

There is a sense of healing in our lives. It's not that we have to serve God. We want to serve God because of who He is. "Personal preferences and fear fade into the background when a person has had the privilege of seeing the glory of the Holy King."[12] The wonder of the sacrifice of Christ should be the driving factor in all we do. If we are not feeling compelled to minister on behalf of the One who has shown Himself to be faithful, we need to start over and rediscover the grandeur of God.[13]

Ellen White connects worship and service: "True worship consists in working together with Christ. Prayer, exhortation, and talk are cheap fruits, which are frequently tied on, but fruits that are manifested in good works, in caring for the needy, the fatherless, and widows, are genuine fruits, and grow naturally upon a good tree."[14] Service is not about riches and honor on Earth but about becoming overwhelmed with appreciation for the One who heals brokenness with love.[15]

RESTORED FOR PROCLAMATION

John Newton took to the seas with his father at the age of eleven, almost five years after the death of his mother. He made a living on the ocean as a navy sailor and then working on a slave ship with his father, transporting slaves from Africa to the New World. He thought he had a good life but soon found himself at odds with the other crew members, who left him in West Africa with a slave trader by the name of Amos Clowe. Clowe gave Newton to his mistress, who cruelly mistreated him as she did her other slaves. Hungry and clothed in rags, Newton was forced to beg for food.[16]

Newton's father commissioned a ship to rescue him. During the voyage home, a terrible storm damaged the ship. This event led him to his spiritual awakening. "Newton prayed to God and the cargo miraculously shifted to fill a hole in the ship's hull and the vessel drifted to safety. Newton took this as a sign from the Almighty and marked it as his conversion to Christianity."[17]

In the mid-1750s, John decided to leave the slave trade and go into a lifelong ministry of preaching the gospel. Later he began fighting against the slave trade. He wrote the song "Amazing Grace" in response to God's power to not only forgive but also to use wretched people for His good.

Like Newton, we must recognize the disparity between our sinfulness and the holy character of God. Our response to His glory must be humility, and our response to His forgiveness must be service. The grace of God penetrates our hearts and works to bring them in line with the heart of God. Service to the King is not about riches and honor on Earth; rather, it is about becoming overwhelmed with appreciation for the One who heals brokenness with love.[18]

CONCLUSION

Isaiah met with God and had a revelation of the greatness of the Lord, and it changed his life. The same Living God is eager to meet with you. Earthly kings come and go, but the King of kings is alive forever, full of power, and willing to reveal Himself.

The King calls us to see Him as He truly is—the holy God. He calls us to see ourselves as we truly are—sinful and in desperate need of Him. He calls us to discover that He can cleanse all sin and give life to those who will receive Him. He commissions us to look on the harvest fields of this world and be His witnesses. He calls us to change the world through the power of Jesus.

Have you had a throne-room worship experience? Have you seen the Lord in the pages of His Word? Have you heard His voice? Are you overwhelmed by your sinfulness in light of His holiness? Have you accepted the salvation He offers, which was purchased with His own blood? Have you accepted His call to service? Open your heart to Him today. Worship Him with praise, thanksgiving, and service. Like Isaiah, allow yourself to be transformed as you meet God face-to-face.

---

1. Portions of this chapter were adapted from S. Joseph Kidder and Kristy L. Hodson, "Meeting God Face to Face," *Adventist World*, last modified March 10, 2016, https://archives.adventistworld.org/2016/march/meeting-god-face-to-face.html.

2. Gary V. Smith, *Isaiah 1–39*, New American Commentary, ed. E. Ray Clendenen, vol. 15A (Nashville, TN: B&H Publishing, 2007), 190.

3. Smoke, as mentioned in Isaiah 6:4, is a symbol of God's presence. See Exodus 24:16 and Revelation 15:8.

4. Ellen G. White, "The Knowledge of Christ and Self Leads to Humility," *Review and Herald*, October 16, 1888.

5. Smith, *Isaiah 1–39*, 192.

6. John Goldingay, *Isaiah*, Understanding the Bible Commentary Series, eds. Robert L. Hubbard Jr. and Robert K. Johnston (Grand Rapids, MI: Baker Books, 2012), 59, 60.

7. Raymond C. Ortlund Jr., *Isaiah: God Saves Sinners*, Preaching the Word, ed. R. Kent Hughes (Wheaton, IL: Crossway Books, 2005), 81.

8. Ellen G. White, *The Desire of Ages* (Mountain View, CA: Pacific Press®, 1940), 172.

9. John N. Oswalt, *Isaiah*, NIV Application Commentary, ed. Terry C. Muck (Grand Rapids, MI: Zondervan, 2003), 132.

10. Goldingay, *Isaiah*, 60; Smith, *Isaiah 1–39*, 194.

11. Smith, *Isaiah 1–39*, 183.

12. Smith, *Isaiah 1–39*, 199.

13. Oswalt, *Isaiah*, 132.

14. Ellen G. White, "Doing for Christ," *Review and Herald*, August 16, 1881.

15. Oswalt, *Isaiah*, 129.

16. "John Newton: Reformed Slave Trader," *Christianity Today*, accessed January 21, 2018, http://

www.christianitytoday.com/history/people/pastorsandpreachers/john-newton.html.

17. David Sheward, "The Real Story Behind 'Amazing Grace,' " Biography, August 11, 2015, https://www.biography.com/news/amazing-grace-story-john-newton.

18. Oswalt, *Isaiah*, 129.

CHAPTER 5

CORPORATE WORSHIP

Praise Him Joyfully Whose Love Endures Forever

Enter his gates with thanksgiving and his courts with praise;
give thanks to him and praise his name. For the L*ord* *is good and his love*
endures forever; his faithfulness continues through all generations.
—Psalm 100:4, 5

Jeff Smith slept in on Sabbath morning. His wife came and woke him up, saying, "You need to get ready to go to church."

Jeff replied, "I am not going to church anymore."

"But you need to go," his wife entreated.

"Why?" he asked. "Give me one good reason why I should go to church." Jeff looked his wife straight in the eyes and continued. "I find it to be boring, predictable, and irrelevant. No one there loves me or cares about me. It does not meet my needs. Just give me one good reason why I should go."

His wife said, "I will give you two reasons. First of all, you are thirty years old, and you need God. Second, people in church expect you to be there. After all, you are the pastor of that church."

Have you ever felt like Jeff Smith as you go to a worship service? Do you find church to be boring, irrelevant, and predictable? Why is church is so boring sometimes? I believe church is boring because it has become a spectator sport: we go to see and hear a program rather than to be engaged and participate. We see God as the producer, the pastor as the actor, and the congregation as the audience. Søren Kierkegaard states that in true worship, God is the audience, the members of the congregation are the actors, and the pastor and the worship leaders are the prompters.[1]

God intends that our worship, private and corporate, should be enthusiastic and participatory and that it should flow out of hearts that have been in touch with Him all week. When we are engaged with God, worship becomes exciting and meaningful.

Psalm 100 gives us powerful insights regarding how and why we are to come to God and connect with His heart. Often referred to as the Old Hundredth, it is a psalm of thanksgiving that was used by early Christians "for morning prayer, while throughout the history of the Christian church it has often been used by the assembled people of God as they engage in communal worship before the Lord."[2]

THE *HOW* OF WORSHIP

Psalm 100 alternates between calls of how to worship and reasons why God is worthy of worship.

Worship the Lord with joy. "Shout for *joy* to the Lord, all the earth. Worship the Lord with gladness; come before him with joyful songs" (Psalm 100:1, 2; emphasis added). Joy should be a significant part of how we worship.

In Hebrew thought, שִׂמְחָה (*simchah*) translates as "gladness" or "joy."[3] Therefore, when we come to worship the Lord, there ought to be an exuberance because the King of kings has come to us and He allows us to come to Him.

Psalm 122:1 states, "I was glad when they said unto me, Let us go into the house of the Lord" (KJV). This joy should not be artificial; it should come out of our hearts because we are in a relationship with God. When God is the center of our lives, our hearts will radiate with joy and enthusiasm because we are His. Authentic worship comes from an overflowing heart.

When we worship God, we are going into the presence of our Creator, who put an infinite value on our lives at the expense of the life of His own Son. When we have our Sabbath, our convocation, our festival, we ought to come with gladness, not dragging our feet, because God is good. The psalmist says it ought to be our delight and joy to come face-to-face with the Lord and bask in His presence.

We must not confuse joy with happiness. While you cannot expect to always have happiness, you can always have joy. There are times in our lives when situations cause sadness, but that does not mean we need to lose our joy (James 1:2, 3). Happiness is a subjective emotion, dependent on happenings and circumstances. However, joy is a state of mind produced by the Holy Spirit dwelling within us: "But the fruit of the Spirit is love, joy, peace, forbearance, kindness, goodness, faithfulness, gentleness and self-control" (Galatians 5:22, 23). Our worship is an outpouring of that joy.

Happiness is advertised as attainable if only we buy this or that. But we can't buy joy. The ability to worship the Lord with gladness has everything to do with our coming to know the Lord. God's joy, person, and character give us reasons to worship with gladness because we are His. Out of that knowledge, we are to worship Him with great joy.

Furthermore, *joy* can be defined as "an inner confidence that God is in control" of every circumstance of our lives.[4] Nehemiah declares that the joy of the Lord strengthens us (Nehemiah 8:10). Our problems may seem insurmountable, but joy says, "I believe God is in control of the issues surrounding my life right now."

He is going to work everything out to His glory and honor and for our good (Romans 8:28). Acts 2:25, 26 states,

> I saw the Lord always before me.
>   Because he is at my right hand,
>   I will not be shaken.
> Therefore my heart is glad and my tongue rejoices;
>   my body also will rest in hope.

When we come to worship our heavenly Father, our hearts should be full of joy. Joy does not depend on what happens to us, how well we do in the world, or the opinion of others. Joy comes to us when God enters our hearts and dwells in us.

I once had a church member who was nearly blind and deaf but never missed a worship service. I once asked, "Why do you come to church? You can't hear or see anything." The church member replied enthusiastically, "I don't need to hear and see to praise the Lord, serve Him, and tell the whole universe that I am on God's side. My heart is full of the things of God, and they spill over in joy, praise, and adoration." We don't need a tongue to praise the Lord, although it is helpful. What we need is a heart fully engaged with the heart of God.

Worship the Lord with enthusiasm. How are we supposed to act when we come together to worship God? Psalm 100:1 states, "*Shout* for joy to the Lord, all the earth" (emphasis added). This is an interesting command because "shout" (רוּעַ; *ruwa'*) is the same word used to refer to a battle cry in Joshua 6:10. It is also a shout of triumph over one's enemies, as in Joshua 6:16, when the Israelites were told to shout victoriously after marching around Jericho.[5] When people get together to worship God, there ought to be a joyful acknowledgment of the victory Jesus accomplished when He conquered death and secured our salvation at the cross.

Psalm 100:1 is also a directive for "all the earth" to come together corporately to worship and praise our Creator. Walter Brueggemann expounds on this concept:

> When the community praises, it submits and reorders life. It is not only a moment of worship but also an embrace of a *doxological life* which is organized differently. So the summons is a summons to reorient life.
> ... A life without praise is more likely a life turned in on self.[6]

We come together to praise the Lord through singing, giving testimonies, and thanksgiving as a reminder that He is the Creator and Giver of life.

As we see in Psalm 100:2, we are to "worship the Lord with gladness; come before him with joyful songs." This is a cry or a song of joy. We start to get the picture that when God's people come together to worship Him, there ought to be enthusiasm and excitement.

Some may counter, "But if we're going to be reverent before the Lord, doesn't it require silence?" There is a choir anthem that says, "The LORD is in his holy temple; let all the earth be silent before him" (Habakkuk 2:20).[7] A study of the context of this verse shows that God is not talking to worshipers but an enemy nation that was about to receive His judgment. God said, "I want you to be quiet, because I am about to execute judgment."

But don't the psalms talk about silence? I once went through the psalms and looked at every reference that talks about silence.[8] Almost every time the book talks about silence it is not in the context of worship but of judgment and death. Silence was something negative.[9] For example, Psalm 115:17, 18 declares,

> It is not the dead who praise the LORD,
>   those who go down to the place of silence;
> it is we who extol the LORD,
>   both now and forevermore.

(See also Psalms 31:17; 107:42.) And the psalmist shows his praise through joyous noises: "That my heart may sing your praises and not be silent. LORD my God, I will praise you forever" (Psalm 30:12).

There are times when we need to be silent to listen, contemplate, and decide to be fully devoted to Jesus. Silence allows us to reflect on what we've read and learned. (Psalm 4:4 contains one such example.) But once we're done with our introspection, we can express exuberance and enthusiasm though singing, sharing testimonies, and generous giving. We come together because all week God has been showing us His mercy and love. Worship is a time to celebrate and share what God has done for us!

Ellen White encourages us to be enthusiastic in our worship. She writes,

> Ardent, active piety should characterize the worshipers. . . .
>   . . . The lifeless attitude of the worshipers in the house of God is one great reason why the ministry is not more productive of good. The melody of song, poured forth from many hearts in clear, distinct utterance, is one of God's instrumentalities in the work of saving souls. All the service should be conducted with solemnity and awe, as if in the visible presence of the Master of assemblies.[10]

But what about reverence? Though we equate reverence with silence, biblical reverence is closely associated with fear, awe, and wonder. "Therefore, since we are receiving a kingdom that cannot be shaken, let us be thankful, and so worship

God acceptably with reverence and awe" (Hebrews 12:28; see also Genesis 31:31; Matthew 10:28; Acts 9:31).[11]

This reverence, fear, or respect for God often is manifested in our actions toward others. In the Old Testament, fearing God is repeatedly associated with showing kindness to those in one's sphere of influence. This carries over to the New Testament. Luke 18:1–4 illustrates that fearing God should lead to respecting people,[12] and Ephesians 5:21 notes that the motivation for submission to others is "reverence for Christ." Biblical reverence is more of an attitude that affects our character and actions rather than the single act of being silent in worship settings. I found no mention of reverence being synonymous with silence in the Bible or in the modern dictionary.[13] When we stand in front of God and have a vision of His grace, love, majesty, awesomeness, and greatness, we are overwhelmed by all that He is, and we say, "Wow, what a God!" This act of wonder leads us to worship the Lord with enthusiasm, for He is worthy of our praise.

Worship the Lord with true thanksgiving. We are to make a joyful noise, but that is not all. Psalm 100:4 says, "Enter his gates with thanksgiving and his courts with praise; give thanks to him and praise his name." This is more than just a simple thank-you.

Let's suppose you have sent out dozens of résumés, have had multiple job interviews, and finally land that perfect job. You know God's hand was in it. In your quiet time, you pray, "God, thank You for providing this job." That's great, but you still haven't provided thanksgiving. You haven't fulfilled this until you're in the presence of God's people and say, "I want to tell you what God has done for me. I finally got the job I needed in order to provide for my family. God is the one who made it all possible!" Now you have accomplished biblical thanksgiving: public acknowledgment—a sharing with others what God has done. In Revelation 12:11, John says, "They overcame him [Satan] by the blood of the Lamb, and by the word of their testimony" (KJV).

Do you have anything to be thankful for? One man I talked to answered a similar question with these words: "Think of what Jesus has done for you, in you, with you, and promised to you." I truly believe that if we would come to church with this kind of attitude, our individual worship would improve dramatically. When we come to church, our worship ought to reflect the thankfulness of our hearts.

Psalm 107:22 states that we need to "sacrifice thank offerings and tell of his [God's] works with songs of joy." We must tell what we are thankful for. When we worship with thanksgiving, we are full of joy and enthusiasm and are ready to shout to and with all the earth about the greatness of God.

WHY DO WE WORSHIP?

There are days we don't feel like coming to the Lord with thanksgiving or joy. If we don't feel like worshiping, if we lack enthusiasm, then what is going to be the driving force to worship? Let's go to the *why* section of Psalm 100.

Because He is God. "Know that the Lord is God. It is he who made us, and we are his; we are his people, the sheep of his pasture" (Psalm 100:3). We worship the Lord because *He is God.* "This is a call to worship that demands that we recognize the real center of life, that we surrender our greed and self-centeredness to Yahweh who is all powerful. . . . When we accept this invitation, we acknowledge and confess all that He is. We also accept Yahweh's definition of our identity; who He is determines who we are."[14] He knows everything about us and still loves us.

Because He is good. Another reason to worship is because the Lord is good (verse 5). It really is that simple. We worship the Lord with joyful song and praise because He has lavished His goodness on us. When we worship the Lord, we are proclaiming His goodness. Psalm 95 gives us many examples of this goodness: He is our salvation (verse 1), He is great (verse 3), He is strong (verse 4), He is our Maker (verse 6), and He is gracious (verse 7).

James L. Mays elaborates on how God's goodness calls for our worship: "The knowledge of Yahweh's *favor* comes through traditions of the past, ever renewed by recurrences of that *hesed* [love] in the present. But that knowledge does not turn back to the past; it summons to the future. The basis of praise is the confidence that the Lord's faithful favor in the past has already opened up the future as the sphere of His goodness. . . . Praise grows out of, and begins to actualize in the present, the vision of the goodness of the Lord, which awaits the worshiping community in the tomorrows of life."[15]

Because His love endures forever. Psalm 100:5 goes on to say, "And his love endures forever." That Hebrew word for "love," חֶסֶד (*hesed*), could be the most important word in the Old Testament, being used in 241 verses.[16] Some Bibles translate it as "lovingkindness" (NASB), "mercy" (KJV), or "gracious love" (ISV). Psalm 103 uses it four times and explains that "for as high as the heavens are above the earth, so great is his love for those who fear him" (verse 11). I like to translate חֶסֶד as "loyal love," because it is a two-pronged word. On the one hand, it is saying that God has affection and passion for us as His people: "Showing love [חֶסֶד; *hesed*] to a thousand generations of those who love [אָהַב; *'ahab*] me and keep my commandments" (Exodus 20:6). On the other hand, it is a covenant word. This love of God is so much greater than the love we offer Him. It has an aspect of commitment or staying power. Time and again, the Israelites turned from God, but He always pursued them and called them back into a relationship with Him. Not only does God have affection for us, but He is committed to us regardless of how we treat Him (Genesis 32:10).

God's love will respectfully pursue you no matter what—no matter what you do, where you come from, or where you go. God loves you no matter who you are. He is madly in love with you. Nothing can separate you from the love of God (Romans 8:38, 39).

ENDURING PRAISE

I have found that when I do not feel like worshiping, I need to take time to reflect on the character of God. This is what inspires me for worship: God is holy, just, loving, gracious, powerful, merciful, and so much more. The more we know about God, the more we experience Him, and the more we are going to *want* to worship Him. He is a great and awesome Lord.

We cannot remain silent in worship but will shout and sing for joy when we see that our awesome God is faithful in all things. "The hand which cleft the sea and brought water from the rock is still with us, working equal wonders. Can we refuse to 'worship and bow down' when we clearly see that 'this God is *our* God for ever and ever, and will be our guide, even to death'?"[17] May God give you the desire to worship Him with gladness, praise, and thanksgiving because He is God, and His love endures forever.

---

1. Emily R. Brink, "Who's the Host? We May Be Getting Carried Away With Kierkegaard's Analogy," *Reformed Worship* 33, September 1994, http://www.reformedworship.org/article/september-1994/whos-host-we-may-be-getting-carried-away-kierkegaards-analogy.

2. Allan Harman, *Psalms*, Mentor Commentary (Fearn, Scotland: Christian Focus, 1998), 329. Psalm 100 has lasting relevance for believers today when they come together for worship.

3. According to the Blue Letter Bible, the Hebrew word שִׂמְחָה (*simchah*) occurs ninety-four times in eighty-nine verses in the Old Testament. In the KJV, it is translated as "joy" forty-four times and as "gladness" thirty-one times. *Strong's Concordance*, s.v. "H8057," accessed January 24, 2019, https://www.blueletterbible.org/lang/lexicon/lexicon.cfm?Strongs=H8057&t=KJV.

4. Don Brackbill Jr., *Surviving the Shadow: Coping With the Crisis of Life* (Bloomington, IN: WestBow Press, 2013), 76.

5. *Strong's Concordance*, s.v. "H7321," accessed January 24, 2019, https://www.blueletterbible.org/lang/lexicon/lexicon.cfm?Strongs=H7321&t=KJV.

6. Walter Brueggemann, "Psalm 100," *Interpretation* 39, no. 1 (January 1, 1985): 65, https://doi.org/10.1177/002096438503900107.

7. The Hebrew word הָסָה (*hacah*), translated in Habakkuk 2:20 as "silent," is only used eight times in the Old Testament (Numbers 13:30; Judges 3:19; Nehemiah 8:11; Amos 6:10; 8:3; Habakkuk 2:20; Zephaniah 1:7; Zechariah 2:13); it is not found in Psalms. This word carries the meaning of a command for silence, often as a means of correction. The context of Habakkuk 2 is very clear that the word is referring to judgment on the nations. After the appearance of the five woes in chapter 2 (verses 6, 9, 12, 15, 19), the command is given to the nations to be quiet in order to receive God's judgment. *Strong's Concordance*, s.v. "H2013," accessed January 24, 2019, https://www.blueletterbible.org/lang/lexicon/lexicon.cfm?Strongs=H2013&t=KJV.

8. Note that Psalm 46:10 uses the word רָפָה (*raphah*), which deals with relaxing or letting go; therefore, "be still" is not about audible sounds but a state of mind. Psalm 131:2 contains the word דָּמַם (*damam*) for "quieted myself," which can mean silence. But based on the verse's context of a weaned child, it deals with quieting one's mind to remove anxiety by putting hope in the Lord (see verse 3). *Strong's Concordance*, s.vv. "H7503," "H1826," accessed January 24, 2019, https://www.blueletterbible.org/lang/lexicon/lexicon.cfm?Strongs=H7503&t=KJV; https://www.blueletterbible

.org/lang/lexicon/lexicon.cfm?Strongs=H1826&t=KJV.

9. Some examples are Psalms 8:2; 39:9; 50:3, 21; 63:11; 107:42. (Psalms 28:1; 35:22; 83:1; and 109:1 deal with humanity's desire for God not to be silent.)

10. Ellen G. White, *Testimonies for the Church*, vol. 5 (Mountain View, CA: Pacific Press®, 1889), 492, 493.

11. For both the Hebrew and Greek, it is the context that determines the meaning. In the Old Testament, the Hebrew word אָרֵי and its derivatives are usually translated as "fear," with connotations of being afraid, respectful, or in awe. *Strong's Concordance*, s.v. "H3372," accessed January 24, 2019, https://www.blueletterbible.org/lang/lexicon/lexicon.cfm?Strongs=H3372&t=KJV.

In the New Testament and the Septuagint, the Greek word φόβος and its derivatives mean "terror, fear, alarm, fright, reverence, respect, awe." W. Mundle, "Fear, Awe," in *The New International Dictionary of New Testament Theology*, vol. 1, ed. Colin Brown (Grand Rapids, MI: Regency Reference Library, 1975), 621.

12. Mundle, "Fear, Awe," 623.

13. *Merriam-Webster* defines *reverence* as "honor or respect felt or shown." *Merriam-Webster*, s.v. "reverence," accessed January 24, 2019, http://www.merriam-webster.com/dictionary/reverence.

14. Craig Bowman, "More Than Routine Words: A Reflection on Psalm 100," *Christian Studies* 20 (Fall 2004): 32, http://austingrad.edu/Christian Studies/CS 20/20.pdf.

15. James L. Mays, *The Lord Reigns: A Theological Handbook to the Psalms* (Louisville, KY: Westminster John Knox Press, 1994), 82; emphasis in the original.

16. See *Strong's Concordance*, s.v. "H2617," accessed January 24, 2019, https://www.blueletterbible.org/lang/lexicon/lexicon.cfm?Strongs=H2617&t=KJV. The importance of this word can be seen in the fact that it is the word God uses to describe Himself in Exodus 20:6.

17. Charles H. Spurgeon, "Psalm 95," in *The Treasury of David*, vol. 4 (London: Passmore and Alabaster, 1874), 320; exposition of verse 7; emphasis in the original.

CHAPTER 6

FAMILY WORSHIP
Praising God Together

Love the Lord *your God with all your heart and with all your soul and with all your strength. These commandments that I give you today are to be on your hearts. Impress them on your children. Talk about them when you sit at home and when you walk along the road, when you lie down and when you get up.*
—Deuteronomy 6:5–7

Family worship is the regular, intentional gathering of a family unit to worship God by reading Scripture, praying, singing praise, and finding ways to be involved in ministry and evangelism together.[1] There are four major components to every family worship: (1) reading, (2) praying, (3) singing, and (4) pursuing mission (see Acts 2:42–47). Every Christian family should have such time daily.

Although George Barna's research shows that 85 percent of parents "believe they have the primary responsibility for the moral and spiritual development of their children," among churched families, fewer than 10 percent "read the Bible together, pray together (other than at mealtimes) or participate in an act of service as a family unit" in a typical week. One out of twenty have a family worship experience outside of church in a typical month.[2] Among active Seventh-day Adventist members, 39 percent of families never have worship at home; 28 percent have worship on a daily basis; and 33 percent have family worship once a week.[3]

Gather the whole family at least one time this week and have family worship. If this is new for the family, keep it very simple. Sit in a circle, read a few Bible verses (for instance, Luke 19:1–10), lead in a short prayer, and sing a simple song (such as "Jesus Loves Me").

Worship of the Lord is first vertical, connecting with God through prayer, worship, and Bible study, and then horizontal, connecting with people through ministry and evangelism, beginning in the home and involving the whole family (Matthew 22:37–39).

In this chapter, I will provide the purpose of family worship and some practical suggestions and methods for family worship. These ideas and examples are gleaned from interviews conducted with twenty-one families regarding the best way to have family worship.[4]

WHAT IS THE PURPOSE OF FAMILY WORSHIP?

There are many reasons for family worship. In this section, we will examine the seven major ones.

The first purpose is to worship God together and learn more of His ways. Children should learn to worship God in their early years, so that they might have respect for Him in their later years. They need to learn how to regard Him and to realize that He is the Creator, the Lord and Savior, who is holy and to be honored in all they say and do. "Bring them up in the training and instruction of the Lord," writes Paul (Ephesians 6:4). The worship of God is beneficial for all ages. It brings the family closer to one another and to God.

The second reason to institute family worship is to honor God's Word, develop respect for it, and live by it. James says, "Do not merely listen to the word, and so deceive yourselves. Do what it says" (James 1:22). Furthermore, Jesus said, "It is written: 'Man shall not live on bread alone, but on every word that comes from the mouth of God' " (Matthew 4:4). Finally, the home is a good place to practice this exhortation: "Let the word of Christ dwell in you richly in all wisdom; teaching and admonishing one another in psalms and hymns and spiritual songs, singing with grace in your hearts to the Lord" (Colossians 3:16, KJV). We need to honor the Bible in our homes and teach our children from it.

The third purpose of family worship is to assist in the faith development of children. George Barna gives the probability of someone accepting Christ as Savior as follows: 32 percent for ages 5–13; 4 percent for ages 14–18; 6 percent for ages 19 and older.[5] This makes it imperative that families do everything they can to be intentionally active in the religious upbringing of their children. Barna also notes that only one-third of white and Hispanic and two-fifths of black teens surveyed expected to stay in the church once they were living on their own.[6] Research shows that children whose families are active in their faith development have a higher probability of staying in the church.[7] It is the desire of parents to raise Christian children who will grow up with a commitment to Christ, good moral standards, and be witnesses for Christ in the community and who not only take the church seriously but enjoy being part of it. Paul acknowledges the value of knowing the Scriptures and living by them from a young age when he addresses Timothy: "But as for you, continue in what you have learned and have become convinced of, because you know those from whom you learned it, and how from infancy you have known the Holy Scriptures, which are able to make you wise for salvation through faith in Christ Jesus" (2 Timothy 3:14, 15).

Family worship's fourth objective is to establish the family in faith, personal convictions, and doctrine. Children, young people, and adults need convictions to stand up against their peers. They must understand their faith and know that it is Bible based. It is important for them to comprehend what they believe and why. The home makes a good Bible school where children can be grounded as they face the humanistic, evolutionary philosophy of modern society.

The fifth reason for having family worship is to pray over problems, needs, and burdens the children may have so that they may have confidence in the God that answers prayers. All family members have personal needs. It would be beneficial if each family member could learn to share them openly and take them before the Lord together. For example, there are school needs, relationship problems, character issues (such as timidity and fears of all kinds), and questions about entertainment (such as television viewing habits and many other areas). Teenagers have deep needs and hate to express them for fear of being misunderstood or embarrassed. Their problems are big to them and must be considered. Parents can model taking their needs to God in prayer. All family members need to know that God will hear and answer them, thus building confidence in Him. Children who learn to pray openly at home will have no problem praying publicly in the church or weekly prayer meetings as they grow.

Family worship's sixth purpose is to pray and intercede for others with regard to their needs or trials. Praying for the spiritual and physical needs of others helps to shift the focus away from self. It also provides an opportunity for the Lord to open the hearts and minds of those praying to be more compassionate. This will result in an increased desire for ministry, mission, and evangelism.

The seventh purpose of family worship is to find relevant and meaningful ways to minister in the home, in the church, and in the world. When a family takes on a project together, it brings the family closer and allows God to use family members to bless the world. Here are some examples of ways families can minister: adopting a less fortunate family to pray over and help out during the holidays, hosting a small group, singing and fellowshiping at nursing homes, helping out at a food pantry, sharing food with the homeless, giving Bible studies, and visiting others as a family.

HOW DO YOU CREATE AN EFFECTIVE FAMILY WORSHIP ENVIRONMENT?

If you are like many parents, you are wondering how you can best create a worship environment in your home that is conducive to the spiritual maturation of your children (as well as your own spiritual well-being). The following details how to provide such an environment.

Pay attention to your own spirituality. One of the most important factors in creating an effective environment for family worship is your own spirituality. If worship is a priority for you, your children will make it their priority as well. Kids pick up on what is really important to parents.

Effective family worship begins by making Jesus a priority in your life. Paul said, "Follow my example, as I follow the example of Christ" (1 Corinthians 11:1). Your family sees what is important to you. If you have a strong relationship with Christ and live His love, others will want to emulate you.

Make family worship practical and relevant. Show the relevance of Scripture to life. Show how you live in the light of the Word of God, how you develop biblical values and a biblical worldview, and how you gain wisdom from Scripture. Show your family how to make decisions that honor God, how to resist temptation, and how to live the Christian life. This is where real change takes place.

Search out methods that will appeal to all age levels. Different ages have different interests. What may appeal to one will not appeal to another. Vary the methods so as to keep family worship from becoming boring and routine. Cultivate children's interest so monotony does not kill it.

Make it interesting. Have a delightful, happy, and intriguing time, filled with enthusiasm so that the whole family looks forward to it. Do not make it a time of forced listening to the Bible or of bitter participation while you drone through whole chapters of the Bible beyond family comprehension. Don't drag the family through a long, dry, routine prayer. If they participate in bitterness, they will abhor family worship. "Fathers and mothers, make the hour of worship intensely interesting. There is no reason why this hour should not be the most pleasant and enjoyable of the day. A little thought given to preparation for it will enable you to make it full of interest and profit. From time to time let the service be varied."[8]

Make it short. Ellen White gives very helpful advice about family worship. She encourages the family to make it short and interesting: "The father, or, in his absence, the mother, should conduct the worship, selecting a portion of Scripture that is interesting and easily understood. The service should be short. When a long chapter is read and a long prayer offered, the service is made wearisome, and at its close a sense of relief is felt. God is dishonored when the hour of worship is made dry and irksome, when it is so tedious, so lacking in interest, that the children dread it."[9]

Do not make worship so long that the children despise the time it takes. It is better to have it short and sweet, vital and satisfying, so their appetites hunger for more. Always finish before they want you to. A good general rule is ten to fifteen minutes.

Let all participate and become involved. Those that can read should take turns reading as well as praying. Even the little ones who cannot read yet can say a few words in prayer. Teach your children songs in which all take part. Take time for discussion and self-expression as well as answering questions and solving problems. Children, especially, are inquisitive and want to know. Every idea needs to be respected and needs attention.

Do not spend time criticizing or gossiping. There is nothing that will sour the family worship environment more than tearing something or someone apart.

This is not time to air church problems except in sincere prayer. Remember, it is worship time.

Let the older children lead out in family worship in whole or in part. Let older kids do it their way and express themselves. It will create interest in worship for them. This is also a good way to develop them spiritually and their self-confidence. They should be encouraged in what they do or say and not belittled.

Have family worship when it is most convenient for all. Suppertime is usually the best time for family worship, before the various activities of the evening begin. Ellen White encourages us to have daily family worship, once in the morning and once in the evening. White notes, "In every family there should be a fixed time for morning and evening worship. How appropriate it is for parents to gather their children about them before the fast is broken, to thank the heavenly Father for His protection during the night, and to ask Him for His help and guidance and watchcare during the day! How fitting, also, when evening comes, for parents and children to gather once more before Him and thank Him for the blessings of the day that is past!"[10]

PRACTICAL EXAMPLES AND METHODS FOR INSPIRING FAMILY WORSHIP

The following are ideas for family worship. Discuss these suggestions with your family and implement the ones that best fit your situation.

Read small sections of the Bible. Rather than reading a whole chapter of the Bible at a time (a whole chapter may be quite long and hard to retain), study just one paragraph or story a day. Let all the family members suggest a title for the paragraph according to its content. Let each one list some things he or she observes in the paragraph, such as places, people, things, special words, meanings, applications, insights, and so on. This can be great fun for children and a real challenge for all. It is like observing things in a room or on an automobile ride. When you have gone through the paragraph in this way, then investigate the spiritual lessons that may be learned. Let each family member make it personal and tell what he or she has learned.

Study the miracles of Christ. Read about one miracle a night, and learn something about Christ from each miracle (especially let each family member learn something). Study the miracle to ascertain where it happened, the occasion, what happened, and who was involved and then discuss its lessons and applications.

Get to know Bible characters. Getting to know Bible characters is a good way to lend variety to worship. Read about the character in the Bible, and study his or her weaknesses and strengths. Discuss how you may learn something from the individual. See yourself in Bible characters, and learn many practical lessons.

Learn Bible doctrine. Everyone should know the basic doctrines of the Bible. All family members should be grounded in the truth. You can find the doctrines by means of a good concordance or from a book on basic doctrines of the Bible.

Study a particular book of the Bible. Select a book of the Bible that is appropriate for your children's ages, and have each family member read two or three verses as you go around the room. You can read anywhere from one to two chapters to an entire book, such as Ruth or Philippians, each night. Let the children help choose what book of the Bible to read. Older children can discover the book's theme, major divisions, lessons, key chapters, and ideas.

Study "great chapters" of the Bible. "Great chapters" include Genesis 1, Exodus

WORSHIP IDEAS FOR DIFFERENT FAMILIES

While the traditional family worship model aims to provide something for a typical nuclear family with parents and kids, it's important to address other family units within the church. Singles; single seniors; dating couples; and married couples without children or with grown, out-of-the-house children can benefit from creative worship ideas, strengthening their personal relationships with God in ways that work with their respective situations.

Singles (young adults, divorced persons, widows and widowers, unmarried seniors)
- If you are a younger single person, study 1 Timothy 4:12, and journal what this verse is saying to a contemporary young person. Read one chapter from Proverbs, and journal your thoughts on Solomon's message to young people. Do this with other chapters or verses that are meaningful to you.
- Regardless of your age, study the 28 fundamental beliefs (especially the ones dealing with key doctrines, such as the Sabbath, baptism, the Second Coming, and the state of the dead).
- Make a new elderly friend in a nursing home, and worship the Lord with them during a visit.
- If other family members live close by, stop in to worship with them. If they are far away, make use of Skype or FaceTime to worship together remotely.
- Find a prayer partner, and work through the Bible or another spiritual book together.
- Read books on personal devotions, and share your thoughts with friends and relatives.
- Read about the Holy Spirit for a few weeks, and pray for change in whatever areas of life you may need a little help in.

Married couples without children or dating couples
- Read through a devotional book or chapters of the Bible together, discussing ideas along the way.
- Write a letter to God, and share it with your spouse or significant other.
- Write appreciation notes to each other, and read what the Bible has to say about love.
- Pick a day of the week to specifically pray for grown children or other family members and friends.
- Use the Bible to study the character of Christ. This will take some time, but as you discover what Christ is really like, pray for the Holy Spirit to help you emulate these same characteristics.

20, Deuteronomy 6, Psalm 23, Isaiah 53, Matthew 24, John 3, Romans 8, 1 Corinthians 13, Hebrews 11, and Revelation 22. Families can go through a book of the Bible chapter by chapter. Families can read a chapter a day if the children are old enough to comprehend it. Learn the key verse in the chapter, get the key word, and break the chapter down into its paragraph parts to find the structure of the chapter. Study special promises, examine how Christ is seen, look at important doctrines in the chapter, and study what sins should be avoided, what things a person should do, and what lessons can be learned.

Read major verses. Major verses include Joshua 1:9; Psalm 46:1; Proverbs 3:5, 6; Isaiah 41:10; Jeremiah 29:11; Matthew 11:28; 28:18–20; John 3:16; Romans 8:28; Galatians 5:22, 23; Philippians 4:13; 2 Timothy 1:7; and Hebrews 12:1, 2. Studying major verses adds variety to family worship. Take one verse a night for a period of time and scrutinize what it means for each individual. For example, families might examine a series of verses on great promises in the Bible, such as prayer, salvation, victorious living, or Christ's second coming. Try to memorize the verses.

Implement a scripture-memorization program. Even a three- or four-year-old can learn ten verses if the right ones are selected, and by the time a child is five years old, he or she can learn Psalm 23. Try it, make it fun, and you will be amazed at what your family can accomplish![11]

Read devotional books for appropriate age levels. Age-appropriate devotional books are available in most bookstores, including Adventist Book Centers. Children enjoy these and find them very interesting. Discernment needs to be used in selecting titles. Think about a book's relevance to every age group.

Play Bible games. Bible games can be quite engaging and add a challenge to family worship. They can appeal to youth and keep family worship from feeling boring. Use Bible games that teach a lesson and from which the family may learn something helpful for Christian living.

Study maps. The understanding of salvation can be enhanced by an awareness of biblical geography. Children might enjoy learning where certain countries, rivers, and mountains are as well as what happened there, such as the giving of the law on Mount Sinai, the Israelites crossing the Red Sea, and Christ walking on the water. Show them where these things took place, and draw some lessons from it.

Use pictures or videos. Visuals are a wonderful way to interest children. Many Bible storybooks have lots of pictures, making the Bible come alive. Use videos that cover Bible events, such as the Exodus or the life of Jesus; use nature videos to show the greatness of God; or use videos of great heroes of faith, such as Martin Luther, John Huss, and others.

Use object lessons. Visual aids of all kinds can be useful in family worship. Be creative, and use whatever object you have handy to teach a Bible truth. Christ readily used everyday objects, such as sheep and goats, rocks, water in the well of Samaria, and others, as object lessons. There is no end to object lessons.

TALKING WITH ELLEN G. WHITE

If we were to interview Ellen White, what would she say about family worship?

Family worship seems like a good idea but is hard to do. What would you suggest?
"By a little thought and careful preparation for this season, when we come into the presence of God, family worship can be made pleasant and will be fraught with results that eternity alone will reveal. Let the father [or mother or children] select a portion of Scripture that is interesting and easily understood; a few verses will be sufficient to furnish a lesson which may be studied and practiced through the day. Questions may be asked, a few earnest, interesting remarks made, or incident, short and to the point, may be brought in by way of illustration. At least a few verses of spirited song may be sung, and the prayer offered should be short and pointed. The one who leads in prayer should not pray about everything, but should express his needs in simple words and praise God with thanksgiving."[13]

"As circumstances permit, let the children join in the reading and the prayer."[14]

"The hour of family worship should be made the happiest hour of the day."[15]

"Let the seasons of family worship be short and spirited. Do not let your children or any member of your family dread them because of their tediousness or lack of interest. When a long chapter is read and explained and a long prayer offered, this precious service becomes wearisome, and it is a relief when it is over."[16]

Family worship sounds like a really good idea for children. What about parents?
"How appropriate it is for parents to gather their children about them . . . to thank the heavenly Father for His protection during the night, and to ask Him for His help and guidance and watchcare during the day! How fitting, also, when evening comes, for parents and children to gather once more before Him and thank Him for the blessings of the day that is past!"[17]

"Each morning consecrate yourselves and your children to God for that day. Make no calculation for months or years; these are not yours. One brief day is given you. As if it were your last on earth, work during its hours for the Master. Lay all your plans before God, to be carried out or given up, as His providence shall indicate."[18]

Any advice for those families with no children? What are your personal devotions like?
"I never choose to begin a day without receiving special evidence that the Lord Jesus is my Helper, and that I have the rich grace that it is my privilege to receive.

"In my morning devotions I have regarded it my privilege to close my petition with the prayer that Christ taught to His disciples. There is so much that I really must have to meet the needs of my own case that I sometimes fear that I shall ask amiss; but when in sincerity I offer the model prayer that Christ gave to His disciples I cannot but feel that in these few words all my needs are comprehended. This I offer after I have presented my special private prayer. If with heart and mind and soul I repeat the Lord's prayer, then I can go forth in peace to my work."[19]

Read or listen to short biographies of godly servants of Jesus. We can learn from those who have gone before us. Missionaries, evangelists, and pastors are a few examples.

Sing. Families should always sing if possible. Have a songbook for each family member, or project the song on a wall. Parents can also use websites, such as YouTube and GodVine, to find songs to sing along with. Learn great hymns of faith. You can also teach from the songs, as there are stories behind the hymns. There are many books that tell the history and meaning of songs. Some great songs are also found in the Bible (see Ephesians 5:19).

Listen to sermons. Listen to the sermons of famous preachers, evangelists, and teachers on CD or via the internet. Parents can even find sermons for children online. The Lord can use His preached Word in the lives of each family member.

Join or create small groups. A small group can discuss the Bible story under consideration, then come up with practical ideas of how it applies to life today. The main idea is to learn about God, the gospel, and godly living.

CONCLUSION

Be intentional about family worship on a consistent basis. Anything you do is better than nothing. Make it interesting, practical, Christ-centered, relevant, and participatory for all.

There will be some common challenges to family worship (e.g., when there are different ages of children in the home; when children are very young; when one parent is less committed; when parents don't feel competent to teach the Bible; and when children are resistant or opposed to family worship). But the more you show your love and commitment to Jesus and the more you live the ideals of the Christian life, the more the children will be interested. There is no substitute for you and your life making the greatest impression on your children.

Finally, pray for your children and family. Leave them in the hands of God, and He will take care of them. "By sincere, earnest prayer parents should make a hedge about their children. They should pray with full faith that God will abide with them and that holy angels will guard them and their children from Satan's cruel power."[12] One man told me that he prayed and fasted for his children and grandchildren every day and claimed them for Jesus. Today all of them are walking with the Lord. "The prayer of a righteous person is powerful and effective" (James 5:16).

---

1. This chapter is adapted from S. Joseph Kidder, "Creating Exciting Family Worship," in *Revival and Reformation: Building Family Memories*, eds. Elaine Oliver and Willie Oliver (Silver Spring, MD: Adventist Family Ministries, 2015), 62–67, https://family.adventist.org/wp-content/uploads/2017/10/FM_Planbook-2015.pdf.

2. George Barna, *Transforming Children Into Spiritual Champions: Why Children Should Be Your Church's #1 Priority* (Ventura, CA: Regal, 2003), 77, 78.

3. S. Joseph Kidder, *The Big Four: Secrets to a Thriving Church Family* (Hagerstown, MD: Review and Herald®, 2011), 128.

4. Seven pastors' families, seven teachers' families, and seven lay members' families.

5. George Barna, *Grow Your Church From the Outside In: Understanding the Unchurched and How to Reach Them*, rev. ed. (Ventura, CA: Regal Books, 2002), 45.

6. George Barna, *Real Teens: A Contemporary Snapshot of Youth Culture* (Ventura, CA: Regal Books, 2001), 113.

7. Jerry W. Lee, Gail T. Rice, and V. Bailey Gillespie, "Family Worship Patterns and Their Correlation With Adolescent Behavior and Beliefs," *Journal for the Scientific Study of Religion* 36, no. 3 (September 1997): 372–381, http://dx.doi.org/10.2307/1387855.

8. Ellen G. White, *Prayer* (Nampa, ID: Pacific Press®, 2002), 202.

9. Ellen G. White, *Testimonies for the Church*, vol. 7 (Nampa, ID: Pacific Press®, 1948), 43.

10. White, *Testimonies for the Church*, 7:43.

11. If you would like more information on how to implement a scripture-memorization program for your family, visit https://www.wholesomewords.org/family/kjvmem.html.

12. White, *Testimonies for the Church*, 7:42, 43.

13. Ellen G. White, *Child Guidance* (Washington, DC: Review and Herald®, 1954), 521, 522.

14. White, *Testimonies for the Church*, 7:43.

15. Ellen G. White, *Christian Service* (Washington, DC: Review and Herald®, 1925), 210.

16. Ellen G. White, *Last Day Events* (Nampa, ID: Pacific Press®, 1992), 84.

17. White, *Testimonies for the Church*, 7:43.

18. White, *Testimonies for the Church*, 7:44.

19. Ellen G. White, *That I May Know Him* (Washington, DC: Review and Herald®, 1964), 261.

PART 3

Journey to the
Heart of God
Through Prayer

CHAPTER 7

THE PRIVILEGE OF PRAYER
Knowing God

"When you pray, say: 'Father, hallowed be your name, your kingdom come. Give us each day our daily bread. Forgive us our sins, for we also forgive everyone who sins against us. And lead us not into temptation.'"
—Luke 11:2–4

Even though we know we should pray constantly, many—if not most—of us would confess we don't pray as often as we should. Could the reason we don't pray more be that we've misunderstood the purpose of prayer?

I want to challenge you to look at your motivation in praying. Almost everyone prays when they are desperate. We sometimes hear the phrase *foxhole prayer*, which, of course, comes from the idea that when we are pinned down in a foxhole, with bullets flying around us, almost all of us are inclined to pray. In other words, we all get to some point where we realize we cannot accomplish something without divine intervention, so we go to God in prayer.

However, the purpose of prayer is not only to depend constantly on God but also to know Him, enjoy Him, build a friendship with Him, and desire Him. Prayer becomes meaningful when we fall in love with God and our souls become united with His. "Unceasing prayer is the unbroken union of the soul with God, so that life from God flows into our life; and from our life, purity and holiness flow back to God."[1]

In the following sections, I want to propose three reasons for meaningful prayer.

WE PRAY TO SEEK TO ESTABLISH A DEEPER RELATIONSHIP WITH GOD
"Jesus responds to the disciples' request to teach them how to pray by starting with how to address God. We begin by saying, 'Father' (Luke 11:2). . . . Prayer begins with a relationship with God, and the primary purpose of prayer is to deepen that relationship."[2] It is when we forget the primary purpose of prayer that we stop praying except in case of emergency.

Most of us grow up viewing prayer as asking for things. We learn to pray by saying, "God, help me with this. God, give me this. God, bless me with this. God, protect me." Or we pray for others, and so we pray the same thing: "God, help them. God, protect them. God, bless them. God, keep them and be with them."

I am sure that many of us could tell about a time when we prayed hard for something and we did not get the answer we wanted. It may have been a prayer for someone to be healed. It may have been a prayer to get a job or to have a baby or to have a relationship restored. But no matter how hard we prayed, the answer did not come. We began to wonder, *Am I asking in the wrong way? Is there some code or combination of words I'm not using?*

"The purpose of prayer is knowing God, not just getting answers."[3] Prayer is intended to be much more than asking for what we want and bringing our needs before God. Prayer is not just asking for Him to bless, protect, or help us. There is a depth of prayer that goes beyond that.

Meaningful praying is when we move from needing God to bless us to wanting a relationship with Him. It is when we long to be with God, whether we ask for anything or not, that praying becomes a deep desire of our hearts and not just something we know we should do.

In the Sermon on the Mount, Jesus tells us that God knows what we need before we even ask. Now some of us ask, "If He already knows everything, what is the point of praying?" In asking this question, we are on the verge of breaking through into what prayer is really all about.

God does not tell us to bring all our needs to Him so that we can inform Him of everything. He already knows. God designed prayer for intimacy that supersedes what we want and what we need. The reason He told us to "go into your room, close the door and pray to your Father, who is unseen" (Matthew 6:6) is that there is a closeness God intends to take place in this thing called prayer that we will miss if we make it all about our lists.

We are not desperate for something; instead, we are desperate for Someone. This is the heart of prayer. Ultimately, God designed prayer for us to enjoy Him and to experience His goodness, grace, and mercy personally—in a way that nothing in the world can even begin to compare with.

The priority of prayer is time, not talk. The most important thing in the world is not our job, finances, football team, family, spouse, or even kids. The most important thing in the world is our personal, intimate relationship with Jesus. It is the most important thing in the world because everything in our lives flows from this one thing.

The Lord's Prayer shows us why Jesus was constantly taking time to be with the Father. There was an intimacy that happened when He was alone with the Father in prayer that would affect every single thing He did. Jesus teaches us that in order to develop that kind of intimacy, we need to set a specific time to be alone with the Father.

At this point, I know the first thing that many of us think is, *Well, I pray all the time, and I pray without ceasing. It says that somewhere in the Bible, doesn't it? So that's what I do. I pray when I'm shaving and driving to work. I pray when I'm cooking and washing dishes. I pray when I'm doing this or that. That's when I pray. I pray all the time. I don't need to set aside a dedicated time.*

Well, that sounds good, but what if you tried that in your marriage? My wife and I are together all the time. We talk all the time as we are running here and there. We are always talking. But there's something about intimacy that just does not happen when you're constantly going here, there, and everywhere. That's why we see Jesus setting aside a specific time to be alone with the Father.

God has designed us to experience unique and fulfilling closeness with Him as we pray. I encourage you to pray everywhere and pray all the time but also to set aside a time to "go into your room, close the door and pray to your Father, who is unseen" (Matthew 6:6). This one practice will revolutionize your life—not just your prayer life but your *whole* life—if you make it your singular goal. It will revolutionize your life because there is a reward that is waiting from your Father in that time that cannot be found anywhere else: to actually know God, not just know about Him. We pray to know God better. Prayer fulfills the command of Jesus: "Love the Lord your God with all your heart and with all your soul and with all your mind" (Matthew 22:37).

Prayer is about establishing a love relationship with God. "Prayer will be no task to the soul that loves God; it will be a pleasure, a source of strength. Our hearts will be stayed upon God, and we shall say by our daily life, 'Behold the Lamb of God, which taketh away the sin of the world.' "[4]

WE PRAY TO SHOW WE ALWAYS NEED GOD

If we look at what the Bible says about prayer, it will reveal that prayer is about recognizing—every moment of every day—that we are completely dependent on God. If Jesus is our model and our mentor in prayer, we should learn from His example how to depend on God.

According to God's Word, our entire lives are intended to be lived with the attitude that unless God intervenes, we cannot do anything. We are to acknowledge our absolute dependence on God—not just in case of emergency but in every moment. Every single thing we do, as followers of Jesus Christ, is not possible without divine intervention.

Jesus prayed in total dependence on God. Immediately after He was baptized, He prayed (Luke 3:21). His ministry began with a face-to-face battle with the devil that involved Jesus praying and fasting (Luke 4:1, 2). Luke tells us about His source of strength: "Jesus often withdrew to lonely places and prayed" (Luke 5:16).

Before Jesus called the twelve disciples, He prayed: "One of those days Jesus

The Privilege of Prayer: Knowing God

went out to a mountainside to pray, and spent the night praying to God" (Luke 6:12).

At the Transfiguration, Jesus' purpose of being alone with Peter, John, and James was prayer: "He took Peter, John and James with him and went up onto a mountain to pray" (Luke 9:28).

Jesus also taught the disciples about persistence in prayer: "Then Jesus told his disciples a parable to show them that they should always pray and not give up" (Luke 18:1).

Finally, one of the most well-known instances of Jesus praying is when He went to Gethsemane right before His arrest and crucifixion (Luke 22:39–42).

" *'Why was Jesus always praying?'* or maybe a deeper question, when you look at Jesus' life and ministry in the Gospels [is this]: 'What did he do on his own, apart from prayer?' NOTHING."[5] There's not one thing Jesus did on His own. He lived His life in dependence on the Father.

Christ said, "The Son can do nothing by himself; he can do only what he sees his Father doing" and "by myself I can do nothing" (John 5:19, 30). These statements prompt this question: If Jesus, God in the flesh, could say, "I can do nothing by myself," then who are we to think there is anything in our Christian lives that we can do on our own? There is nothing we can do apart from total dependence on God.

The life-giving power of prayer is "why the disciples came to Jesus and asked him to teach them to pray. It's not that they had never been taught to pray"; they knew how to pray in the synagogue and on the Sabbath, and they knew how to pray in various circumstances and how to follow religious rituals. "But they saw in Jesus something very different. They saw in his life something more than just a religious ritual. Prayer was something that literally nourished Jesus."[6] It was a necessity for Him, and His life was dependent on it. The disciples saw the difference, and they said, "Lord, teach us to pray—like *You're* praying" (see Luke 11:1).

The early church prayed in complete reliance on God. It wasn't just Jesus who emphasized praying all the time; the early church followed His example (Acts 1:14). When the apostles were persecuted by the Sanhedrin, they did not get together and complain about how hard it was to be a Christian. They *prayed* (Acts 4:24). Later in Acts 4, we see the power of praying with absolute dependence on God. The believers' prayers caused them to be filled with the Holy Spirit, and they spoke the Word with boldness (verse 31).

When Peter was imprisoned, what was the church's response? Prayer (Acts 12:5). When the church at Antioch wanted to make the gospel known in all nations, how did they start? By praying (Acts 13:2, 3). When the new churches needed leaders, what did they do? "Paul and Barnabas appointed elders for them in each church and, with prayer and fasting, committed them to the Lord, in whom they had put their trust" (Acts 14:23).

In Acts, the fundamental conviction of the church was that the believers could do nothing without God—so they prayed. That is why *we* must pray, because we are dependent on God and we can do nothing without Him. The early church knew this. They did not just pray before meetings or after meetings. Prayer was the very purpose of their meeting together!

In our lives, is prayer essential or optional? Some of us might think, *I don't need to learn to pray. Prayer is just talking to God.* We need to learn to pray because if we can do nothing without God, that means we cannot pray without Him, which is why the disciples came to Jesus. We don't see them asking Jesus to teach them to witness or teach or even heal. All we see them saying is, "Teach us to pray," because prayer is the stabilizing force on which our Christianity is dependent. We pray to show we always need God.

WE PRAY TO SURRENDER TO GOD'S PLAN

In talking about prayer, it is easy to focus on the *have to* and the *need to*, but there is also a *get to* aspect of prayer. That is to say, God has designed prayer as the means for us to be involved in what He is doing in the world.

The power of prayer is in our relationship with God. All of my life, I have heard phrases such as "prayer changes things" or "there's power in prayer." In order for prayer to have power, we must connect with the God of the universe.

In our prayers, we connect with the Living God who is the Lord and Creator of the universe and who has infinite and unstoppable power. Prayer in and of itself is powerless. But when prayer is a means by which we connect in a vital relationship with God, we will see incredible power. God is the one who has all power—not us in our praying. The way we connect with that power is through surrender.

By *surrender*, I mean that our attitude reflects that of Jesus in Gethsemane. We pour out our hearts and ask God for what we want, but ultimately we say, "Yet not my will, but yours be done" (Luke 22:42). That is surrender, and it grows out of a relationship of absolute trust. As we recognize our desperate need for God, and as we seek to know Him better and better, we will grow to understand that His plan is always best, and we will grow to the point of surrender to His will in all things. That is where life gets exciting because that is where God begins to use us.

CONCLUSION

In his book *Prayer*, Timothy Keller shares that after September 11, 2001, he and his wife were both experiencing serious illnesses in addition to the shock of the terrorist attacks. His wife, Kathy, came to him with a request, saying:

> Imagine you were diagnosed with such a lethal condition that the doctor told you that you would die within hours unless you took a particular medicine—a pill every night before going to sleep. Imagine that you

were told that you could never miss it or you would die. Would you forget? Would you not get around to it some nights? No—it would be so crucial that you wouldn't forget, you would never miss. Well, if we don't pray together to God, we're not going to make it because of all we are facing. I'm certainly not. We *have* to pray, we can't let it just slip our minds.[7]

Prayer is a necessary gift that God has given to us because He loves us. "God is interested in your prayers because He is interested in you. Whatever matters to you is a priority for His attention. Nothing in the universe matters as much to Him as what is going on in your life today."[8]

As we pray our hearts will be united, our relationships will be strengthened, and blessings will overflow. As Ellen White wrote, "It is prayer that unites hearts. It is prayer to the Great Physician to heal the soul that will bring the blessing of God. Prayer unites us with one another and with God. Prayer brings Jesus to our side, and gives new strength and fresh grace to the fainting, perplexed soul to overcome the world, the flesh, and the devil. Prayer turns aside the attacks of Satan."[9]

---

1. Ellen G. White, *Steps to Christ* (Nampa, ID: Pacific Press®, 2000), 98.
2. Elements City Church, "Why It Matters—Week 6: Why Prayer Matters," Bible.com, accessed January 28, 2019, https://www.bible.com/events/277216#!.
3. Elements City Church, "Why It Matters."
4. Ellen G. White, *Gospel Workers* (Battle Creek, MI: Review and Herald®, 1892), 437.
5. Elements City Church, "Why It Matters"; emphasis in the original.
6. Elements City Church, "Why It Matters."
7. Timothy Keller, *Prayer: Experiencing Awe and Intimacy With God* (New York: Penguin Books, 2014), 9, 10; emphasis in the original.
8. S. Joseph Kidder, *Out of Babylon: How God Found Me on the Streets of Baghdad* (Nampa, ID: Pacific Press®, 2018), 83.
9. Ellen G. White, *Our High Calling* (Hagerstown, MD: Review and Herald®, 2000), 177.

CHAPTER 8

PRAYER

Releasing the Power of the God of the Impossible

"Truly I tell you, if you have faith as small as a mustard seed, you can say to this mountain, 'Move from here to there,' and it will move. Nothing will be impossible for you."

—Matthew 17:20

A few years ago, I led a training session for a group of pastors visiting India. During our time together, we spent one afternoon sight-seeing along the Bay of Bengal. Our bus stopped in one of the cities, and as soon as we stepped foot outside, we were surrounded by children. Their outstretched hands were seeking any gifts we were willing to give. In the midst of the crowd, I saw a beautiful little girl, who was about ten years old. She reminded me of my own daughter, and I couldn't help but feel a tug on my heart.

I approached her and reached into my pocket. Her eyes grew wide as she watched me pull out my wallet. Inside was a single rupee and a twenty-dollar bill. Twenty dollars would have easily been a few days' worth of wages—maybe even several weeks' worth! Removing the twenty-dollar bill, I handed it to her, but she didn't take it. Instead she pointed to the single rupee coin, which she could see in my other hand. I shook my head, trying to tell her that the twenty-dollar bill was the much better gift. But she just shook her head and pointed more insistently at the coin.

Like this child, how often do we plead for the single-rupee blessing, even as God is extending a better gift? We may think He is holding out on us, but what if there are greater blessings He offers? What if they just look different than those we're expecting? We may believe God only has the power to give us the rupee, when in fact, He has all the power in the world to give us anything we want. We may even doubt He can answer our prayers at all! But Jesus has promised that whatever we ask according to His name, big or small, He will supply: "And I will do whatever you ask in my name, so that the Father may be glorified in the Son" (John 14:13; see also John 15:16; 16:23). Whatever your request or need might be, do you daily bring it to God in earnest prayer, believing He will intervene and make all things work together for good?

In *Testimonies for the Church*, Ellen White highlights the value of prayer:

> There are few who rightly appreciate or improve the precious privilege of prayer. We should go to Jesus and tell Him all our needs. We may bring Him our little cares and perplexities as well as our greater troubles. Whatever arises to disturb or distress us, we should take it to the Lord in prayer. When we feel that we need the presence of Christ at every step, Satan will have little opportunity to intrude his temptations. It is his studied effort to keep us away from our best and most sympathizing friend. We should make no one our confidant but Jesus. We can safely commune with Him of all that is in our hearts.[1]

In *The Circle Maker*, Mark Batterson asserts, "*Bold prayers honor God, and God honors bold prayers.* God isn't offended by your biggest dreams or boldest prayers. He is offended by anything less. If your prayers aren't impossible to you, they are insulting to God. Why? Because they don't require divine intervention. But ask God to part the Red Sea or make the sun stand still or float an iron axhead, and God is moved to omnipotent action."[2]

BELIEVING GOD'S POWER

Of course, we have heard that God answers prayer. We may even say we know He answers prayer. But do we truly *believe* it?

Many people tend to pray superficially, just praying about a request, a need, or a desire. But soon the words turn hollow as the same phrases are repeated over and over again. What may have started with good intentions becomes shallow and empty.

Perhaps it is easier for us to pray without passion than to have our sincere hopes dashed. We can believe God loves us and desires our good, but what if He *can't* do what we ask? Often our prayers stop short because—either consciously or unconsciously, beneath our knowledge and professed trust—we believe God will stop short too.

Though it is well established that the Creator of the universe is capable of handling whatever problem we bring to Him, for our benefit, we must personally ask so that we can see His power proven in our lives. In fact, Ellen White states in *The Ministry of Healing* that we honor God when we believe that He will bless us: "As you ask the Lord to help you, honor your Saviour by believing that you do receive His blessing. All power, all wisdom, are at our command. We have only to ask."[3]

The miracles of Heaven are free to those who seek them with believing hearts. Jesus reminded His disciples on numerous occasions to have faith in the words they prayed. If they desired something from God, big or small, they were to believe that He would provide for their needs: "Therefore I tell you, whatever you ask for in prayer, believe that you have received it, and it will be yours" (Mark 11:24). "And whatever you ask in prayer, you will receive, if you have faith" (Matthew 21:22, ESV).

We must resist the temptation to stop our prayers short of our true requests. Rather, fully believing in God's power and goodness, we are to ask boldly and expect wholeheartedly that God will deliver.

PRAYING FOR A MIRACULOUS DELIVERANCE

Following the outpouring of the Holy Spirit at Pentecost, the believers set out to proclaim the message of Christ's resurrection and soon return. Thousands of people were converted to this new religious movement, causing concern for both the Jewish leaders and the Roman officials. If they couldn't stop these Christians, they might soon find their authority threatened.[4]

In Acts 12, we find the story of Herod Agrippa's imprisonment of Peter, and the pagan governor's attempt to disrupt the Christian movement. Peter was thrown into prison during the Festival of Unleavened Bread, which meant that Herod, out of respect for the local Jewish traditions, had to wait until the end of the festival week to execute the apostle. Concerned that some Christians might try to break in and free Peter, Herod stationed additional prison guards at the apostle's side; one chained to his left wrist and one to his right. Peter had no way of escape.[5]

Herod rightly surmised that the local Christians would be concerned. They gathered secretly to discuss the matter, but rather than planning a prison break, they fell to their knees and prayed for a miracle. They knew no human being could free Peter—only God could save him. Only God could do the impossible.

The evening before the appointed execution, anxious Christians met together again for an all-night prayer meeting. Meanwhile, Peter, who remained confident in Christ even as he faced death, slept peacefully between the guards. Suddenly, he was roused by an angel of the Lord, "Quick, get up" (Acts 12:7). Immediately, the chains fell from Peter's wrists. He stood up and quickly put on his cloak and sandals. "Follow me," the angel instructed. Together, they slipped out of the prison. Once they were out on the street, the angel departed, leaving the newly freed Peter dazed and alone. Suddenly realizing his miraculous freedom, he hurried to find his fellow believers, who at that very moment were praying for his deliverance.

Hearing a knock at the door, a servant girl went to see who was visiting so late at night. When she heard the familiar voice of Peter, she was so overjoyed that she left him at the door and ran back inside to tell the others of his arrival. "They said to her, 'You are out of your mind.' But she kept insisting that it was so, and they kept saying, 'It is his angel!' " (verse 15, ESV).

Even though the believers had been praying for Peter's release, they could hardly believe it was true. Peter was free? We marvel at their surprise, but stories like this abound in Scripture. When God's people pray for His intervention, they are often incredulous when He acts!

In Exodus 6, God promised His people that He would deliver them from Egyptian slavery:

> "Say therefore to the people of Israel, 'I am the Lord, and I will bring you out from under the burdens of the Egyptians, and I will deliver you from slavery to them, and I will redeem you with an outstretched arm and with great acts of judgment. I will take you to be my people, and I will be your God, and you shall know that I am the Lord your God, who has brought you out from under the burdens of the Egyptians. I will bring you into the land that I swore to give to Abraham, to Isaac, and to Jacob. I will give it to you for a possession. I am the Lord.' " (Exodus 6:6–8, ESV)

But even after God gave this promise and assurance, the Israelites still did not believe: "Moses reported this to the Israelites, but they did not listen to him because of their discouragement and harsh labor" (verse 9).

The oppressed Israelites found it impossible to trust the words of deliverance God gave them. Like the Christians who later gathered to pray for Peter, they did not truly believe He would miraculously rearrange circumstances to answer their cries. But He did. He rewarded their incomplete faith—not by comforting them in their sorrow but by altering history.

Christians today face a similar obstacle. We pray for a miracle; yet in our hearts, we do not believe anything will come of it. If something miraculous actually occurs, it seems too good to be true! We often try to explain the miracle away, finding other reasons to account for God's intervention. But we should be careful not to allow difficult circumstances to keep us from seeing God do the impossible.

FACING THE IMPOSSIBLE

In *Out of Babylon*, I tell about the difficulties I faced in getting a college degree:

> In 1976, I had a major crisis in my life. During that time, I had already lost two years of education because of the Sabbath and my schooling situation in Iraq, which caused me to leave the country and attend Middle East College. Because of . . . [the Lebanese] civil war, I was forced to go back home to Iraq. What I really wanted was to go to Walla Walla College to study engineering.
>
> Unfortunately, I was faced with four major problems. First off, I had no money. At that time, the cost of Walla Walla was seven to eight thousand dollars a year, and I had a total of about five dollars saved up. I was told that I was totally out of my mind to even think of going to Walla Walla College.

There would be no way for me to afford it. It was impossible.

The second major problem was the strained relationship between Iraq and the US. The Iraqi government had strictly forbidden people from going to the US for any reason, and the US was not giving visas to Iraqi citizens. For many years, there has been a mutual distrust between the two governments.

The third issue was also related to the Iraqi government—mandatory army service. Since I was not in school, the Iraqi army had sent a notice that I was required to enlist in the army.

The fourth problem that seemed to have no solution was that I needed to find someone to guarantee that I would come back to Iraq if I went to Walla Walla. If I didn't come back, this person would have to pay $10,000. I didn't know of anyone who would be willing and able to take on this responsibility.

As I reflected on these problems, they seemed impossible to resolve. My heart sank. What could I do about it? . . .

As I was going through this time of major crises, I went to church one week with a very long face—I wanted people to know I was discouraged. At the end of Sabbath School, Muneer and Selma [some friends] stopped and asked me why I looked sad. I explained that [my difficulties] had not gone away. I was still struggling with the four issues. They asked, "Did you pray about it?" In my heart, I knew that they were going to ask me this since we had already talked about the power of prayer the previous Sabbath.

"Of course I prayed about it," I said.

They went on to say, "But have you really prayed about it? Have you agonized over it? Do you believe that God is able to find a solution? What you describe to me sounds very difficult if not impossible. Yet think about it this way: You want God to change the policies of governments. You want God to change the policies of the army. You want Him to find thirty-two thousand dollars to help with your education and then find someone to guarantee you for ten thousand dollars. These seem like four impossibilities.

"You are kind of like the Israelites with the Red Sea in front and the Egyptian army behind, with no place to go. God is left with three options, all of which seem impossible. He can fly you over to where you want to go, kill the Egyptian army, or split the Red Sea."

Then they pressed the question, making it deeply personal, "Do you believe that God is able to do something in your life? Do you believe that He can change circumstances? Can He alter policies and history? Provide money? Can He change the hearts of people?"

I thought about it. They were right. It was going to take a miracle. The question now became, *Do I believe that God is able to perform that miracle? Do I have enough faith to believe that?*[6]

FROM HEAD CONCEPTS TO HEART CONVICTIONS

In my head, I started to believe that God is all powerful and has the ability to do anything. Yet this belief had not settled in my heart.[7] I knew that God is all powerful, but I wasn't sure He would demonstrate His power in my life.

Muneer and Selma took me to their home and started to share many verses about the power of God. First, we looked at God's power over the natural world:

- When God decided certain bodies of water needed parting, He parted them (Exodus 14; Joshua 3).
- When His people were hungry, God provided food from heaven (Exodus 16).
- When the Israelites were thirsty, Moses brought their request to God, and God brought water out of a dry rock (Exodus 17:1–7).
- When Israel's troops needed more time in battle, God extended the daylight hours (Joshua 10:12–14).[8]
- When Elijah prayed on Mount Carmel, God brought rain to the parched land (1 Kings 18).
- When Jonah was in the sea, God commanded a fish to swallow him to keep him safe (Jonah 1).
- When a wedding ran out of wine, Jesus changed ordinary water into delicious wine (John 2:1–12).
- When a storm endangered the lives of the disciples, Jesus stilled it (Mark 4:35–41).
- When thousands of people came to hear Jesus speak, He used a few morsels to produce more than enough food for everyone (Matthew 14; 15).
- When sick people were brought to Jesus, He healed them, demonstrating His power over sickness and disease (Matthew 21:14; Mark 1:40–45).

Next, we studied Bible passages that revealed God's power to change people's hearts. "God had the power to make shy Moses a leader (Exodus 3–4), to soften cruel Pharaoh's heart (Exodus 11:1–8), to keep discouraged Elijah from quitting (1 Kings 19:15) and to turn the fanatical persecutor Saul into a globe-trotting apostle (Acts 9:1–31)."[9] God also had the power to

- encourage Joshua to fill the shoes of his predecessor (Joshua 1:9),
- change the cowardly Peter into a man of boldness and courage (Luke 22:54–62; Acts 4:1–12), and
- humble James and John, the proud sons of Zebedee (Matthew 20:20–28).

In studying God's power in the natural world and in human lives, I could see that He could do whatever He wanted. He could change nature as easily as He could change a person's heart. History is full of God's powerful interventions in the world. But as I studied all these passages, I didn't want to simply have God's power as a concept in my head. I wanted to be fully convicted of His power in my heart. I wanted to resonate completely with the psalmist's words when he wrote:

> Praise the Lord from the earth,
>   you great sea creatures and all ocean depths,
> lightning and hail, snow and clouds,
>   stormy winds that do his bidding,
> you mountains and all hills,
>   fruit trees and all cedars,
> wild animals and all cattle,
>   small creatures and flying birds,
> kings of the earth and all nations,
>   you princes and all rulers on earth,
> young men and women,
>   old men and children.
> Let them praise the name of the Lord,
>   for his name alone is exalted;
>   his splendor is above the earth and the heavens.
> And he has raised up for his people a horn,
>   the praise of all his faithful servants,
>   of Israel, the people close to his heart.
> Praise the Lord. (Psalm 148:7–14)

The entire Bible is a testimony to the power of God. He has always been able to accomplish the impossible. Malachi 3:6 says plainly, "I the Lord do not change." Hebrews 13:8 declares that "Jesus Christ is the same yesterday and today and forever." If He could control nature and alter the circumstances of His people, then I could have confidence that He had the power to do so in my life now.[10]

A frequent refrain in Scripture is the powerful theme that *God is able*.

He was able to save three of his followers from a fiery furnace in Daniel 3. He was able to save Daniel from the lions' mouths three chapters after that. He was able to conceive a child in a ninety-year-old womb, Romans 4 testifies. He was able to give his followers all they could possibly need, says 2 Corinthians 9. He was able to save completely those who come to God through Jesus, according to Hebrews 7. And he is "able to do immeasurably more than all we ask or imagine," according to the words of Ephesians 3.[11]

Ellen White echoes this truth: "Keep your wants, your joys, your sorrows, your cares, and your fears before God. You cannot burden Him; you cannot weary Him. He who numbers the hairs of your head is not indifferent to the wants of His children. 'The Lord is very pitiful, and of tender mercy.' James 5:11. His heart of love is touched by our sorrows and even by our utterances of them. Take to Him everything that perplexes the mind. Nothing is too great for Him to bear, for He holds up worlds, He rules over all the affairs of the universe."[12] There is nothing you will ever face that God cannot handle.

If doubt has eroded your belief in the power of God, do not give up. Search the scriptures, and the power of God will bring conviction to your heart. And when that conviction arrives, your prayers will take on new meaning as you begin believing that God can do something about your circumstances.

THE GOD OF THE IMPOSSIBLE

As in Peter's case, God rescued me from an impossible predicament. After I had pored over Scripture and studied until my heart was in awe of His incredible power, I began to sincerely pray over my four impossibilities: I needed money to pay for school; I needed permission to leave my country; I needed to be released from my obligation to the army; and I needed someone who could guarantee my return. For several months, I spent hours every day agonizing in prayer, pleading for God to make my impossibilities possible.

It wasn't long before I noticed several changes in myself. I began to see the power of God in my life. I could sense His presence. I could feel His strength everywhere I went. My faith was strengthened. My words were spoken with conviction. Like never before, I could say with certainty that God was a real and powerful force in my life. I had complete confidence in what He was going to do.[13]

In faith, I applied to Walla Walla College and was accepted to study engineering. A friend of mine from the United States, whom I met while we were both in Lebanon, found someone to pay for part of my first year of schooling. Soon afterward,

> I received a letter from Walla Walla College stating that my finances for the first year were taken care of by an unknown individual. God has thousands of ways—not one, five, fifty, or one hundred—to provide for our needs, of which we know nothing. Some of them are unlikely, if not unbelievable. He sent food to Elijah through ravens, rained manna from heaven, brought forth water from rocks, and had an anonymous person pay for my schooling.
>
> One day, a man from church came up to me and said, "I know you need someone to guarantee your return in order to leave the country. I'd like to do that." While I was praying, God was working on this man's heart. God has the power to soften hearts and influence them. . . .

Because this man stepped up to guarantee me, the United States granted me a student visa. As for the Iraqi government letting me leave, my request reached the desk of the prime minister, Saddam Hussein. . . . Iraq would have to make some changes to the law to allow me to leave. Thankfully, they made an exception and granted me the exit visa. God is in control of the destinies of the nations and of individuals.[14]

Additionally, because I was going to an accredited college, I was exempt from joining the army. I don't know how to explain it, except to say God is able. If He was able to split the sea, save Israel, and drown the Egyptian army, then exempting me from army duty is no problem. All of my impossibilities were solved in miraculous ways.

Ellen White reminds us that Jesus continues to make the impossible possible even today. "Were not miracles wrought by Christ and His apostles? The same compassionate Saviour lives today, and He is as willing to listen to the prayer of faith as when He walked visibly among men. The natural cooperates with the supernatural. It is a part of God's plan to grant us, in answer to the prayer of faith, that which He would not bestow did we not thus ask."[15]

ACCEPT THE INVITATION

God is inviting you to call on Him. In fact, He wants to hear from you as often as possible. He urges believers to "pray without ceasing" (1 Thessalonians 5:17, ESV). In *Steps to Christ*, Ellen White writes, "We should have the door of the heart open continually and our invitation going up that Jesus may come and abide as a heavenly guest in the soul."[16] Keep the line of your heart open, and remain in constant contact with God.

When you pray, God wants you to approach Him with confidence. "Let us therefore come boldly unto the throne of grace, that we may obtain mercy, and find grace to help in time of need" (Hebrews 4:16, KJV). There is no need for timidity or uncertainty, nor is there need for stress and concern. God wants you to release your worries to Him and trust that He will take care of your problems. "Do not be anxious about anything, but in every situation, by prayer and petition, with thanksgiving, present your requests to God" (Philippians 4:6). God is delighted to bear your burdens and see your anxiety turned into joy.

In the book *In Heavenly Places*, Ellen White writes the following:

Make your requests known to your Maker. Never is one repulsed who comes to Him with a contrite heart. Not one sincere prayer is lost. Amid the anthems of the celestial choir, God hears the cries of the weakest human being. We pour out our heart's desire in our closets, we breathe a prayer as we walk by the way, and our words reach the throne of the Monarch of the universe. . . . It is God to whom we are speaking, and our prayer is heard. You who feel the most unworthy, fear not to commit your case to God.[17]

When you choose to trust wholeheartedly in the One who is able to do more than you can ask or think, then you will begin to see His hand at work in your life. Miracles become realities for those who believe in Him. You need only accept the invitation God is extending. Come, bring your heart's deepest desires before Him, and just as He intervened in the lives of the Israelites and early Christians, He will intervene in your life today.

The God of the impossible can only be discovered through the power of prayer. So why not pray as you have never prayed before? Pray as if your life depends on it. Persevere. Be convinced that God is all powerful—that He has the power to do anything, to change anyone, and to intervene in any circumstance.

---

1. Ellen G. White, *Testimonies for the Church*, vol. 5 (Mountain View, CA: Pacific Press®, 1889), 200, 201.
2. Mark Batterson, *The Circle Maker, expanded ed.* (Grand Rapids, MI: Zondervan, 2016), 15; emphasis in the original.
3. Ellen G. White, *The Ministry of Healing* (Mountain View, CA: Pacific Press®, 1905), 514.
4. Bill Hybels, *Too Busy Not to Pray: Slowing Down to Be With God*, 3rd ed. (Downers Grove, IL: InterVarsity Press, 2008), 38, 39.
5. Ellen G. White, *The Acts of the Apostles* (Mountain View, CA: Pacific Press®, 1911), 145, 146.
6. S. Joseph Kidder, *Out of Babylon: How God Found Me on the Streets of Baghdad* (Nampa, ID: Pacific Press®, 2018), 73–75.
7. Hybels, *Too Busy Not to Pray*, 37.
8. Hybels, *Too Busy Not to Pray*, 39.
9. Hybels, *Too Busy Not to Pray*, 41.
10. Hybels, *Too Busy Not to Pray*, 42.
11. Hybels, *Too Busy Not to Pray*, 43.
12. Ellen G. White, *Steps to Christ* (Mountain View, CA: Pacific Press ®, 1892), 100.
13. Kidder, *Out of Babylon*, 81.
14. Kidder, *Out of Babylon*, 82.
15. Ellen G. White, *The Great Controversy* (Mountain View, CA: Pacific Press®, 1911), 525.
16. White, *Steps to Christ*, 99.
17. Ellen G. White, *In Heavenly Places* (Washington, DC: Review and Herald®, 1967), 82.

CHAPTER 9

PRAYER

Connecting With God

Pray continually, give thanks in all circumstances;
for this is God's will for you in Christ Jesus.
—1 Thessalonians 5:17, 18

As we look at the life of Christ, we see a life of continual connection with God. He often withdrew to pray alone (Luke 5:16; Matthew 14:23).[1] He also spent entire nights in prayer (Luke 6:12). As Ellen White reminds us, "His humanity made prayer a necessity and a privilege. He found comfort and joy in communion with His Father. And if the Saviour of men, the Son of God, felt the need of prayer, how much more should feeble, sinful mortals feel the necessity of fervent, constant prayer."[2] Yet we, who look to Christ as an example, ask, How can anyone possibly pray all day, or even for an entire hour?

Before we begin praying, time should be given to quiet our minds and remove distractions as we come into God's presence (Psalm 37:7; Lamentations 3:25, 26). This may be done through the reading of a devotional book or listening to spiritual songs and music. It may involve going to a special corner of your home—one that is set aside for time with God. This preparation involves simply taking time to let God love you as you bask in His presence.

THE TEN ASPECTS OF PRAYER

The following sections offer guidelines on structuring quality time in prayer with ten scripturally based aspects. "Some of these aspects may require only a minute, whereas others—such as intercessory prayer for the world—will require far more."[3]

1. *Praise and adoration (Exodus 15:1, 2; Psalm 63:1–5; Matthew 6:9, 10; Revelation 4:6–11; 5:12; 19:6).* "All prayer should begin with recognition of God's nature. The Lord's Prayer—our model for all praying—begins with 'Our Father which art in heaven, Hallowed be thy name' " (Matthew 6:9, KJV).[4]

"The first idea Jesus gives us for making contact with God is captured by the words: 'Our Father in heaven: May your holy name be honored' [Matthew 6:9,

GNT]. Jesus is talking about praise."[5] We begin connecting with God by praising and worshiping Him.

What is praise? Praise is thanking God for who and what He is. It means to value and to esteem Him. It means to declare, "God, You are good! There's no one as good as You!"

"Why should I praise God? Because it gets my focus off myself and onto God so I can talk to him and not at him. . . . If you want help learning how to praise God, read through the Book of Psalms. Many of them were written simply to praise God. If you read them aloud, you'll learn a lot about praising God in prayer."[6]

In my own devotions, I always read one of the psalms in addition to another scripture I am reading. They thrill my heart and motivate me to worship God.

Praise is that aspect of prayer that vocally values God for His virtues and accomplishments. Ellen White expresses, "The soul may ascend nearer heaven on the wings of praise. God is worshiped with song and music in the courts above, and as we express our gratitude, we are approximating to the worship of the heavenly hosts. 'Whoso offereth praise glorifieth' God. Let us with reverent joy come before our Creator, with 'thanksgiving, and the voice of melody.'"[7]

There are 4 reasons for adoration:

- Adoration sets the tone for the entire prayer.
- Adoration reminds us of God's identity and inclination.
- Adoration purifies the one who is praying.
- God is worthy of adoration.[8]

2. Confession (Psalms 51; 139:23, 24; Jeremiah 3:12, 13; Acts 2:38; 3:19; 1 John 1:9, 10). "The Psalmist asked God to search his heart for unconfessed sin [Psalm 139:23]. He knew sin was one of the greatest roadblocks to answered prayer. Early in prayer we need to make time for confession. This clears the way for powerful praying."[9]

It is a joy to have our conscience cleansed, thus feeling free to pray and knowing that God has forgiven us, for Jesus' blood will plead on behalf of our repentant souls. Ellen White writes, "True repentance will lead a man to bear his guilt himself and acknowledge it without deception or hypocrisy. Like the poor publican, not lifting up so much as his eyes unto heaven, he will cry, 'God be merciful to me a sinner,' and those who do acknowledge their guilt will be justified, for Jesus will plead His blood in behalf of the repentant soul."[10]

Confession has two aspects to it: one to God and one to other people. All of our sins should be confessed to God, but we must be discerning about sharing our faults with others. Ellen White advises, "True confession is always of a specific character, and acknowledges particular sins. They may be of such a nature as to be brought before God only; they may be wrongs that should be confessed to individuals who have suffered injury through them; or they may be of a public character, and should then be as publicly confessed. But all confession should be definite and to the point, acknowledging the very sins of which you are guilty."[11]

There are several benefits to confession:

- Your conscience will be cleaned.
- You will be flooded with relief that God has a forgiving nature. . . .
- You will feel free to pray.[12]

3. The Word (2 Samuel 22:31; Psalm 119; Jeremiah 23:29; 2 Timothy 3:16). "The commandment of the Lord [His Word] is pure, enlightening the eyes" (Psalm 19:8, ESV). "When we bring God's Word into our prayer, we are opening our eyes to new possibilities in God."[13] Here we bring actual Scripture into our prayers. We take the example of Peter and John in Acts 4:23–30 as they prayed for the fulfillment of an Old Testament prophecy, acknowledging the power of God against those who wanted to harm them.

Read God's Word and pray God's Word. We can never pray outside of God's will when we pray Scripture. The Bible will bring us closer to God and will reveal His will to us. "The study of the Scriptures is the means divinely ordained to bring men into closer connection with their Creator and to give them a clearer knowledge of His will. It is the medium of communication between God and man."[14]

The Bible is the Word of God. It contains the mind of God and His will for each of our lives. Proverbs 4:5 states, "Get wisdom, get understanding; do not forget my words or turn away from them." And Psalm 119:130 declares, "The unfolding of your words gives light; it gives understanding to the simple." As we study God's Word, we will be given wisdom and understanding to navigate this life and its challenges.

There are a few reasons we should study Scripture: First, the Word of God is totally authoritative. The book of Psalms affirms this fact. Psalm 33:4 states, "For the word of the Lord is right and true; he is faithful in all he does." And Psalm 119:160 says, "All your words are true; all your righteous laws are eternal." The Bible is the only source for absolute divine authority. This divine authority is for you and me as servants of Jesus Christ.

Second, God's Word is totally sufficient for the Christian life. "All scripture is given by inspiration of God, and is profitable for doctrine, for reproof, for correction, for instruction in righteousness: That the man of God may be perfect, throughly furnished unto all good works" (2 Timothy 3:16, 17, KJV). The Word of God equips us for everything we do.

Third, Scripture will accomplish what it promises. Isaiah 55:11 states, "So shall my word be that goeth forth out of my mouth: it shall not return unto me void, but it shall accomplish that which I please, and it shall prosper in the thing whereto I sent it" (KJV). There are so many promises given to us in the Bible. These promises reassure us and bring comfort to our lives in our times of trial.

4. Intercession (Psalm 2:8; Matthew 9:35–39; John 17; 1 Timothy 2:1, 2). "Our prayer now centers on intercession for a lost and dying world. This concerns praying for others who have desperate needs."[15]

Jesus and Paul give us the perfect examples of intercessory prayer. Jesus prayed for us, saying, "My prayer is not that you take them out of the world but that you protect them from the evil one. They are not of the world, even as I am not of it. Sanctify them by the truth; your word is truth. As you sent me into the world, I have sent them into the world. For them I sanctify myself, that they too may be truly sanctified" (John 17:15–19). The Bible records about forty instances of the apostle Paul praying for the church.[16] He prayed for a variety of things, such as the endurance of faith, joy and peace, spiritual gifts, and comfort.

When we pray for other people, we are identifying with them as part of the human family. "In calling God our Father, we recognize all His children as our brethren. We are all a part of the great web of humanity, all members of one family. In our petitions we are to include our neighbors as well as ourselves. No one prays aright who seeks a blessing for himself alone."[17]

In our prayers for others, we can pray for family, friends, coworkers, our ministries, and the spiritual and physical needs of people in the church and around the world.

5. Petition (Matthew 6:11–13, 33; 7:7–11; Luke 11:1–13; James 4:2, 3). "This aspect of prayer concerns our personal needs. Petition is included in the Lord's Prayer in the expression: 'Give us this day our daily bread" [Matthew 6:11, KJV]. To petition God is to open our need to God through prayer."[18] "We know that God hears us if we ask according to His will. But to press our petitions without a submissive spirit is not right."[19]

Jesus taught us that prayer can move mountains and change situations. But if the situation remains the same, He will strengthen us to go through it. And eventually, He will teach us why. Oswald Chambers says, "We hear it said that 'Prayer alters things'; prayer not so much alters things as alters the one who prays."[20]

Ellen White gives us reasons to petition God: "Prayer to the Great Physician for the healing of the soul brings the blessing of God. Prayer unites us one to another and to God. Prayer brings Jesus to our side, and gives new strength and fresh grace to the fainting, perplexed soul. By prayer the sick have been encouraged to believe that God will look with compassion upon them. A ray of light penetrates to the hopeless soul, and becomes a savor of life unto life. Prayer has 'subdued kingdoms, wrought righteousness, obtained promises, stopped the mouths of lions, quenched the violence of fire.' "[21]

We can petition for our needs—healing, strength, encouragement, and hope—our family's needs, the salvation of our loved ones, and our church's needs.

6. Thanksgiving (1 Chronicles 16:34; Psalms 100; 106; 118; 136; 1 Thessalonians

5:18). "The Bible is filled with commands to give thanks to God (Psalm 106:1; 107:1; 118:1; 1 Chronicles 16:34; 1 Thessalonians 5:18)."[22] "When Paul wrote to the Philippians, he instructed them to offer prayer and supplication 'with thanksgiving' [Philippians 4:6]."[23] Most Bible writers "list reasons why we should thank Him, such as 'His love endures forever' (Psalm 136:3), 'He is good' (Psalm 118:29), and 'His mercy is everlasting' (Psalm 100:5[, KJV]). Thanksgiving and praise always go together. We cannot adequately praise and worship God without also being thankful."[24] "Thanksgiving differs from praise in that praise recognizes God for who He is, and thanksgiving recognizes God for specific things He has done."[25]

There are several reasons why we should be thankful to God: First, thanksgiving removes arrogance and self-centeredness from our lives. Gratitude and selfishness cannot coexist.

Second, thanksgiving keeps our hearts in a right relationship with the Giver of all good gifts. It reminds us that He is responsible for everything good in our lives.

Third, thanksgiving reminds us of how much we have. It helps us to realize that we could not exist without the merciful blessings of God. "We don't thank Him for harm He did not cause, but we thank Him when He gives us the strength to endure it (2 Corinthians 12:9)."[26]

Fourth, thanksgiving keeps bitterness away. We cannot be both thankful and bitter at the same time. "Rejoice always, pray continually, give thanks in all circumstances; for this is God's will for you in Christ Jesus" (1 Thessalonians 5:16–18).

Fifth, thanksgiving keeps our hearts receptive to God's peace. It "saves us from a host of harmful emotions and attitudes that will rob us of the peace God wants us to experience (Philippians 4:6-7)."[27]

We can thank God for answered prayers, spiritual blessings, relational blessings, and material blessings.

7. Singing (Psalms 111–113; Colossians 3:16). "Sing and make music from your heart to the Lord" (Ephesians 5:19). Many Christians have learned the beauty of singing a new song to God during prayer. These songs may be psalms or hymns, or they may come straight from the heart with the Holy Spirit creating the melody.

To sing to the Lord is to worship Him. We learn in the Old Testament that the combination of singing and prayer was an integral part of worship. Through songs and prayer, we can express our adoration to God. Some psalms are specifically called prayers (Psalms 17; 86; 90; 102; 142).

In 1 Chronicles, we are told that four thousand of the thirty-eight thousand Levites chosen for temple service were musicians (1 Chronicles 15:16; 23:5). They were singers who played musical instruments (harps, lyres, and cymbals; 1 Chronicles 15:16) to raise sounds of joy in their worship of God. They were singing in the temple as the incense of prayers went up into the heavens.

As part of my worship of God, I incorporate singing. I always start my worship by listening to songs and end my worship by singing to the Lord.

8. Listening (1 Kings 19:11–14; Psalms 37:7; 40:1; Ecclesiastes 5:1–3; John 10:2–4). "Whether through His written Word or by [the] inner 'still small voice' of His Holy Spirit, God speaks to praying Christians. But we must take time to listen."[28]

In order to hear from God, we must do two main things: First, we must "make ourselves available to God with the proper attitude":

> There are many things that can distract us from spending time with God [such as busyness, a wandering mind, and lack of motivation]. . . . Making quiet time, free from as many distractions as possible, is difficult but important. The proper attitude is also important. Attitudes such as humility and courage are important. We have to humbly recognize that we don't have all the right answers. We also need to prepare our hearts so we have courage to do what is right, no matter how our fears or selfish ambitions may try to persuade us otherwise.[29]

Second, we need to "learn discernment; that is, the ability to tell whether we have really heard from God":

> Someone who knows what God is like knows His voice. Therefore, we must make time to improve our knowledge and relationship with God, through study of scripture, quiet prayer, and learning from fellow Christians. Emotions are a part of discernment, but making a choice because you feel it is right is only one piece of the equation. We shouldn't entirely discount how we feel, but at the same time we must be careful to separate what is God's will for us and what are our own desires (which aren't necessarily His). The first test is that God's voice will never contradict His word, the Bible. That is one reason why study of scripture is so important. Quiet, dedicated prayer time is also important in order to try to block out the distractions of everyday life.[30]

As I learn to hear God's voice, I practice the following three principles:

1. Don't be uncomfortable with silence.
2. What you hear from God will be in harmony with His Word.
3. Act on what you hear. God may tell you of personal changes to be made, of people to reach, or He may just tell you that He loves you.

9. Commitment (Psalms 31:5; 37:5; Proverbs 16:3; John 13:17). When we pray, we should take time to recommit and dedicate ourselves to "seek first his kingdom and his righteousness" (Matthew 6:33). Each day should be a new commitment to walk with our Creator and submit to His will.

10. Praise and adoration (Psalms 135; 150; Matthew 6:13, KJV). "We begin our prayer by recognizing God's nature, and we end in similar fashion. Jesus taught this when He ended His prayer with the statement, 'For thine is the kingdom, and the power, and the glory, for ever' " (Matthew 6:13, KJV).[31]

THE HEART OF THE MATTER
Developing a prayer life will lead you into a ministry that changes you and the world around you. We've just talked about ten aspects of prayer. C. S. Lewis captured the significance of many of them: "Prayer in the sense of petition, asking for things, is a small part of it; confession and penitence are its threshold, adoration its sanctuary, the presence and vision and enjoyment of God its bread and wine."[32]

HOW I END MY PRAYER TIME
I always finish my worship time with God with this prayer:

> Lord, You are my senior partner. I want You to go with me everywhere. I am going to meet a lot of people today. Give me words of hope for some, encouragement for others, and wisdom for those in need.
>
> I am going to be teaching classes today. I want You to take over and teach these classes for me. I want to decrease, but I want You to increase.
>
> I am going to be preaching today. I want You to be the one who is going to be preaching, and I want to step aside. I want the message to come from You and not from me or anyone else.
>
> I am going to be facing temptations today. Lord, give me victory over them. Lord, whatever I do today, I want to do it for Your glory and Your honor. I want to be mindful of Your presence in my life.
>
> When I face difficulties today, help me see them from Your perspective and to grow from them.
>
> Father, I choose to be 100 percent committed to You. Neutralize my own ideas and opinions. I want the spirit of a learner.
>
> Reveal Your plans for my life today. Jesus, I choose to implement what I learn today, both by practicing it and by sharing it.
>
> "Whatever is true, whatever is noble, whatever is right, whatever is pure, whatever is lovely, whatever is admirable—if anything is excellent or praiseworthy"—may I think about such things. Whatever I have learned or received or heard from You, may I put it in practice. God of peace, be with me (Philippians 4:8, 9).
>
> "Let the words of my mouth, and the meditation of my heart, be acceptable in thy sight, O Lord, my strength, and my redeemer" (Psalm 19:14, KJV). Amen.

---

1. This chapter was adapted from S. Joseph Kidder, "How to Spend an Hour in Prayer," Kidder's

Column, *Elder's Digest* 22, no. 2 (April–June 2016): 28, 29.

2. Ellen G. White, *Steps to Christ* (Mountain View, CA: Pacific Press®, 1892), 94.

3. Dick Eastman, "How to Spend an Hour in Prayer," NAD Prayer Ministries, accessed January 29, 2019, http://www.nadprayerministries.org/wp-content/uploads/2012/01/How-to-Spend-an-Hour-in-Prayer-Focus-Points.pdf.

4. Eastman, "How to Spend an Hour in Prayer."

5. Rick Warren, "When You Pray, Begin With Praise," Bible.com, accessed January 29, 2019, https://www.bible.com/reading-plans/135-rick-warrens-daily-devotional/day/273#!.

6. Warren, "When You Pray, Begin With Praise."

7. Ellen G. White, *My Life Today* (Hagerstown, MD: Review and Herald®, 2015), 33.

8. S. Joseph Kidder, comp., "7 Steps to Effective Prayer," NAD Prayer Ministries, accessed January 30, 2019, http://www.nadprayerministries.org/wp-content/uploads/7StepsToEffectivePrayer-2-ups.pdf.

9. Eastman, "How to Spend an Hour in Prayer."

10. White, *Steps to Christ*, 40, 41.

11. White, *Steps to Christ*, 38.

12. Kidder, "7 Steps to Effective Prayer."

13. Eastman, "How to Spend an Hour in Prayer."

14. Ellen G. White, *The Great Controversy* (Mountain View, CA: Pacific Press®, 1911), 69.

15. Eastman, "How to Spend an Hour in Prayer."

16. Craig Carr and S. Joseph Kidder, "The Secret Life of the Pastor," *Ministry*, January 2018, 26.

17. Ellen G. White, *Sons and Daughters of God* (Hagerstown, MD: Review and Herald®, 2003), 267.

18. Eastman, "How to Spend an Hour in Prayer."

19. Ellen G. White, *The Ministry of Healing* (Nampa, ID: Pacific Press®, 2003), 230.

20. Oswald Chambers, *Biblical Ethics*, in *Biblical Ethics, the Moral Foundations of Life, the Philosophy of Sin* (Grand Rapids, MI: Discovery House, 2015), 103.

21. Ellen G. White, "Pray Without Ceasing," *Review and Herald*, October 30, 1900.

22. "Why Is Giving Thanks to God Important?" Got Questions, accessed January 30, 2019, https://www.gotquestions.org/giving-thanks-to-God.html.

23. Eastman, "How to Spend an Hour in Prayer."

24. "Why Is Giving Thanks to God Important?"

25. Eastman, "How to Spend an Hour in Prayer."

26. "Why Is Giving Thanks to God Important?"

27. "Why Is Giving Thanks to God Important?"

28. Eastman, "How to Spend an Hour in Prayer."

29. "Learning to Listen to God," The Life, accessed January 30, 2019, https://thelife.com/learning-to-listen-to-god.

30. "Learning to Listen to God."

31. Eastman, "How to Spend an Hour in Prayer."

32. C. S. Lewis, "The Efficacy of Prayer," in *The World's Last Night, and Other Essays* (San Diego: CA: Harvest Books, 2002), 8.

PART 4

Journey to the
Heart of God
Through Feeding
on His Word

CHAPTER 10

FEEDING ON GOD'S WORD
Knowing God Through His Word

Your word is a lamp for my feet, a light on my path.
—Psalm 119:105

I grew up in Baghdad at a time when it was very difficult to get a Bible: It cost about one hundred dollars, and sometimes it took up to a year to get one. I was about sixteen when I decided to own my own Bible. I did not want to ask the church to give me one because I didn't want to cost them money. I wanted to work for my own Bible so that it would be special to me. I worked hard for my dad and earned one hundred dollars and gave it to the government, registering my name to get a Bible. After eight months, I got a notice that my Bible was ready to pick up. After school one day, I went to pick it up. I was so excited that I immediately went home, hoping to read it.

My mother, who was a very loving woman, was also very strict when it came to homework. We couldn't do anything—no television, no sports, no playing outside—unless our homework was done first. She would help us and make sure we did it correctly. I got home around 4:00 P.M. after picking up my Bible and worked on my homework until 10:00 P.M. My mom inspected my work and then told my brother and me it was time for bed. I really wanted to read my Bible, so after my brother had fallen asleep, I went to the kitchen and got a flashlight. I got back into bed with my Bible, pulled the covers over my head, and turned on the flashlight. Someone had told me to start reading in the book of John. I fumbled my way through and found it. I just happened to land on John 8:12, which reads, "When Jesus spoke again to the people, he said, 'I am the light of the world. Whoever follows me will never walk in darkness, but will have the light of life.' " When I read these words, I was filled with so much joy and excitement that my heart started beating really fast. My thoughts began to change, and I determined in my heart that Jesus would be the light of my life!

As I was immersed in reading, I didn't notice that my mom had gone to the kitchen to prepare the meals for the next day. On her way back to her bedroom, she decided to check on us. When she opened our door, she saw the beam of light shining through the blanket. She was terrified, wondering what her son was reading. She pulled back the blanket, and to her surprise, she found me reading my Bible. She let out a huge sigh of relief and said, "You have twenty minutes to read, then go to sleep."

That was my first personal encounter with the Bible, and I fell in love with the Word of God. After this, I read it consistently and with passion. . . . I looked forward to reading it every day! I learned all of the stories of the life and teachings of Jesus, the stories of Acts, the teachings of the apostle Paul, and all the stories of the Old Testament. The result was that I fell in love more deeply and passionately with my Lord and Savior, Jesus Christ.[1]

THREE TRANSFORMING TRUTHS

I want to look at three truths from God's Word that have transformed my life and will change your life and bring you closer to Christ.

1. We study God's Word to know the truth. We study the Bible because it is our authority for faith. It cannot fail—it is the truth. "Sanctify them by the truth; your word is truth" (John 17:17). The Bible is the truth because it is the Word of God: "And we also thank God continually because, when you received the word of God, which you heard from us, you accepted it not as a human word, but as it actually is, the word of God, which is indeed at work in you who believe" (1 Thessalonians 2:13).

Second Peter 1:20, 21 also emphasizes that Scripture is the Word of God as the verses state, "No prophecy of Scripture comes from someone's own interpretation. For no prophecy was ever produced by the will of man, but men spoke from God as they were carried along by the Holy Spirit" (ESV). We have the words of humans in Scripture, but ultimately we are told in these verses that they are the words of God. These people were inspired by the Holy Spirit, so they spoke God's Word, not their own words. Therefore, these words are authoritative and truthful. Jesus said, "Scripture cannot be broken" (John 10:35, ESV).

In Matthew 5:17, 18, Jesus said, "Do not think that I have come to abolish the Law or the Prophets; I have not come to abolish them but to fulfill them. For truly I tell you, until heaven and earth disappear, not the smallest letter, not the least stroke of a pen, will by any means disappear from the Law until everything is accomplished." Our Lord Jesus Christ believed the Old Testament was the Word of God. Six times in the book of Matthew Jesus replied to those who questioned Him with the words "Have you not read . . . ?"[2]

The authority of Scripture is clear in the life of our Lord. He always trusted the Word of God—it was His authority. And if it was His authority, it should be our authority. The authority of Scripture reigns over reason and tradition. So we study God's Word because it is inspired and authoritative.

Scripture tells us what to believe by what it teaches. As we believe in a personal God who has manifested Himself in Scripture, our faith is revealed to us supernaturally. Ellen White reminds us:

> The Bible is of the highest value because it is the word of the living God. Of all the books in the world it is the most deserving of study and attention, for it is eternal wisdom. . . .
>
> . . . But the beauty and excellence of these diamonds of truth are not discerned by the natural eye.[3]

Scripture does not only tell us what to believe but also what to do practically. It corrects and trains us in righteousness so that we are equipped to live lives that please God. We do not rely on only our own reason or intuition for what we should believe or how we should live. We rely on God's authoritative revelation.

2. We study God's Word to help us grow in knowledge. All Christians should be growing in their knowledge of the Scriptures. In Acts 20:27, Paul says, "For I have not hesitated to proclaim to you the whole will of God." Neither should we hesitate in seeking to understand the Bible. We must not only read the parts that we especially like or that we already know but the Bible in its entirety. "For everything that was written in the past was written to teach us, so that through the endurance taught in the Scriptures and the encouragement they provide we might have hope" (Romans 15:4).

We need a plan to study God's Word. We have routines for eating, working, and sleeping. The same should apply to studying the Bible. In fact, most of us work best if we have patterns and consistency in our lives. We need habits to read God's Word. Less than 20 percent of churchgoers read the Bible daily.[4] We may have a desire to read it, but we may fail to do so because it's not a habit in our lives.

When I got my first Bible, I resolved in my heart to study it constantly so that I would grow in my knowledge of Jesus. I personally have my own devotions from six to seven in the morning. During that time, I start with prayer that the Lord will bless me and help me experience His presence in my life. Each day I read one chapter (starting with the Old Testament) and one chapter from Psalms. I do this every day until I finish reading the whole Bible, and then I repeat the cycle. I frequently compliment studying the Bible with reading the Conflict of the Ages series, especially the portions that are pertinent to what I am reading in Scripture.

Sometimes, I go deeper with just a portion of the chapter or one word that catches my attention, such as *loving-kindness, justified,* or *cleansed.* This will often send me to commentaries, dictionaries, or the internet for more study. I also incorporate praise into my worship by listening to music and singing during my devotions. I always finish my devotions with an extended time of prayer, including petition and intercession. Then I sit in solitude and listen for the voice of God. Sometimes I have felt Him saying, *"I love you,"* and sometimes I hear Him saying, *"There is something you need to pay attention to in your life so it can help you grow spiritually."* Many times, He has placed the names of people to call or visit on my heart. When I call or visit, they will ask how I knew they needed someone to talk with. My answer is, "I didn't, but the Lord did."

Most days I go for an hour prayer walk before noon and will listen to Scripture and pray. During that time, I pursue intercessory prayer, praying for at least five people every day. In the evening, I have a short devotion with my wife. It took me a while to develop this routine. My suggestion is to start with thirty minutes in the morning—twenty minutes for Scripture and ten minutes for prayer. It is better to start small and fulfill your goal than to start big and crash.

Part of what we should do with the knowledge we gain from the Bible is pass it on to others, especially our family and children. We read in Deuteronomy 6:6, 7 how diligently parents are to teach their children the Scriptures: "These commandments that I give you today are to be on your hearts. Impress them on your children. Talk about them when you sit at home and when you walk along the road, when you lie down and when you get up." God's people were instructed to talk about the Bible at home with their children, when they walked along the road, when they were lying down, and when they got up. We will do that if we know God's Word and are excited about God's truth. We naturally talk about what we are excited about. If the Word is thrilling to us, we will talk about it with our families and anyone we know.

Another example of passing on one's knowledge of Scripture is from the story of the Samaritan woman at the well in John 4. When the woman realized who Jesus was and what this living water was that He was talking about, she dropped everything and ran into town to tell everyone about Him. This is the power of the gospel. It penetrates our hearts and makes us want to share with others. John 4:14 says, "Indeed, the water I give them will become in them a spring of water welling up to eternal life."

3. We study God's Word because it is transformational. The Bible was given not only for our information but for our transformation. Second Timothy 3:16, 17 says, "All Scripture is God-breathed and is useful for teaching, rebuking, correcting and training in righteousness, so that the servant of God may be thoroughly equipped for every good work."

Applying Scripture to your life is transformational. "You must expose yourself to Scripture from every source so that you can grasp its principles and understand how to apply it to your life. . . . You don't catch it by reading a few favorite texts now and then. . . . You need to read it over and over, comparing Scripture with Scripture so that you have the balance of the whole counsel of God. You need to study it in more depth. You need to memorize key verses. And you need to meditate on God's Word."[5]

If we sincerely study the Scriptures and ask God to change us, His purposes will be accomplished in us. God proclaims,

> My word that goes out from my mouth:
>   It will not return to me empty,
> but will accomplish what I desire
>   and achieve the purpose for which I sent it. (Isaiah 55:11)

The truth of the Word of God will affect the heart just as much as the sun and rain affect the earth. God's Word is never spoken in vain and will always produce the effect He intends. Those who are willing to receive His Word will be filled with a transformational knowledge and love of God.

We need more than theoretical knowledge. We must encounter Jesus within the pages of Scripture and allow the Holy Spirit to transform us. Ellen White comments on an encounter between Jesus and Nicodemus in which there was a contrast between information and transformation: "Nicodemus had come to the Lord thinking to enter into a discussion with Him, but Jesus laid bare the foundation principles of truth. He said to Nicodemus, It is not theoretical knowledge you need so much as spiritual regeneration. You need not to have your curiosity satisfied, but to have a new heart. You must receive a new life from above before you can appreciate heavenly things. Until this change takes place, making all things new, it will result in no saving good for you to discuss with Me My authority or My mission."[6]

The following are some transformational steps in Bible study that have helped me in my spiritual growth:

A. *Application to self.* Application is going to depend on where I am on my journey with God, the issues I am struggling with, the hindrances to my spiritual growth, and the insights I have gained from Scripture on that day.

Scripture records the lives of many people who were disobedient to God (such as Adam and Eve). As I study, I ask myself, *In what way am I displaying disobedience and rebellion against God?* I then ask the Lord to reveal that to me. I ask Him, "What in my life is mirroring the lives of those I am reading about in Scripture?" When I start asking these questions, the story goes from being a historical story to becoming *my* story.

In addition, I may ask if I am prejudiced like Jonah was toward the Ninevites. Is there a group that I harbor resentment toward or that I am prejudiced against? Although I know God is merciful and compassionate, do I feel threatened or jealous of others when God shows them favor?

The application to self will vary from time to time, but the main point is that

I see the parallels between the biblical story and my story. The ultimate goal of transformational Bible study is application, not just interpretation.

B. Sharing with others. I have always determined to share at least one idea that I have uncovered in Scripture each day. This can take the form of encouraging someone. Or I can be excited about a new discovery and I may just want to share some insights or blessings that I have gained from the text. I try to do it in a natural way, without forcing it. I get tremendous blessings from doing this, and many people have told me they have been blessed by the insights I have shared with them.

C. Memorization. Memorization is an art that is not often exercised. Children are told to memorize verses for Sabbath School, but when they become adults, they stop doing it. I believe that we should commit Scripture to memory, even if it is just the main thought of the text. "The mind must be restrained, and not allowed to wander. It should be trained to dwell upon the Scriptures; even whole chapters may be *committed to memory*, to be repeated when Satan comes in with his temptations."[7]

"Colossians 3:16 tells us to 'let the word of Christ dwell in us richly' [author's translation]. Deuteronomy 6:4-9 tells us to bind God's law on our foreheads, teach it to our children, talk about it wherever we go, and make it an integral part of our lives. We must know Scripture first before we can teach it or apply it as God desires."[8]

Jesus quoted the Old Testament frequently in His life and ministry. He quoted from books such as Exodus, Deuteronomy, Psalms, and Isaiah. "It's clear that he thought of the Scriptures as the ultimate authority in life and a way to understand the heart and desires of God."[9] Let us follow Jesus by knowing and trusting Scripture the way He did.

"When we know God's Word and obey it, we are able to experience God at a deeper level and experience the freedom that comes only through obedience (John 8:31-32, 14:21). The deeper we know God, the deeper we know his will for us. Romans 12:2 says that when we renew our minds and are transformed, we will be able to 'discern what is the will of God, what is good and acceptable and perfect' " (ESV).[10]

D. Transformation. After I have gone through the preceding stages of studying the Scriptures, I ask for the Holy Spirit to bring about the changes in my life that will make me more like Jesus in character, worldview, and thinking. In transformational Bible study, the purpose is to walk with God and be changed by His Spirit.

CONCLUSION

Ultimately, we read the Bible for the purpose of knowing God. "You will seek me and find me when you seek me with all your heart" (Jeremiah 29:13; see also Deuteronomy 4:29).

Ellen White urges us to " 'search the Scriptures.' No other book will give you such pure, elevating, ennobling thoughts; from no other book can you obtain a deep, religious experience. When you devote time to self-examination, to humble prayer, to earnest study of God's word, the holy Spirit is near to apply the truth to your heart. As you feed upon the heavenly manna, you will find comfort and joy, and will be inspired to tell others of the wonderful experience you have received."[11]

Start with a plan. Make adjustments as you go and find what works for you. Then focus on cementing your routine and making time with God in His Word a habit. It is easy for other things to crowd out your time in the Word, so guard your time with Him. Stick with it, and you will be changed.

---

1. S. Joseph Kidder, *Out of Babylon: How God Found Me on the Streets of Baghdad* (Nampa, ID: Pacific Press®, 2018), 19, 20.

2. When the Pharisees questioned what Jesus did on the Sabbath, He said, "Haven't you read what David did?" (Matthew 12:3); "Haven't you read in the Law that the priests on Sabbath duty in the temple desecrate the Sabbath and yet are innocent?" (verse 5). When Jesus was questioned on divorce, He responded, "Haven't you read . . . that at the beginning the Creator 'made them male and female'?" (Matthew 19:4). When the religious leaders questioned Jesus as children in the temple courts were shouting "Hosanna to the Son of David" in reference to Him, Jesus said, "Have you never read, 'From the lips of children and infants you, Lord, have called forth your praise'?" (Matthew 21:16). When Jesus told the parable of the wicked vineyard tenants to the religious leaders, He concluded by saying, "Have you never read in the Scriptures: 'The stone the builders rejected has become the cornerstone'?" (verse 42). Finally, when the Sadducees doubted the resurrection, Jesus replied, "Have you not read what God said to you?" (Matthew 22:31).

3. Ellen G. White, *Counsels to Parents, Teachers, and Students* (Nampa, ID: Pacific Press®, 2011), 421.

4. Ed Stetzer, "New Research: Less Than 20% of Churchgoers Read the Bible Daily," Exchange, *Christianity Today*, September 13, 2012, http://www.christianitytoday.com/edstetzer/2012/september/new-research-less-than-20-of-churchgoers-read-bible-daily.html.

5. Steven J. Cole, "Lesson 17: Why You Need the Bible (2 Timothy 3:16-17)," Bible.org, April 15, 2013, https://bible.org/seriespage/lesson-17-why-you-need-bible-2-timothy-316-17.

6. Ellen G. White, *The Desire of Ages* (Nampa, ID: Pacific Press®, 2002), 171.

7. Ellen G. White, *Gospel Workers* (Battle Creek, MI: Review and Herald®, 1892), 418; emphasis added.

8. Kevin Halloran, "Ten Biblical Reasons to Memorize Scripture," Unlocking the Bible, November 1, 2016, https://unlockingthebible.org/2016/11/ten-biblical-reasons-to-memorize-scripture/.

9. Halloran, "Ten Biblical Reasons to Memorize Scripture."

10. Halloran, "Ten Biblical Reasons to Memorize Scripture."

11. Ellen G. White, "Bible Religion," *Review and Herald*, May 4, 1897.

CHAPTER 11

FEEDING ON GOD'S WORD
How to Read the Bible for Transformation

"I desire to do your will, my God; your law is within my heart."
—Psalm 40:8

Paul said in Romans 12:2: 'Be *transformed* by the renewing of your mind' (emphasis added). The word Paul uses here is the word we use for the metamorphosis of a butterfly. The change in the end is something completely different than was there before."[1] This is a spiritual transformation that can happen to us through the reading of the Bible. This complete character transformation involves matching our thinking, thoughts, and behavior to God's.[2]

Oftentimes Christians read the Bible with a focus on information. Their goal is to learn the content of the Scriptures, including historical data, personal stories, practical principles, important truths, and so on. . . .

However, it's also important for Christians to understand that the Bible is not a textbook for history and philosophy. It's much more significant:

For the word of God is living and effective and sharper than any double-edged sword, penetrating as far as the separation of soul and spirit, joints and marrow. It is able to judge the ideas and thoughts of the heart. (Hebrews 4:12, HCSB)[3]

The Greek word *energēs* ("effectual"; "active") is where we get our word *energy*. It means that the Word is effectual and will accomplish what God intends it to do.[4]

"The primary purpose of the Bible is not to communicate information to our brains. Instead, the primary purpose of the Bible is to change and transform us at the level of our hearts. In other words, in addition to reading the Bible for the purpose of information, Christians must also commit to regularly reading God's Word for the purpose of transformation."[5]

Nothing is more vital to our ability to understand and be transformed by Scripture than wholehearted devotion to Christ. When we are out of tune with

God, our inner world is cluttered with self-centered sin, harbored resentments, and neglected spiritual opportunities. In contrast, a clean inner life sharpens our ability to hear the message of Scripture so that we can escape the enslavement of what is to move on to what can be.

To help move toward that goal, the following are twelve practical steps for reading the Bible, with a focus on transformation. Determine to do as many steps as possible; however, remember that you cannot do them all every day.

1. Read in spite of feelings. Everyone has fluctuating moods. To keep from being victimized by your moods, you should determine to read the Bible when you feel like it, when you don't feel like it, and when you have no feelings at all. How encouraging it is during "down" moods to read in the Bible, "My soul is weary with sorrow; strengthen me according to your word" (Psalm 119:28). I determine in my heart to read the Bible even when I don't feel like it. The amazing thing is, after I read it, I feel blessed and encouraged. It is a matter of simply diving in—the Word will get hold of you and change you.

2. Take time. I know of many people who wake up early in the morning to read Scripture. Others read sometime during the day or at night. Though their practices do not offer precise patterns, they do demonstrate that spiritual development requires us to take quality time for reading the Bible. It is time well spent because every relationship and responsibility is better after we have saturated our minds and souls with God's point of view and expectations.

I start the day with my devotions at six in the morning for one hour. It is very important for me to start the day with God: I want thoughts of God to be with me for the rest of the day. I want His guidance, His will, and His power with me throughout the day. I am going to face challenges, but I know that if God is with me, I am going to face them with confidence.

A couple of years ago I got sick and stayed home. The first day I was bored, so I watched television in the morning. I found myself thinking about the programs I was watching the rest of the day. The following day I decided to start the day with my devotions, and I found myself thinking about the things of God throughout the day. This demonstrated to me the importance of starting every day with God, so His presence and His thoughts are with me for the rest of the day.

3. Find the right place. It may sound strange to worry about where you study the Bible, but this is an important step. If your goal is to have a significant encounter with God's Word, you need to concentrate. That means you need to be proactive about getting rid of distractions—no smartphones beeping, no kids demanding attention, no television, no internet, and so on.

> Even Jesus had to eliminate distractions when He sought out a deeper encounter with God. . . .
>
> *Very early in the morning, while it was still dark, [Jesus] got up, went out, and*

made His way to a deserted place. And He was praying there. . . . [Mark 1:35, HCSB]
Find yourself a quiet, peaceful place where you can realistically dive into the Bible and stay there for awhile.⁶

4. Prepare your heart. Just as it is important to minimize external distractions when you study God's Word, it's also important to prepare yourself internally. Reading the Bible for transformation is a spiritual experience. It involves your heart and emotions—your inner being.

This kind of "internal preparation means different things to different people at different times. For example, if you're buckling under the weight of stress or negative emotions, you may need to spend significant time in prayer before you even approach the Bible. Pray for peace. Pray for a calm heart. Pray for release from stress and anxiety."⁷ "Never should the Bible be studied without prayer. Before opening its pages we should ask for the enlightenment of the Holy Spirit, and it will be given."⁸

At other times you may prefer to worship God in advance of studying His Word. Or, you may want to encounter the reality of God by getting into nature and immersing yourself in the beauty of His creation.

Here's the point: before you even begin flipping pages in the Bible, spend a few moments in contemplation and self-evaluation in order to prepare yourself for a transformational experience.⁹

5. Start simply. If you are a beginner, you should think of the Bible as a library of books. At the outset of a spiritual quest, it is useful to browse through this sixty-six-book library until a section captures your interest and speaks to your need.

Those who are new to Scripture might begin with Matthew 5–7 (the Sermon on the Mount); Psalms 23, 24, 100, 122, 139; Isaiah 35, 55; the Gospels of Mark and Luke; or Paul's letter to the Philippians. Next, begin cultivating a friendship with the Old Testament prophets and books such as Genesis, Exodus, Isaiah, Jeremiah, and Jonah. Then turn to the Acts of the Apostles in the New Testament for exciting accounts of the early church. After completing these sections, you will be ready for almost any passage.

6. Read with anticipation. To counteract boredom, count on receiving a fresh word from God each time you read. Anticipation nourishes readiness to listen and learn. People who look for a fresh word from Scripture are seldom disappointed. Receptivity always expands as new truths are allowed into the shady nooks and obscure corners of life. If you expect the Bible to speak to your situation, you will usually discover a gold mine of resources.

As you read the Bible and worship God, anticipate that He will show up, bless you, reveal Himself to you, and guide and direct you.

7. Evaluate what the text says. When you're ready to read through a passage of Scripture for transformation, decide to spend time to find out what God is telling you in the text. Seek its meaning, and how it can be useful in your life.

"Spend time identifying the truths contained" in the specific passage of Scripture you are reading. Find and note "the major themes and principles contained in the verses you read."[10]

Keep reading in spite of difficult passages. Ellen White writes, "We should come with reverence to the study of the Bible, feeling that we are in the presence of God. All lightness and trifling should be laid aside. While some portions of the word are easily understood, the true meaning of other parts is not so readily discerned. There must be patient study and meditation and earnest prayer. Every student, as he opens the Scriptures, should ask for the enlightenment of the Holy Spirit; and the promise is sure that it will be given."[11]

Take time to seek clarification from commentaries, atlases, dictionaries, and other study aids. But keep reading. Think of Scripture as God's personal word to you for each new day.

8. Enter Scripture as an active participant. Look at a miracle, an event, a parable, a relationship, or even a single word from the Bible through the eyes of the people who were there. Allow its first meaning to take root in you. Seek to apply all your senses to help you live the experience and listen for its contemporary significance. How did Lazarus feel as he threw off his graveclothes? What would it be like to spend time with Peter and John? As you read Jeremiah, think how troubled his times seemed to him. How would it feel to be in prison with Paul? What was the leper's reaction when Jesus healed him?

Be an active participant who views the incident as if it happened yesterday or this morning. For example, in your mind, climb into the tree with Zacchaeus to get a better view of Jesus. Try to imagine every detail of that event. See, hear, and smell the pressing crowd. Feel the burning heat. Grip the tree limb. Sneeze because of the swirling dust. Then allow your heart to melt with devotion as Jesus calls your name and invites Himself to your home.

9. Paraphrase a passage. This exercise helps you learn more about life from Scripture because it requires you to carefully consider the meaning of every word in a passage. Ask yourself as you read, *What does the passage say to me?* To be most effective, this approach requires that paraphrases be written—writing encourages organization and precision of thought.

Some people keep a journal in which they record paraphrases and jot down new thoughts for future reading. Writing your paraphrase now, and then reading it later deepens its impact and makes you deal with the passage at least twice. In reality, two or more thoughtful encounters with a passage make it reverberate in one's inner world for a long time. This practice will likely lead to the joyous discovery that obedience to Scripture is more than a duty—it is also a gloriously satisfying adventure.

A young boy in juvenile detention came up with a creative paraphrase of the first verse in Psalm 23: "The Lord is like my Probation Officer. He will help me. He tries to help me make it every day. He makes me play it cool."[12] A pilot might say, "The Lord is my Pilot." A sailor might say, "The Lord is my Captain." A mother might say, "The Lord is my Counselor as I raise my kids." This technique can make Scripture relevant to each person's situation.

10. Determine the implications for your life. Read the text until you receive a word that speaks to your situation. Put your name in the promise as you read: "I will never leave [your name], nor forsake [your name]" (Hebrews 13:5, KJV). "Who shall separate [your name] from the love of Christ? Shall trouble or hardship or persecution or famine or nakedness or danger or sword?" (Romans 8:35). "I will not leave [your name] as [an orphan]; I will come to [your name]" (John 14:18).

Another way to make Scripture your own is to pray it back to God. On your knees, with your Bible open to a passage, simply pray, "Lord, I think this passage promises help for my present problem." Or "Lord, this passage makes demands I cannot meet. I need Your help now." Or "Lord, open the meaning of this passage for me. Overcome my slow mind and active resistance. I want the mind of Christ." This method harmonizes belief with behavior as you move from merely reading the Bible to actually living it.

11. Determine how you will obey.

It's not enough for us to know what we need to do.
We need to actually do something. We need to obey what the Bible says through our daily actions and attitudes.
Do not merely listen to the word, and so deceive yourselves. Do what it says (James 1:22, NIV).
. . . [We need to prayerfully] make a specific, concrete plan about how you will obey and apply the truths you discover.[13]

Since character development is not a one-time event but an ongoing experience in the life of believers, we should continually be reading the Bible for transformation, allowing the Holy Spirit to bring us closer to the will of God.

12. Share it. One gifted Bible teacher said, "It was by teaching that I learned what I know about the Bible." Home Bible studies, family devotions, Bible classes, and even casual conversations offer opportunities to encourage others with Scripture. A shared word from the Bible frequently relieves personal perplexity. To offer a promise from Scripture provides a lift for the giver and keeps the receiver thinking about the passage for a long time, so both are energized by its message.

Each day I always try to share at least one thought from what I have read in Scripture with someone. I have noticed it brings encouragement and hope to others. Sometimes it moves people to think about issues they have never thought about before. It reminds them of the love of God.

CONCLUSION

In this chapter, we covered twelve steps to studying the Bible. To encourage lifelong growth, remember two characteristics of Scripture that stand forever: the Bible is (1) simple enough that anyone can find their way to God and (2) challenging enough to stimulate the most brilliant mind. Wherever you are in your spiritual growth, the Bible is for you.

The study of Scripture has to be bathed in earnest prayer for the Holy Spirit to reveal His will to us and through His power change us to become more and more like Him. May we take the time to immerse ourselves in God's Word.[14]

---

1. Tobin Crenshaw, "Transformation Starts in the Mind," Christian Bible Studies, *Christianity Today*, February 16, 2010, https://www.christianitytoday.com/biblestudies/articles/theology/thatisreallylife.html.

2. Portions of this chapter originally appeared in S. Joseph Kidder, "How to Study the Bible for Transformation," Kidder's Column, *Elder's Digest* 22, no. 3 (July–September 2016): 30, 31.

3. Sam O'Neal, "How to Study the Bible for Transformation," ThoughtCo, last updated March 6, 2017, https://www.thoughtco.com/how-to-study-the-bible-for-transformation-363284; emphasis in the original.

4. Steven J. Cole, "Lesson 13: God's Powerful Word (Hebrews 4:12-13)," Bible.org, May 20, 2013, https://bible.org/seriespage/lesson-13-god's-powerful-word-hebrews-412-13.

5. O'Neal, "How to Study the Bible for Transformation."

6. O'Neal, "How to Study the Bible for Transformation," emphasis in the original.

7. O'Neal, "How to Study the Bible for Transformation."

8. Ellen G. White, *Steps to Christ* (Nampa, ID: Pacific Press®, 2000), 91.

9. O'Neal, "How to Study the Bible for Transformation."

10. O'Neal, "How to Study the Bible for Transformation."

11. Ellen G. White, *Testimonies to Ministers and Gospel Workers* (Nampa, ID: Pacific Press®, 2003), 107, 108.

12. Carl F. Burke, *God Is for Real, Man* (New York: Association Press, 1966), 39.

13. O'Neal, "How to Study the Bible for Transformation"; emphasis in the original.

14. See appendix 1 at the end of this book for a guide to journaling that combines many of the steps detailed in this chapter.

PART 5

Journey to the
Heart of God
Through Outrageous
Forgiveness

CHAPTER 12

OUTRAGEOUS FORGIVENESS
Unpayable Debt

Then Peter came to Jesus and asked, "Lord, how many times shall I forgive my brother or sister who sins against me? Up to seven times?" Jesus answered, "I tell you, not seven times, but seventy-seven times."
—Matthew 18:21, 22

There is a story told about a man that was bitten by a dog that was discovered to have rabies. The man was rushed to the hospital, and tests revealed that he, too, had contracted the dreaded disease. The doctor came in to see the man and said, "I am sorry to say you have rabies. Your situation is incurable and terminal. All I can suggest is that you get your affairs together as quickly as possible." The man was stunned. Finally, after a few moments, he summoned the strength to ask for a piece of paper and a pen, and he began to write furiously. About an hour later, the doctor came back to check on his patient. The man was still writing. The doctor said, "Well, I'm glad to see you're getting your will together." The man looked up and said, "Doc, this ain't no will. It's a list of all the people I'm going to bite before I die."

If you've lived on this earth for any period of time, you likely have your own list of people you want to bite before you die. On your list, there may be a fellow church member who relentlessly criticizes you. There may be a coworker who berates you. There may be a close friend who betrays you. You cannot control the offenses that come into your life, but you can control what you do with those offenses. You can hold on to them until they metastasize into bitterness and destroy you and your family, or you can make the choice to let go of and forgive those offenses. I personally believe that the single greatest choice any Christian makes is whether to forgive those who wronged him or her.

Why should I forgive people who have hurt me deeply, and how can I let go of those wounds that have scarred my life?

UNPAYABLE DEBT

Peter comes to Jesus one day and says, "Lord, how many times shall I forgive my brother or sister who sins against me? Up to seven times?" (Matthew 18:21).

> Peter is expecting Jesus to say that such magnanimity would be beyond the call of duty. The rabbis used to say there was an obligation to forgive someone three times; Peter here is doubling it and throwing in a bonus round for good measure.
>
> The concern behind Peter's question has been felt by everyone who has ever been hurt. Why should I forgive? What if the other person doesn't deserve it? I might get hurt again. Forgiveness looks like a pretty risky business. Forgiveness looks to Peter like one of those activities that Jesus is always talking about, and it is probably a pretty spiritual thing to do, but it doesn't always work out so well for those of us who live in the real world.
>
> Imagine Peter's response when, instead of commending him, Jesus tells him he still has seventy acts of forgiveness to go: "I tell you, not seven times, but seventy-seven times."[1]

Perhaps this is an allusion to a character in the book of Genesis named Lamech, who takes the concept of revenge to its ultimate extreme.[2] He says to his wives,

> I have killed a man for wounding me,
> a young man for injuring me.
> If Cain is avenged seven times,
> then Lamech seventy-seven times. (Genesis 4:23, 24)

But Jesus replaces seventy-seven times of vengeance with seventy-seven times of forgiveness. This doesn't mean that on the seventy-eighth violation Peter can let the offender have it. Jesus is "making a point that there are two ways to live with hurt: the way of vengeance and the way of forgiveness. The first way leads to death, and the second to life."[3]

Then Jesus goes on to tell a story to illustrate the magnitude of forgiveness.

> Therefore, the kingdom of heaven is like a king who wanted to settle accounts with his servants. As he began the settlement, a man who owed him ten thousand bags of gold [ten thousand talents] was brought to him. Since he was not able to pay, the master ordered that he and his wife and his children and all that he had be sold to repay the debt.
>
> At this the servant fell on his knees before him. "Be patient with me," he begged, "and I will pay back everything." The servant's master took pity on him, canceled the debt and let him go.

But when that servant went out, he found one of his fellow servants who owed him a hundred silver coins. He grabbed him and began to choke him. "Pay back what you owe me!" he demanded.

His fellow servant fell to his knees and begged him, "Be patient with me, and I will pay it back."

But he refused. Instead, he went off and had the man thrown into prison until he could pay the debt. When the other servants saw what had happened, they were outraged and went and told their master everything that had happened.

Then the master called the servant in. "You wicked servant," he said, "I canceled all that debt of yours because you begged me to. Shouldn't you have had mercy on your fellow servant just as I had on you?" In anger his master handed him over to the jailers to be tortured, until he should pay back all he owed.

This is how my heavenly Father will treat each of you unless you forgive your brother or sister from your heart. (Matthew 18:23–35)

Now, in our culture, we don't know much about talents, so we may miss the enormity of this debt. A talent was the equivalent of 15 years' wages, so the servant owed his master 150,000 years' wages or just under 55 million days' wages.

This is an unbelievable sum of money. It is a debt that is impossible to pay. To give you a point of context, the total annual revenue collected by the Roman Empire from the whole land of Palestine averaged about nine hundred talents as opposed to the ten thousand talents the servant owed. We also know that Solomon's temple was famous for its incredible amounts of gold. In fact, according to 1 Chronicles 29:4–7, all the gold contained in the temple was eight thousand talents, which is still less than this man owed his master![4]

Do you get the idea? This poor servant stands before the king with an absolutely impossible debt. Jesus' first listeners would have perked up at this point in His story and said, "Wait a minute. That is impossible!"

But that's the way Jesus tells the story. The poor servant is standing in front of his master with a debt that would take 150,000 years to repay, and he doesn't have the money to repay it. He has to stand there and say, "Sorry, but I don't have it." Is it any wonder the king commands that the servant, his wife, and children all be sold into slavery?

The servant falls on his knees and begs for mercy. "Master, have patience with me, and I will repay you everything." How in the world could he ever do that? Certainly, the king knew better. But the king had compassion. He decided to forgive the whole debt, and the servant went out with a clean slate, completely forgiven.

YOU OWE, YOU PAY

John Ortberg, in his book *Everybody's Normal Till You Get to Know Them*, writes,

Jesus' listeners would know that such a thing would never happen. When it comes to debt, every economy that has ever existed has been built on one simple rule: *You owe, you pay.* Certain people who lend money are always quite touchy about this. They keep careful accounts. . . .

It is crucial here to grasp what Jesus is saying about the heart of God. When the CEO [master] forgives the debt, it doesn't simply disappear. There is still the loss of a vast fortune to be accounted for. Who absorbs it? The answer, of course, is the owner. When he forgives the embezzler [servant], it is not a casual thing. Forgiveness comes with a price tag that no one in the room but the old man [master] can ever fully understand. He comes up with a whole new system for handling the unpayable debt: *You owe, I'll pay.*

Imagine the embezzler's [servant's] response. "I can't believe it. I didn't have a prayer. It was a total long shot—and it paid off! I threw myself on the mercy of the court, and he took the loss. I got grace. I'm free!". . .

. . . Now we need to step back from the story for a while. The master in Jesus' story, of course, is a stand-in for God. The other character, the embezzler [servant], represents you and me. Jesus says we have accumulated a moral debt before a just and holy God, and it's been growing for years. Every time we are less than honest or fudge an expense account or tax return or treat a five-year-old too harshly or make a cutting remark we shouldn't or should speak truth in love but don't or gossip or tell a racist joke or have sexually impure thoughts—each act adds to a mountain of moral debt. All human beings owe that enormous debt.[5]

YOU OWE, GOD PAYS

What we owe God is an unpayable debt. David said, "I was sinful at birth" (Psalm 51:5). We sin from the moment we are conscious. Many times we look at the sin in terms of the act, but in the eyes of God, even our immoral desires, thoughts, and motives are sin.

For instance, Jesus redefined adultery from the act itself to the contemplation of the act when He said, "You have heard that it was said, 'You shall not commit adultery.' But I tell you that anyone who looks at a woman lustfully has already committed adultery with her in his heart" (Matthew 5:27, 28).

He also redefined murder from the physical act of killing someone to being angry at that person: "You have heard that it was said to the people long ago, 'You shall not murder, and anyone who murders will be subject to judgment.' But I tell you that anyone who is angry with a brother or sister will be subject to judgment" (verses 21, 22).

Then He changed the definition of love from just loving the people who love us to loving the people who hate us and are our enemies: "You have heard that it was said, 'Love your neighbor and hate your enemy.' But I tell you, love your enemies and pray for those who persecute you, that you may be children of your Father in heaven" (verses 43, 44).

The Bible has many words for *sin*, with meanings such as "missing the mark," "transgression," and "going astray." One word, though—`avah* in Hebrew—means "to distort," "to make crooked," or "to pervert" and includes sin and its consequences. It is manifested in thought, word, and deed as we show the twisting of our souls (Job 33:27; Psalm 106:43; Isaiah 30:13).[6]

We live in a state of sin. Even the good things we want to do might have mixed motives. For example, we want to help someone, but we also want recognition. We often love just so we can be loved. We worship God for the blessings and not for who He is.

Ellen White saw that sin is much deeper than we ever thought. Even our good motives, actions, and religious services are not acceptable to God because they are passing through sin-tainted humanity. She writes, "The religious services, the prayers, the praise, the penitent confession of sin ascend from true believers as incense to the heavenly sanctuary, but passing through the corrupt channels of humanity, they are so defiled that unless purified by blood, they can never be of value with God. They ascend not in spotless purity, and unless the Intercessor, who is at God's right hand, presents and purifies all by His righteousness, it is not acceptable to God."[7]

Our debt to God is infinite and unpayable, but we do not have to despair because the blood of Jesus Christ took care of everything. Ellen White continues, "All incense from earthly tabernacles must be moist with the cleansing drops of the blood of Christ. He holds before the Father the censer of His own merits, in which there is no taint of earthly corruption. He gathers into this censer the prayers, the praise, and the confessions of His people, and with these He puts His own spotless righteousness. Then, perfumed with the merits of Christ's propitiation, the incense comes up before God wholly and entirely acceptable. Then gracious answers are returned."[8]

So God Himself pays the debt. We owed, and He paid. He forgave. "In him we have redemption through his blood, the forgiveness of sins, in accordance with the riches of God's grace" (Ephesians 1:7; see also Galatians 3:13).

FORGIVEN TO FORGIVE

Let's return to Jesus' parable of the unmerciful servant. The servant hadn't gone very far when he met a man who owed him money, about a hundred denarii (the equivalent of one hundred days' wages). He was so adamant to get it back that he grabbed the debtor by the throat and growled, "Pay back what you owe me" (Matthew 21:28).

This second debtor begged for mercy with the same words the first debtor had used with the king: "Be patient with me, and I will pay it back" (verse 29). But the king's servant would have none of it. He put his debtor in prison. Some of his fellow servants saw the whole thing, recognized the injustice, and reported it to the king.

Jesus concluded the story by saying:

> Then the master called the servant in. "You wicked servant," he said. "I canceled all that debt of yours because you begged me to. Shouldn't you have had mercy on your fellow servant just as I had on you?" In anger his master handed him over to the jailers to be tortured, until he should pay back all he owed.
>
> This is how my heavenly Father will treat each of you unless you forgive your brother or sister from your heart." (verses 32–35)

We all have been wronged at some time or another. Someone, no doubt, has hurt us deeply—an unfaithful spouse, an abusive parent, a disloyal friend. It's hard to forget those hurts. They aren't trivial—they're real—and it's hard to forgive. It's easy for these things to loom so large that they overpower us and fill us with bitterness and the desire for revenge.

If anyone had the right to feel resentment, it would have been Stephen when he was unjustly stoned. But he surrendered his bitterness to the Lord; before he died, he prayed, " 'Lord, do not hold this sin against them.' When he had said this, he fell asleep" (Acts 7:60).

THE COST OF AN UNFORGIVING HEART

John Ortberg writes about one of the reasons we are to forgive others:

> True forgiveness is never cheap. Hurt is deep; hurt is unfair. You want the offenders to know the pain they have inflicted on you. You want them to get paid back.
>
> In fact, only one thing I know costs more than forgiving someone. Know what it is?
>
> Not forgiving them. Non-forgiveness costs your heart.[9]

Forgive and your anger will be removed. Bit by bit, joy will come back to you. You will be able to trust again, and compassion will be restored to your heart.

Forgive and the powerful grudge you nurse will grow smaller and weaker. It will no longer be a monster of hostility, ruining your life. Bitterness and hate will flee. This is life with forgiveness. God calls us to "get rid of all bitterness, rage and anger, brawling and slander, along with every form of malice. Be kind and compassionate to one another, forgiving each other, just as in Christ God forgave you" (Ephesians 4:31, 32).

JESUS SHOWS US THE WAY OF FORGIVENESS

You and I are the debtor in this story. Every one of us has sinned and failed to live up to God's ideal for us, and in a very real sense, that puts us in debt. We owe something that we cannot pay. We are hopelessly bankrupt.

Jesus' story, however, shows us that God is willing to forgive us completely. David defines forgiveness as follows:

> Blessed is the one
>   whose transgressions are forgiven,
>   whose sins are covered.
> Blessed is the one
>   whose sin the Lord does not count against them
>   and in whose spirit is no deceit. (Psalm 32:1, 2)

Another Bible translation puts it this way: "What happiness for those whose guilt has been forgiven! What joys when sins are covered over! What relief for those who have confessed their sins and God has cleared their record" (verses 1, 2, TLB).

God is willing to wipe the slate clean. He accepts us. He doesn't say, "We will work out an installment plan, so you can pay back the debt." He doesn't say, "We will lower the debt so that you have to pay only a part of it." No. He says, "I forgive you totally. The debt is canceled. You are free." When we grasp the enormity of the gift of forgiveness that has come to us in Jesus Christ, it makes a difference. The meaning and reality of that gift, when we understand it, enables us to forgive those who have wronged us.

The servant in Jesus' story never really comprehended the gift of grace that he had received. You can tell that from his response to the king: "I will pay back everything." As if he ever could! Our debt of sin is far too great for us ever to atone for it. But on the cross, Jesus Christ carried it for us. There's no way to measure what He has given us.

When we realize that we have been forgiven an impossible debt, it's hard for us to get terribly excited about the one somebody owes us. This doesn't mean that we will ignore wrongs and injustices, but we will see fellow sinners from a different perspective when we realize what God has forgiven us.

God knows that a heart filled with gratitude for His forgiveness will inevitably forgive as it has been forgiven. Understanding that God has forgiven us an impossible debt overwhelms us, gives us a new perspective, and opens our hearts to forgive as we have been forgiven.

TRANSFER OF CREDIT

After accepting the call to teach at Andrews University, I started receiving many invitations for speaking engagements all over the world. In one of those early days of frequent flying, I was traveling from South Bend International Airport in Indiana to Chicago O'Hare International Airport. (At this time, O'Hare was the busiest airport in the world.) I arrived in Chicago at 6:00 A.M., hungry and sleep deprived. Upon my arrival in Chicago, the crowd was elbow to elbow, and the bathroom was unclean; being a germaphobe, I decided not to use it. I kept walking, and to my right, I saw an oasis in the middle of the desert: a sign that read "United Club."

I fly United, so I went to the lobby of the club. I looked around, and I saw the breakfast bar on my right: bagels, muffins, yogurt, eggs, many fruits, and cereals. The seats were leather and looked comfortable. I looked to my left and saw a sparkling, clean bathroom with flowers. Even the view was beautiful. I said to myself, "This is the place where I belong. I need to be here."

A woman at the front desk stopped me and asked, "Do you have a membership?"

"What do you mean?" I said. "I fly United, and this is a United Club."

"No, this is for our elite fliers who pay extra," she retorted.

I replied, "I fly a lot."

She looked at my record and said, "Mr. Kidder, you don't even have enough miles to use our bathroom. You do not belong here. This is for our elite fliers who fly hundreds of thousands of miles. You must pay one hundred dollars for one day or seven hundred dollars for a yearly membership. I am sorry, I have to send you outside."

I left, heartbroken. About three weeks later, I was flying the same route back to Chicago. This time Niels-Erik Andreasen, the then-president of Andrews University, happened to be sitting next to me. When we arrived in Chicago, he invited me to breakfast at the club, but I said, "No, I would love to, but I tried going three weeks ago and was rejected."

He replied, "Just come with me."

We walked to the club. I was behind him, trying to remain unnoticed. I saw the same woman working behind the desk. He showed her his card, and she said, "It is so good to have you, Dr. Andreasen. The food is on the right. The bathroom's on the left, and here is the code for the internet. Let me check the status of your flight and see if you have been upgraded to first class." Then she saw me, and my heart started beating quickly. I knew I would be rejected once again. She looked at me, remembering my face from before and said, "I told you before, you do not qualify to be here." Then Dr. Andreasen looked at her and said, "This is Dr. Joseph Kidder from Andrews University. Today, he is going to be my guest of honor." Her facial expression immediately changed, and she said, "Dr. Kidder, it is good to have you with us. The food is on your right. The bathroom's on your left, and here is the code for the internet. Do you want me to check on the status of your flight?"

What made the difference was the fact that Dr. Andreasen invited me to be his guest of honor, and everything changed. I was able to enjoy the club and be there for several hours because of the credit of somebody else.

One day each one of us will stand in front of the Judge of the whole universe. He will ask for your qualification to be in heaven. You might say, "I have been an Adventist all my life. I went on a mission trip to Africa, and I helped the homeless." Then He will say something like, "All of this amounts to forty points." You think you need one hundred points, so you continue. "I read my Bible every day." Another ten points. You are on your way up. "I pray a lot, and I am a youth director." Another thirty points. "I decided to be vegan recently." Another twenty points. Now you are up to a hundred, but then you are disappointed. He tells you that you need a trillion points to get into that place. In order to be there, you must have always been perfect and pure, thinking the right thoughts and doing the right things from the day you were born.

Suddenly, Jesus shows up and says, "This person is going to be my guest of honor," and you get to go in. Not because of anything you have done, but because of Jesus and His righteousness. His sinless and perfect life becomes yours. All He has done is credited to you. Our enormous debt was paid by the enormous credit of Jesus Christ.

As Jesus has chosen to forgive us, we also have a choice: forgiveness or bitterness, vengeance or mercy, hatred or grace, life or death. Choose wisely. "Therefore, as God's chosen people, holy and dearly loved, clothe yourselves with compassion, kindness, humility, gentleness and patience. Bear with each other and forgive one another if any of you has a grievance against someone. Forgive as the Lord forgave you" (Colossians 3:12, 13).

---

1. John Ortberg, *Everybody's Normal Till You Get to Know Them* (Grand Rapids, MI: Zondervan, 2003), 152.

2. Ortberg, *Everybody's Normal*, 151.

3. Ortberg, *Everybody's Normal*, 152.

4. John F. MacArthur, *The Freedom and Power of Forgiveness* (Wheaton, IL: Crossway Books, 1998), 104.

5. Ortberg, *Everybody's Normal*, 154–156.

6. Colin Brown, ed., *The New International Dictionary of New Testament Theology*, vol. 3 (Grand Rapids, MI: Regency, 1971), 573–587; see also *Baker's Evangelical Dictionary of Biblical Theology*, s.v. "Sin," accessed February 4, 2019, http://www.biblestudytools.com/dictionary/sin/.

7. Ellen G. White, *Selected Messages* (Hagerstown, MD: Review and Herald®, 2006), 1:344.

8. White, *Selected Messages*, 1:344.

9. Ortberg, *Everybody's Normal*, 165.

CHAPTER 13

OUTRAGEOUS FORGIVENESS
The Miracle of Starting Over

Get rid of all bitterness, rage and anger, brawling and slander, along with every form of malice. Be kind and compassionate to one another, forgiving each other, just as in Christ God forgave you.
—Ephesians 4:31, 32

Kevin Tunell spent New Year's Eve in 1982 celebrating. Before he got in his car, Tunell's friends urged him not to drive, but he bragged, "Nothing will ever happen to me." While driving drunk, he lost control of his car and smashed into a young woman's vehicle. Susan Herzog was pronounced dead at the scene.

Seventeen-year-old Tunell pleaded guilty to involuntary manslaughter and drunk driving. He was sentenced to three years' probation and a year of community service lecturing about the dangers of drinking and driving. To settle a civil lawsuit, Tunell agreed to the unorthodox stipulation set by the Herzog family: sending a check for one dollar every Friday for eighteen years to Susan's parents, Lou and Patty Herzog. The Herzogs chose this penalty because Susan, the youngest of their three daughters, was eighteen when she was killed that Friday. In total, Tunell had to pay $936. The drastic drop from a $1.5 million fine to $936 shows either the Herzogs' interest in teaching Tunell a lesson or their vindictive spirit for him to remember the act he committed.

The punishment was harder on Tunell than he expected. The Herzogs took him to court for failing to send checks regularly. Tunell tearfully told the judge that the pain and guilt he felt each time he wrote Susan's name on a check had become too excruciating. He was sentenced to thirty days in jail for contempt of court. Susan's father responded to Tunell's jail time by saying, "Susan's death is there every waking moment. . . . But every time we don't get a check, there's only one thing that comes to our mind: He doesn't remember."

But this was not the case. Tunell had performed his community service duties. He spoke out in two videos on the dangers of drunk driving, and after his year of

101

speaking to schools and other groups was finished, he continued volunteering his time for six more years.

Tunell described that he was tormented by the reminder of what he'd done when he had to send the checks. At one point in the proceedings, Tunell offered the Herzogs two boxes full of prewritten checks carrying dates through 2001, which was a year longer than required by the original settlement. Susan's parents refused them.

The Herzogs maintained that their actions did not originate from a place of vindictiveness. "We do want him to remember," said Susan's mother, Patty. "But that doesn't mean we don't want him to accept it—and get on with his life." The Herzogs seemed to believe that Tunell could palliate his guilt only through being accountable. During an interview, Tunell stated, "From now on, without fail, I will write the checks. All I can do . . . is to try to go on living—and to live as productively as possible."[1]

Most people would understand the Herzogs' anger. But were 936 payments sufficient penance for them to demand? Was the family truly able to put the matter to rest in 2000? Was eighteen years' worth of reparation and remorse sufficient? By the end of the eighteen years, did the Herzogs truly forgive Tunell and have peace?[2]

How many payments do we require? No one makes it through life free of injury. Like Susan and her parents, we all have been victims of someone who has hurt us. Have we truly forgiven that person and do we have peace about him or her and the situation?

COMMON MISCONCEPTIONS ABOUT FORGIVENESS

"What is it that we do, exactly, when we forgive? Lewis Smedes . . . says we must start by understanding what forgiveness is *not* and then look at the three stages that are part of what forgiving *is*."[3]

1. Forgiving is not the same thing as excusing. "Forgiving does not mean tolerating bad behavior or pretending that what someone did was not so bad."[4] Forgiving someone who breaks our trust does not mean that we give them back their position in our lives. Forgivers are not doormats; to forgive a person is not a signal that we are willing to put up with what someone does.[5]

God did not excuse Moses when he struck the rock of Kadesh when he was told to speak to it, but He still forgave him (Numbers 20:1–13).

2. Forgiving is not forgetting. "Scripture writers sometimes use the language of 'forgetting' to describe how God deals with our sin, but this doesn't mean that God has a memory retrieval problem."[6] (For example, God said, "And their sins and iniquities will I remember no more" [Hebrews 10:17, KJV; see also Psalm 103:12].) This means that God does not bring up our past sins and hold them against us. John MacArthur makes the observation that God does not forget our sins. He is an omnipotent God. He chooses not to remember them and use them against us.[7] The Bible says that love "does not dishonor others, it is not self-seeking, it is not easily angered, it keeps no record of wrongs" (1 Corinthians 13:5). Forgiveness is what's required precisely when we *cannot* forget. Forgiveness is not a way to avoid or forget the pain but to heal it.[8]

3. Forgiving is not the same thing as reconciling. Forgiveness and reconciliation are two separate things. "Forgiveness takes place within the heart of one human being. It can be granted even if the other person does not ask for it or deserve it."[9] When we wait for someone to repent before we forgive, we are surrendering our future to the person who wronged us.

"Reconciliation requires that the offender still be alive and be sincerely repentant for the wrong he or she committed. Reconciliation requires the rebuilding of trust, and that means good faith on the part of *both* parties."[10]

WHAT FORGIVENESS IS

Even though King Saul tried to destroy David, David responded with kindness and forgiveness to Saul's household. When David became king, he showed kindness to Saul's grandson Mephibosheth. He restored to him and his family the land owned by the former king and paid to have the land farmed and cared for. David also made a place for Mephibosheth at his own table so that he was accepted as part of the king's family (2 Samuel 9). David forgave Saul without ever reconciling with Saul himself.

Dick Tibbits, in *Forgive to Live*, defines forgiveness as "the process of reframing one's anger and hurt from the past, with the goal of recovering one's peace in the present and revitalizing one's purpose and hopes for the future."[11]

Forgiveness has been defined as "giving up my right to hurt you, for hurting me. It is impossible to live on this fallen planet without getting hurt, offended, misunderstood, lied to, and rejected."[12] But learning how to respond properly by forgiving, being healed, looking at the offender through the eyes of God, and wishing them well is one of the basics of the Christian life.[13]

The apostle Paul defines forgiveness as follows: "God was in Christ reconciling the world to himself, no longer holding people's misdeeds against them" (2 Corinthians 5:19, REB). The word *misdeeds* can be translated as "offenses or harmful acts for which the perpetuators are obligated to atone for."[14] But in this case, it was God in Christ who atoned for them and reconciled the world to Himself. He showed us forgiveness by His decision to relinquish His claim of retribution and judgment on us and to declare us righteous. That is what we need to do to others.

When we forgive, we are to wipe the slate clean, to pardon, and to cancel a debt.

It is important to remember that forgiveness is not granted because a person deserves to be forgiven. Instead, it is an act of love, mercy, and grace.

How we act toward that person may change. It doesn't mean we will put ourselves back into a harmful situation or that we suddenly accept or approve of the person's continued wrong behavior. It simply means we release them from the wrong they committed against us. We forgive them because God forgave us (Ephesians 4:31-32 and Romans 5:8).[15]

THE STAGES OF FORGIVENESS

According to Lewis B. Smedes's *The Art of Forgiving*, there are three stages of forgiveness.

1. Surrendering our right to get even. Forgiveness is a decision not to try to inflict a reciprocal amount of pain on everyone who has caused you hurt. "See that no one repays anyone evil for evil, but always seek to do good to one another and to everyone" (1 Thessalonians 5:15, ESV). "When I forgive you, *I give up the right to hurt you back.* . . . I set you free from the little prison I have placed in my mind."[16] By the same token, when we forgive, we discover that we are set free as well from the prison of pain and grudges we have created for ourselves.[17]

In the Bible, Joseph models this kind of forgiveness. Joseph was treated very badly by his brothers and sold into slavery, eventually ending up in jail. Then he became second in command to the pharaoh of Egypt. He was in a position to get even with his brothers, but he chose to forgive them (Genesis 50:15–21; see also Genesis 45:1–28).

2. Accepting the humanity of the person who has wronged us. Recognizing the humanity of the offender involves a new way of seeing and feeling. When we are deeply hurt, we equate the totality of the person with the wrong that they have done. Instead of looking at them as a human being, we look at them as the scum of the world.[18]

"When we forgive each other, we begin to see more clearly. We do not ignore the hurts, but we see beyond them. We rediscover the humanity of the one who hurt us."[19] "So from now on we regard no one from a worldly point of view. Though we once regarded Christ in this way, we do so no longer" (2 Corinthians 5:16). The one who hurt us "is no longer just an uncollected debt of pain. . . . He is lonely or hurting or weak or nearsighted"—just as we are. "He is also a bearer of the image of God"—just as we are.[20]

In the eyes of the early church, Saul was a persecutor to be feared. After his conversion, God used Ananias to change the perspective of the church to see Saul as a chosen vessel to spread the gospel to the Gentiles (Acts 9:10–19).

3. Revising our feelings and wishing the offender well. Moving into the third stage of forgiveness, "you hope for good things for them. You can hear someone say a kind word about them without inwardly screaming for rebuttal time. You genuinely hope that things are well between them and God, that their relationships are healthy. . . . Of course, this does not happen all at once. And it usually doesn't happen once-for-all; you will have some backsliding, some moments when you would like to hear" they've gone through unexpected pain or trouble. "But the trajectory of the heart is headed in the right direction. When you want good things for someone who hurt you badly, you can pretty much know that the Great Forgiver has been at work in your heart."[21]

In spite of the fact that Jesus was treated badly and was then crucified, He prayed for His enemies (Luke 23:34; see also Matthew 5:43–48). When we forgive, we walk in stride with the forgiving God. The apostle Paul urges us to "get rid of all bitterness, rage and anger, brawling and slander, along with every form of malice. Be kind and compassionate to one another, forgiving each other, just as in Christ God forgave you" (Ephesians 4:31, 32). This is only possible when God makes us into new people by giving us new desires and attitudes toward others.

THE MIRACLE OF FORGIVENESS

"We are always to pursue forgiving people who have hurt us, even when the offenders don't ask for or deserve it. God commands us to forgive because it is the best way to live. He commands us to forgive others because he has forgiven us; he is the Great Forgiver."[22] When we forgive, we break away from a prison of hurt. The chains of bitterness and resentment are broken when we forgive the one who has hurt us. No human beings are more joyful than the forgiving.

"God commands us to forgive whenever we're hurt, and reconcile whenever we can, because life is too short not to do so. . . . If you don't forgive—if you let pride, resentment, stubbornness, and defensiveness stand in your way—you become a hard and bitter person. You carry a burden that will crush the humanity out of your spirit. You will grow a little colder every day."[23] But if we forgive, we will live in joy, our wounds will be healed, and we will be set free.[24]

After David stole another man's wife and had him killed on the front lines of battle, God sent the prophet Nathan to rebuke him. David realized the enormity of his sin and asked God for forgiveness. At that moment, God gave him a pure heart and restored to him the joy of His salvation (Psalm 51:10–12).

Forgiveness is a journey; the deeper the wound, the longer the journey. If your spouse says something hurtful, you may get over it quickly. But if your spouse cheats on you, it is going to require a lot more time for you to heal. Though all sins in the eyes of God cause us to fall short of His glory and miss the mark, their effects on us are not all the same. The deeper the wound that sin inflicts on us, the harder it is to recover.

On the other hand, the deeper the relationship with God, the quicker the forgiveness journey. The more we surrender our hurts to God, the more we pray about it, asking God to heal our broken hearts and relationships, the quicker we will feel His healing power.

FINAL THOUGHTS

There is much more to be said about the miracle of forgiveness, but let's wrap things up with two final thoughts.

> 1) Forgiveness is not an optional part of the Christian life. It is a necessary part of what it means to be a Christian. If we are going to follow Jesus, we must forgive. We have no other choice. And we must forgive as God has forgiven us—freely, completely, graciously, totally. The miracle we have received is a miracle we pass on to others.
>
> 2) We will forgive to the extent we appreciate how much we have been forgiven. The best incentive to forgiveness is to remember how much God has already forgiven you. Think of how many sins he has covered for you. Think of the punishment you deserved but that did not happen to you because of God's grace. Jesus said, "He who has been forgiven little loves little" (Luke 7:47). Your willingness to forgive is in direct proportion to your remembrance of how much you have been forgiven.
>
> . . . You are never more like Jesus than when you forgive. And you will never be set free until you forgive.
>
> Release them, and you will be set free.[25]

Of this we can be sure: we all have been cut deeply by someone in our lives. We have been cheated, criticized, abused, and abandoned. Some of our wounds are fresh and overwhelming. Some of us have scars from things that took place in our childhoods. They appear to have healed over time, but occasionally we are reminded of the unbelievable trauma we faced.

To be sure, the conflict and trauma we undergo in life disfigures us. It does not often disfigure us physically, but it disfigures us emotionally and spiritually. It twists the deepest parts us and makes us unable to engage in relationships the way God intended. We might be critical, cynical, vengeful, or judgmental.

The gospel has the incredible power to redeem even the darkest kinds of evil in your life and mine. That is what people such as Corrie ten Boom and Margaret Achero discovered, and that is what we can experience too. At the cross of Jesus Christ, we can discover that we can be restored and reconciled and that we can forgive. It is at the cross of Jesus where we can be healed. The cross of Jesus is the instrument of our restoration and our reconciliation with God, and God uses it to enable us to overcome conflict and trauma, to forgive one another, and reconcile with one another.

---

1. Bill Hewitt and Tom Nugent, "Kevin Tunell Is Paying $1 a Week for a Death He Caused and Finding the Price Unexpectedly High," *People*, April 16, 1990, http://people.com/archive/kevin-tunell-is-paying-1-a-week-for-a-death-he-caused-and-finding-the-price-unexpectedly-high-vol-33-no-15/.

2. Max Lucado, *In the Grip of Grace* (Dallas: Word Publishing, 1996), 149, 150.

3. John Ortberg, *Everybody's Normal Till You Get to Know Them* (Grand Rapids, MI: Zondervan, 2003), 157; emphasis in the original.

4. Ortberg, *Everybody's Normal*, 157.

5. This section is based on Lewis B. Smedes, *The Art of Forgiving* (New York: Ballantine Books, 1996), 87–94.

6. Ortberg, *Everybody's Normal*, 157.

7. John F. MacArthur, *The Freedom and Power of Forgiveness* (Wheaton, IL: Crossway Books, 1998), 189.

8. Leroy T. Howe, *Guilt: Helping God's People Find Healing and Forgiveness* (Nashville: Abingdon Press, 2003), 89.

9. Ortberg, *Everybody's Normal*, 158.

10. Ortberg, *Everybody's Normal*, 158; emphasis in the original.

11. Dick Tibbits, *Forgive to Live: How Forgiveness Can Save Your Life* (Nashville: Integrity Publishers, 2006), 45.

12. "Definition for Forgiveness," All About God, May 3, 2007, https://www.allaboutgod.com/definition-for-forgiveness-faq.htm.

13. This section is adapted from S. Joseph Kidder, "Forgiveness: What It Is," Kidder's Column, *Elder's Digest* 24, no. 3 (July–September 2018): 30, 31.

14. Howe, *Guilt*, 99.

15. "Definition for Forgiveness."

16. Ortberg, *Everybody's Normal*, 158; emphasis in the original.

17. Smedes, *The Art of Forgiving*, 3–12.

18. Smedes, *The Art of Forgiving*, 3–12.

19. Ortberg, *Everybody's Normal*, 159.

20. Ortberg, *Everybody's Normal*, 159, 160.

21. Ortberg, *Everybody's Normal*, 160.

22. Ortberg, *Everybody's Normal*, 160.

23. Ortberg, *Everybody's Normal*, 163, 164.

24. MacArthur, *Freedom and Power*, 172.

25. Ray Pritchard, "Forgiveness: Healing the Hurt We Never Deserved," Keep Believing Ministries, May 4, 2003, https://www.keepbelieving.com/sermon/forgiveness-healing-the-hurt-we-never-deserved/.

CHAPTER 14

OUTRAGEOUS FORGIVENESS
Loving and Praying for Our Enemies

"You have heard that it was said, 'Love your neighbor and hate your enemy.'
But I tell you, love your enemies and pray for those who persecute you,
that you may be children of your Father in heaven."
—Matthew 5:43–45

In a sermon titled "When Your Enemy Prospers," Bruce Larson asks us to participate in a thought experiment:

> Think of the one person or family or group of people in the world or the land that you hate the most. Think of your ultimate enemy at this moment in your life.
> "Ah," you say, "but I'm a Christian. I don't hate anybody!" God bless you. If you don't hate anybody, I'll give you a second choice. Think of the person you love the least. Some of you say, "I'm a Christian. I love everybody.". . . Think of the person you *like* the least. . . .
> . . . I want you to think of the person you know is your enemy, the person who does not mean you well, the person who has not done you well. Think of that person right now—your enemy.
> Suppose you had it in your power to help that person or that group of people to prosper enormously, spiritually and materially. If it were in your power, would you do it? Or if without your help they prospered, how would you feel right now if this enemy—this group of people or this person—suddenly flourished spiritually, were healed, were abundantly blessed financially?
> Now you understand Jonah's situation.[1]

THE STORY OF JONAH

God asked Jonah to go preach to Nineveh. "The word of the LORD came to Jonah son of Amittai: 'Go to the great city of Nineveh and preach against it, because its wickedness has come up before me' " (Jonah 1:1, 2). "Imagine how Jonah felt when he heard the Spirit say, '[G]o to Nineveh.' He didn't like it at all."² He decided to disobey God and go in the opposite direction. He boarded a boat headed for Tarshish. Jonah resisted, but God found a way to send him to Nineveh. Jonah preached repentance, the people responded positively, and God withheld His judgment on them. However, this forgiveness made Jonah angry.

Why didn't Jonah want to go to Nineveh? Maybe because he was afraid for his life. The Ninevites were a cruel people. "Nineveh was the capital of the Assyrians, an inhumane people that scoured the earth [See Nahum 3:1–4]. The Assyrians had a strict 'take no prisoners' policy. They would pull out the tongues of their captives and then skin them alive. As they left a conquered city, they piled the skulls of their victims outside the ruins."³ Jonah, who was afraid for his life, knew that if he went to Nineveh, he would certainly face a brutal death.

Another explanation is that Jonah didn't want to lose his credibility as a prophet. "Jonah, the man whose name means 'dove,' had grown popular as the prophet that denounced the Assyrians. And now he feared he would lose credibility with the Israelites if he went to preach the offer of grace to the Assyrians."⁴

I believe the main reason Jonah did not want to go to Nineveh is the one he gave in Jonah 4: "Isn't this what I said, Lord, when I was still at home? That is what I tried to forestall by fleeing to Tarshish. I knew that you are a gracious and compassionate God, slow to anger and abounding in love, a God who relents from sending calamity" (verse 2). Jonah had a good understanding of the nature of God. He knew that God was merciful and that if Nineveh repented, God would spare it from destruction. Jonah wanted the Ninevites' destruction. Over the years, he had grown to hate the Assyrians because of what they had done to his people. Jonah wanted God to execute His judgment on them, not spare them. They were Jonah's enemies, and he did not want any blessing on them. In today's world, this would be the equivalent of a father being asked to pray for a terrorist group when his son was killed by them, a woman being asked to pray for someone who raped her, or parents being asked to pray for the drunk driver who killed their daughter.

This story of Jonah illustrates the redemptive work of God in the world. He loves the people of the world as represented by Nineveh and sends us to them.

> The love of God is available to the wicked and vile as well as the civil and self-righteous.
>
> . . . The Assyrians represent the unconverted that desperately need to know both God's love and their impending judgment.
>
> . . . The prophet represents the one sent to share God's love. He was glad to speak for God to the good people—but refused to speak to those that appeared to need the gospel the most.
>
> Our indifference to the lost is an indicator that we need to return to God.⁵

We return to God by understanding and showing His loving nature to others. He wants us back, but we must take that first step toward Him by repenting and confessing our prejudice toward our enemies. Repentance without obedience results in failure. True repentance requires change.

What matters to God is people. That is what God was trying to communicate to Jonah in Jonah 4. God showed compassion on Jonah by giving him a plant for protection from the sun. Thus, Jonah experienced what he loathed, which was to show the Assyrians the forgiveness and mercy of God. We need to see our enemies as God sees them—candidates for grace and blessing.

Jonah was mad because he knew God was always good. Jonah did not grasp the greatness of God's love for a sinful world. He wanted God to be merciful to him and his nation but not to others, especially those who didn't deserve Him.

Have you ever become angry in your spirit because God blessed someone who did not deserve it?

LOVE YOUR ENEMIES

God asked Jonah to bless Nineveh by preaching to the inhabitants. God is asking us to love our enemies. "Love your enemies" is a clear message throughout the New Testament. We see it in the fulfillment of God's gracious plan for our lives through Jesus Christ. "But God demonstrates his own love for us in this: While we were still sinners, Christ died for us" (Romans 5:8). By demonstrating this kind of love, God is commanding us to do the same for others: "But I tell you, love your enemies and pray for those who persecute you" (Matthew 5:44).

We see the principle of loving our enemies in the Old Testament as well. For example, God loved the Ninevites so much that in order to spare them from destruction, He sent Jonah to preach to them (Jonah 1; 2).

Love is an act. Love means working for the other person's well-being. That is how we love our enemies. If we love them, we will cause them to prosper through our prayers, through some direct intervention, or maybe, like Jonah, through our witness. Jonah stood among his enemies and said, "Listen, God doesn't like what you are doing. Change!" And they changed. His witness was used by God to bless his enemies. If we are faithful and obedient, God will bless our enemies through us.

PRAYER AND RECONCILIATION

One year I preached a sermon on intercessory prayer as a part a series of sermons on the importance of connecting with God. About two months later, Mary,* a woman who attended my church, came to me and said that the sermon on intercessory prayer had had a great impact on her life. She said, "On Sabbath evening, I asked the Lord who I should pray for. The Lord told me to pray for a friend." This friend, Paige, was a member of the same church, but they had experienced a severe falling

---

* All names in this story have been changed.

out. Mary told me she'd told God, "Lord, she is the last person I want to pray for. Paige stabbed me in the back. I don't want to pray for her, not after what she did to me." She asked the Lord the following day who she should pray for, and He said, "Paige." She told Him she would pray for anyone in the world but Paige. She still remembered the pain and anguish Paige had caused her and her family. On the third day, Mary asked God, "Who do You want me to pray for?" Again He said, "Paige." Finally, Mary surrendered to God and started praying for Paige. After praying for a few weeks, God gave Mary a love for Paige that she thought could never be possible.

After several weeks of praying for Paige, God told Mary, "You need to reconcile." Mary said, "Lord, it is enough to pray. I can't reconcile." On the following day, He again said to reconcile with Paige. Mary said, "Not now, not today." And in her heart, she said, *I don't think I'll ever be ready.* A few days later God said the same thing, "Go and make things right with Paige." Mary had to swallow her pride and surrender to God's will. She called Paige and made an appointment to meet at a restaurant. When they met, Mary told Paige the whole story about how God had told her to pray for her and changed her own heart to be more forgiving, loving, and accepting. Paige said that she was listening to the same sermon on intercessory prayer, and God had told her to pray for Mary! Paige had prayed for Mary, and God convicted her of the wrong she had done. They both expressed willingness to leave the past behind and start fresh. They embraced each other, and their friendship got a second chance. This is an example of what the power of forgiveness does. It allows you to start again.

God asked Jonah to pray for Nineveh, He asked Mary to pray for Paige, and He is asking us to pray for our enemies.

GOD BLESSES OUR ENEMIES WITH HIS GRACE

The story of Jonah is an excellent illustration of the grace of God. There are many other examples in the Bible that demonstrate how God's grace and blessings should extend to our enemies.

> Think of the prodigal son and the elder brother [Luke 15:11–32]. Who is the enemy to the elder brother who stays home, works the farm, is dutiful, is moral, is obedient to the father? It's the younger brother, who goes off and squanders in riotous and debauched living his half of the inheritance and then comes home and wants to share in what's left. . . . Could the elder brother bless him? No. He did not. The tragedy of that story is not that the younger one stayed lost; he comes home. The elder grinds his teeth and is angry; he could not bless his enemy.
>
> Think of that incredible story of the laborers in the vineyard [Matthew 20], in which a man goes out and hires a bunch of workers, and each hour of the day as he finds more unemployed, he hires them. At the end he pays

them all the same wage, and the ones who worked all day for a *fair* wage said, "This is not fair."[6]

"These who were hired last worked only one hour," they said, "and you have made them equal to us who have borne the burden of the work and the heat of the day."

But he answered one of them, "I am not being unfair to you, friend. Didn't you agree to work for a denarius? Take your pay and go. I want to give the one who was hired last the same as I gave you. Don't I have the right to do what I want with my own money? Or are you envious because I am generous?" (Matthew 20:12–15)

The preceding parable shows that the blessings of God are not dependent on what people do, think, or achieve but on the grace and will of God.

What if you have lost money invested with a friend? "Whether he squandered the money, he was evil, or he stupidly went bankrupt, it doesn't really matter. The money is gone. . . . In God's eyes it doesn't matter. . . . [I may think this person] is my enemy; he betrayed my trust. But God says, 'Forgive. Forgive.' That's a hard word for any of us."[7] But it is essential for us to forgive in order to be healed. In the Lord's Prayer, we pray, "Forgive us our debts, as we forgive our debtors" (Matthew 6:12, KJV).

> Maybe it's [your enemy is] your parents, who failed you because maybe they died on you when you were born; you never had a mom or dad. Or maybe they were abusive—sexually, verbally, emotionally. . . . Maybe they lied to you and said you were the darling of the universe, and spoiled you—indulged you—for real life.
>
> Maybe it's an ungrateful and rebellious child, a child in whom you poured everything you had—love and caring and money and help—and that child now has done the unspeakable and turned on you or betrayed you.
>
> Maybe it's a spouse, who withholds his or her love from you, knowing how desperately you need that one to hold you and cherish you and care for you when you least deserve it. But he or she doesn't. Maybe your enemy is your spouse who cheats on you. Maybe your enemy is your spouse who left you for somebody else.
>
> Maybe your enemy is a friend whom you trusted and who betrayed you, told about you, gossiped about you. . . . Maybe your enemies are theological, ecclesiastic enemies: people in the church who do not call truth what you and I call truth. So we say these people are polluting, diluting the church, and they become our enemies.[8]

Maybe your enemies are conservative or liberal, or those who don't take a stand.

Maybe your enemies are the people who make heavy demands on your time. You have a busy life and job. People keep knocking on your door and interrupting your schedule, pulling you away from the things you need to get done.

THE BLESSING OF OUR ENEMIES SHOULD CAUSE US TO REJOICE

"Let me give you a test for spiritual maturity. How do you feel about your Nineveh, that person you have a hard time praying for, blessing, or being a blessing for? Do you rejoice in that person's blessing? If you do, you have come a long way in the grace of Jesus Christ."[9] You are spiritually mature.

"Jonah—this man of God—did not pass the test" of spiritual maturity. He began his journey defying God's will. He rose to greatness when he went to Nineveh and preached to its people and then goes back full circle to being angry with God for sparing Nineveh from destruction. This is our story. This is my story. I have moments of greatness when I love, pray for, and bless my enemies. Then I come back full circle to defying God's will and "flunk the test of believing in grace. So the sad thing is, Jonah has become like Nineveh." We also become like Nineveh when we behave like Jonah. When we fight our enemies and do not wish them well, we become like the people we are fighting.[10]

The theme of the book of Jonah is to see our enemies through God's eyes of love, forgiveness, and salvation. God says to Jonah, "Should not I pity Nineveh, that great city, in which there are more than 120,000 persons who do not know their right hand from their left?" (Jonah 4:11, ESV). God cared about Nineveh and sent Jonah to preach to its inhabitants. He saved them from utter destruction in spite of their wickedness, harsh treatment of other people, and rebellion against God. God still wanted to show mercy toward the Assyrians and offer them the gift of salvation. In fact, this theme of salvation permeates the whole book of Jonah. In chapter 1, God saved the lives of the sailors. In chapter 2, God saved Jonah from the belly of the fish. In chapter 3, God showed His mercy toward the Ninevites and saved them. In chapter 4, God showed His desire to save all humankind as demonstrated in the salvation of Nineveh. Jonah 2:9 sums up the theme of the book:

> But I, with shouts of grateful praise,
>   will sacrifice to you.
> What I have vowed I will make good.
>   I will say, "Salvation comes from the LORD."

God wants us to see our enemies as worthy of love, worthy of forgiveness, worthy of grace, and worthy of salvation.

HEALING OUR WOUNDS

I saw a demonstration of how God's grace helps us to not only love our enemies but to also heal the hurt and pain we carry in our hearts.

Shortly after arriving at a new church, I visited one of the elders. As we sat in the living room with his family, his wife, Jane, started talking about her son. He had been playing ball outside with a friend, and the ball was kicked into the street. When her son ran into the street to get the ball, a drunk driver struck him and killed him.

Jane told the story in vivid detail and was completely distraught. I assumed by her reaction that the incident had happened recently. However, when I asked her when it took place, she said that it had occurred ten years ago. For ten years, she had carried hate and animosity toward this man who had killed her son and wanted nothing more than absolute justice. She was enraged, resentful, and inconsolable. She lived without peace or joy, with a bitter heart, for ten years.

I wanted to help Jane experience what it meant to forgive the man who had killed her son. I started visiting with the couple and talking with them about forgiveness. I shared how in spite of all that we have done, God has forgiven us through Jesus Christ. I talked to her about how forgiveness brings peace and liberates us. It sets prisoners free, and we discover through forgiveness that we are the prisoners who are set free.

I gave examples of stories about forgiveness from the Bible, such as the story of Jesus on the cross when He prayed to His Father for the people who were crucifying Him. I told about Joseph, who was in a position to harm his brothers (who had inflicted pain on him by selling him into slavery, which led him to being jailed in a foreign land). Instead of making them suffer, he forgave them, helped them, and blessed them. I shared that one of the ways we really know we have forgiven others is when we surrender our rights to get even and start praying for the people who have hurt us and wishing them well.

Then one day when I was visiting with the couple and talking about these issues, I asked if we could kneel down to pray. After prayer, Jane's husband and I started to get up. Jane pulled us back down, and for the first time ever, I heard her pray. She prayed for the man who killed her son, that in spite of all that had happened, this man would come to a place where he could know Jesus. She wished him well and that he would have God's blessing. We got up from our knees, and when she looked at me, she was crying. She said, "For the first time in ten years, I have peace and joy in my heart. I have surrendered my resentment and anger to God."

That is what forgiveness does—it gives us a new beginning in God. We cannot change the past and have no control over what other people do to us. We cannot reverse the effects of what they have done, but through forgiveness and the power of God's grace, we can be healed and have a new beginning.

WE LOVE OUR ENEMIES BY HELPING THEM TO PROSPER

In the book of Jonah, God is saying, "Give your enemies your prayers and blessings. Give them your witness, and help them prosper for your own sake." If there is one thing you take away from the story of Jonah, it is this: "Don't turn down the grace of God, which we see fulfilled in Jesus' life, death, and resurrection. . . . Don't turn down the grace of God or deny it to another. That sums up everything about the Word of God."[11] Even in our darkest times, God gives us the power of grace, which we can extend to our worst enemy.

PASSING THE TEST

The gospel was being taught to Jonah. I can imagine God saying, "Jonah, now you are Nineveh, and I want to forgive you. Go back and forgive your enemies." God still loved Jonah, who was stingy with God's grace. God was still interested in him and talking to him. As God forgave Nineveh, He forgave Jonah also and said: "Jonah, don't you understand it's My nature to forgive and to bless? You do the same. Love your enemies."

Like Jonah, we may have flunked the test of praying for and blessing our enemies. But God says, "I am giving you a second chance to become more like Me in loving and blessing your enemies."

---

1. Bruce Larson, "When Your Enemy Prospers," *Preaching Today*, August 2005, https://www.preachingtoday.com/sermons/sermons/2005/august/078.html; emphasis in the original.
2. Jerry Gifford, "Sermon: Six Signs We Need to Return to God—Jonah 1," LifeWay, January 1, 2014, https://www.lifeway.com/en/articles/sermon-returning-to-god-six-signs-jonah-1.
3. Gifford, "Sermon: Six Signs."
4. Gifford, "Sermon: Six Signs."
5. Gifford, "Sermon: Six Signs."
6. Larson, "When Your Enemy Prospers"; emphasis in the original.
7. Larson, "When Your Enemy Prospers."
8. Larson, "When Your Enemy Prospers."
9. Larson, "When Your Enemy Prospers."
10. Larson, "When Your Enemy Prospers."
11. Larson, "When Your Enemy Prospers."

PART 6

Journey to the
Heart of God
Through Christian
Fellowship

CHAPTER 15

CHRISTIAN FELLOWSHIP
God's Venue for Transformation

Every day they continued to meet together in the temple courts.
They broke bread in their homes and ate together with glad and sincere hearts,
praising God and enjoying the favor of all the people.
And the Lord added to their number daily those who were being saved.
—Acts 2:46, 47

One of my seminary students described her transformational fellowship this way:

Every Friday evening I meet with fifteen to twenty friends for a small-group Bible study. I look forward to seeing them every week to have spiritual and authentic conversations, thought-provoking Bible study, and to eat delicious food together. We also spend time together on Saturday nights by playing games, going bowling, or doing team-building activities. Sometimes during the week, we go to the beach or out to eat together.

We support one another. When a friend is moving, we help him or her clean and move their things. If one of us is preaching somewhere, we pray for them and attend the service. We are a community of like-minded believers that are there for one another. They have helped me grow spiritually and have given me tons of love. Their insights into the Bible have caused me to expand my mind upward. Their prayers have encouraged my heart, and their acceptance and support have made me feel loved even when I do not feel deserving.

Recently, we were visiting a church to support someone from our group who was preaching that Sabbath. During the potluck meal after the service, my friends got up to leave. I was on the other side of the fellowship hall talking to one of the elderly church members when they slipped out. Only one of my friends came over to me to say goodbye. I told him I appreciated him coming to say farewell and asked where the others were. He said they were already in the car, so I told him I was going to go out with him to say goodbye to them.

When I got to the car, my friends rolled down the window, and I kindly

Christian Fellowship: God's Venue for Transformation

teased them about not saying goodbye to me. Then I confessed with a smile that sometimes I had low self-esteem and felt they were too popular to be my friends. In unison, they all said that was not so! One of my friends said in all sincerity, "Naomi, look me in the eyes. *You are loved.*" Immediately, my heart was warmed, and I silently thanked God for giving me this life-changing community that I had never experienced before.

FROM ORDINARY TO EXTRAORDINARY

One of the things that strikes me about the fellowship in Naomi's story and the fellowship I read about in the book of Acts is that it is transformational fellowship. It is life-changing fellowship. It has power and influence. It is about ordinary people who, under the influence of the Holy Spirit and in the joy of Christ, were transformed into extraordinary people who did great things for the cause of God. John Piper writes,

> I want to belong to this kind of fellowship because life is too short and . . . the people outside are too broken and hopeless for us to settle for a notion of fellowship as a kind of comfortable togetherness that has no transforming, empowering, explosive effect when we meet. . . .
>
> Believe me, I love fellowship. I love to be with people of like mind and heart. I love my main support group, . . . and our hours together each week. But my life is so short, and my meeting with the Lord face to face is so imminent and so real, and my desires to make a 100% return on God's investment of grace in my life are so strong, that I am just not interested in any kind of fellowship that does not help people explode with more love, more compassion, more joy, more holiness, and more zeal for God, and more boldness in witness, more power in ministry, more vision for missions. . . . I think . . . [this desire is] an echo in my heart—and yours—of the explosive fellowship we hear about in the book of Acts.
>
> . . . I want every person in this church to know the sweet taste of camaraderie and belonging . . . and unity of spirit and oneness of mind that is the heart in New Testament, Christian fellowship. . . . But I want everything we do in our groups—whether we are studying Scripture, reading a book, focusing on singles issues, marriage issues, supporting a missionary, targeting the inner-city, praying for children—whatever the focus is, I pray that everything that happens in the small groups will be explosive. . . . I hope that the mindset of every small group is to serve an explosion of love and compassion and truth and joy and worship and power and ministry.
>
> . . . This is the kind of fellowship that carried the Christian movement from 120 disciples on the day of Pentecost to 5,000 Christians in Jerusalem alone in a matter of months, and then planted that movement all over the known world in a few short decades.[1]

When I read about fellowship in the book of Acts, I get excited and want God to help me live the life of power and grace the believers lived in the first century. I want more power in my life. I want more love in my heart. I desire more commitment in following Jesus. I want the Holy Spirit to dwell in me in His fullness. I want to experience the joy of the Lord always and make it my strength. I want Jesus to be my Senior Partner every day and empower me in whatever I do, say, or think. That is why it is so important for me to be part of a transformational, Christ-centered fellowship.

TRANSFORMATIONAL FELLOWSHIP

When I read the book of Acts, I learn about the power of biblical fellowship. We read about "ordinary Christians who meet together with such expectancy and fervency of prayer . . . that the Spirit is poured out, and people are added to the church daily."[2] They need this fellowship so desperately that they meet regularly to break bread and worship together. Those who have abundance give to those who do not have enough. They read the Scriptures with one another and pour their hearts out in prayer. We read about lives being changed, bold witnesses, missionaries being called and going forth, and prison doors opening. "This is just Christian fellowship—explosive Christian fellowship. . . . My prayer is that we will not be . . . so content with business as usual" but boldly demand transformational fellowship.[3]

How many of you have been in a place where you were dissatisfied? Well, that's a good place to start moving toward change. I believe the dissatisfaction in our lives is an indicator that something is out of order. The important thing is not to ignore that uncomfortable feeling. Many of us make the mistake of looking for ways to be comfortable in a place of dissatisfaction. That dissatisfaction is presented to us by the Holy Spirit, so we will seek answers and move toward change, but we have to be willing to let God change our circumstances.

There are some of us who were born into situations and others of us who have allowed ourselves to become entangled with circumstances that have obstructed our true identities. It may take God connecting us with the right people to bring change into our lives. It is through these powerful relationships that we will discover who we really are—and, ultimately, where we are destined to soar.

Church fellowship "is what takes place when Jesus Christ unites us together in the body of Christ. It is much more than just having a good time. No, Church fellowship helps us to be the people of God."[4] There are many people today who think they do not need this transformational fellowship. They miss out on being the kind of Christians God wants them to be. It is impossible to do what God has called us to do "without other Christians in our lives. When we are together, we can become stronger Christians."[5]

"What will make us truly grow in the depths of our faith"? We start by surrounding ourselves with people who are exhibiting the characteristics we see in the book of Acts: people who are praying earnestly, worshiping passionately, and serving wholeheartedly. We surround ourselves with those "who serve the difficult cases, the difficult people, the difficult situations." We surround ourselves with "people who see their world as Jesus sees it."[6]

HOW DOES TRANSFORMATION WORK?

The authentic Christian transformational community that Mark and Lisa belonged to provided a great foundation for them to grow closer in their walk with Christ—and eventually it saved their marriage. They had multiple discussions about how completely different their lives would have been if it had not been for their support group. They even believed they could have ended up divorced if not for the prayers and encouragement of members of their faith community.

Mark and Lisa's story starts out like many others. They had a good marriage, good jobs, two children, a great church, and a comfortable home. On the outside, they appeared to have it all; however, within their four walls, things were not as they appeared. They struggled with communication and bottled up their feelings, which led to unnecessary stress, hurt feelings, resentment, disappointment, and anger. The strain of this took a toll on their relationship and could have sent them down a very sad path, but their lives in the community and their commitment to their marriage covenant played a huge role in saving their marriage. The small group they belonged to was loving, accepting, encouraging, and nonjudgmental, allowing Mark and Lisa to open up about their difficult problems and ask for help.

As they shared their lives with the group, they received support and prayers from others who had a personal relationship with Jesus. Eventually, this led Mark and Lisa to make God the center of their lives. They felt encouraged and sought professional help to guide them through the process of putting their marriage back together. The example that others lived out in the community through their love and acceptance for one another was a witness to the transformational love of God.

This transformational experience enabled Mark and Lisa to live their lives more within God's will. This kind of living was more satisfying and rewarding than the path they could have taken. Their lives and their marriage were not perfect, but they were overcoming their struggles together with the support of their fellow believers. Being in a faith community was instrumental in deepening their relationship with God and each other.

The community provided a place for them to stay connected to God personally and unite with Him through like-minded people who lived His love. Mark says, "What we have experienced in our small group has been fertile soil for us to live and grow in our walk with the Lord. It became the place where we could grow into more of the fullness of life God has for us." That is fellowship. That is the church. That is life the way God intended it to be.

MY VISION FOR OUR FELLOWSHIP

As a community of believers who follow Jesus and trust Him fully, "our shared life and ministry will be marked by these six aims":

1. Know and serve one another persistently. (1 Thessalonians 2:7–8; Hebrews 3:12–13)

Week-in and week-out, we will work to know each other more and more deeply—sharing our hearts and lives, praying for one another, asking questions, and bearing each other's burdens. We will be persistent learners of one another. And with everything we learn—good, bad, or otherwise—we will strive to love and serve one another—meeting each other's needs, encouraging growth, and helping one another thrive.

2. Depend on the Lord prayerfully. (Philippians 4:6–7; Hebrews 4:14–16)

Prayer will be the regular, visible engine of our community. We need God every hour, every minute of every hour, so prayer will be our means to everything. We will look to God for everything we need, never taking his provision for granted. When we're alone and when we're together, we will be a people of prayer—always adoring, always confessing, always thanking, always asking.

3. Meet God through his word faithfully and expectantly. (Psalm 19:7–11; 2 Peter 1:3–4)

The Bible will play a central role in our community because it holds the words of life. We need those pages more than we need food, and there are always more riches to be seen, enjoyed, and applied in our lives. We read faithfully—meaning regularly and with the eyes of faith—and we read expectantly—anticipating God to speak and move each time we open his book.

4. Pursue disciples for Jesus boldly and globally. (Matthew 28:19–20; Acts 1:8)

Our commission from Jesus is clear: Go, and make disciples. God saved us in order to send us. We are lights in a world of darkness that is desperately in need. We are God's chosen means of spreading good news and winning worship for himself in every corner of this earth. Therefore, we are to be bold where we are, and we are to be behind what God is doing among the nations. We will witness for Jesus where we are, and send and support witnesses where we are not.

5. Rest in the gospel confidently and humbly. (Romans 8:1, 32, 37–39; 1 Corinthians 15:1–4)

Everything we think, say, and do as a small group stands on the firm foundation of the gospel. We have been saved by grace through faith, wholly apart from anything we have done or earned. We do not deserve God's love, but in Christ we have it. We want our relationships, our meetings, and our ministry together to be shaped by and soaked with the gospel. This message should produce the boldest confidence and courage, and it should produce the most tender and compassionate humility.

6. Work out our salvation soberly and joyfully. (Philippians 2:12–13; Galatians 5:1, 13, 25)

Lastly, we are committed to living more and more like Christ. It is the joyful privilege of God's people to be conformed to the image of his Son. It is not pretty or easy, but it is undeniably good and important. Year by year, week by week, even day by day, we will be identifying areas of weakness or failure, receiving forgiveness because of the finished work of Christ, and then working together for change.[7]

My vision for our church is that we all will be part of a transformational fellowship. It is my vision that we will take community very seriously and live to honor, love, encourage, and pray for one another. My vision is that as a community we will solve problems, do ministry, change the world, and worship and exalt Jesus.

WHAT IS YOUR DECISION?

What can you do to begin experiencing a transformational community? Let me list five things that can move you toward a greater involvement in God's family and make transformational decisions:

1. Find and join a small group or Sabbath School like the ones described in the book of Acts.
2. Take the risk to share your struggles with the group and trust your fellow believers to pray for you and support you.
3. Share your faith with other believers who can give you encouragement and insight.
4. Look for people to encourage in the ministry of Jesus Christ.
5. Handle with great care and prayer every burden that someone shares with you.[8]

Individually, we can't do much. But no matter how wounded or imperfect we may be, when we are together, we make beautiful music and beautiful ministry, and we capture the attention of a world that needs the hope we have.

---

1. John Piper, "Explosive Fellowship," Desiring God, September 9, 1990, https://www.desiringgod.org/messages/explosive-fellowship.
2. Piper, "Explosive Fellowship."
3. Piper, "Explosive Fellowship."
4. "Christian Fellowship (the Church)—Why You Need It," HigherPraise.com, accessed February 6, 2019, http://higherpraise.com/outlines/Sermons/Sermon03.html.
5. "Christian Fellowship."
6. "Christian Fellowship."
7. Marshall Segal, "Every Small Group Needs a Vision," Desiring God, February 26, 2015, https://www.desiringgod.org/articles/every-small-group-needs-a-vision; emphasis in the original.
8. "Christian Fellowship."

TRANSFORMATIONAL FELLOWSHIP IN ACTS

The following examples of transformational fellowship in Acts accomplished nine things:

1. Brought about revival.
When the apostles and disciples, numbering about 120, prayed in the upper room for ten days, the Holy Spirit came upon the church and brought a radical revival and empowered them to be bold witnesses for Jesus and change the world (Acts 1; 2).

2. Culminated in meaningful and joyous worship.
When the early church devoted themselves to fellowship, prayer, and the study of Scripture, the result was praise and joyful worship (Acts 2:42–47).

3. Resulted in many miracles that the believers performed.
They healed the crippled (Acts 3:1–10), raised the dead (Acts 20), and survived a fierce storm and a shipwreck (Acts 27), to name a few miracles.

4. Increased their love and service for others.
They followed Jesus' teaching and became more and more like Jesus, who came to serve and not to be served. They sold property and possessions to give to anyone who had need. They broke bread in their homes and ate together (Acts 2:42–47).

5. Helped them grow in boldness and courage (Acts 4:29).
The same disciples who denied Jesus and ran away from Him turned the world upside down after the Holy Spirit came upon them (Acts 4:13, 31).

6. Gave them more power in prayer.
When Peter was in jail, the whole church, in small groups, prayed for him, and miraculously, the Lord delivered him (Acts 12:1–17).

7. Set apart missionaries.
With prayer and under the direction of the Holy Spirit, the early church appointed Paul and Barnabas for the spreading of the gospel and the work that God called them to do (Acts 13:2).

8. Brought the believers into unity.
In earnest prayer and under the guidance of the Holy Spirit, the early believers resolved the contention about what to do with the Jewish law (Acts 15).

9. Led to praise and deliverance from jail.
When Paul and Silas were in jail in Philippi, they did not complain, but they had the fellowship of worship and praise, resulting in their deliverance by God (Acts 16:16–40).

CHAPTER 16

CHRISTIAN FELLOWSHIP

God's Design for Growth

*And let us consider how we may spur one another on toward love and good deeds,
not giving up meeting together, as some are in the habit of doing,
but encouraging one another—and all the more as you see the Day approaching.*
—Hebrews 10:24, 25

A friend of mine named Kari* once told me why she left the church and how she came back. She grew up going to church and Sabbath School with her parents because it was required. She loved Jesus, but the judgmental attitude some members had and the hypocrisy many others displayed pushed her further and further away. When she graduated from high school and gained her independence, she drifted away from the church very quickly. There was no longer the mandatory attendance pulling her back, nor was there any form of fellowship or community within the church to keep her there. The legalistic, judgmental attitude that Kari had seen was not something she wanted to be part of, so she left.

Ten years later, while she was still out of the church, she got married and had her first child. She and her husband, Joe, wanted to raise their daughter in a Christ-centered atmosphere. They also felt drawn to the church and to God. They made it a mission to find a church that valued Jesus, grace, love, and friendship.

For four years, Joe and Kari would attend a different Adventist church in the area from time to time, praying before each visit that it would be a fit. Although many of the churches had *some* of their required qualities, there was always something missing. One day Kari's counselor recommended they go to his church. When they arrived, they noticed the church was friendly, vibrant, and welcoming, with greeters at every door. They felt at home right away.

After the service, they had the opportunity to speak with Kevin, one of the church members. He happily answered all of their questions and helped them feel comfortable and at ease. Kari told him about their struggle to find a church that would accept them in spite of their past, which wasn't squeaky clean. Finally, she

---

* These names have been changed.

asked the big question: "Can we come here?" She expected a judgmental response, but Kevin's response was simple: "We all have pasts, and this is a great church for sinners. Everyone is welcome."

This conversation with Kevin was the launching pad for many opportunities for fellowship that included Bible studies, small groups, Sabbath School, and retreats. This church took Joe and Kari in as part of their family and helped them grow in their love for Jesus through relationships, mentoring, and discipleship.

As Kari and Joe grew in the Lord, the church gave them many opportunities for ministry in and out of the church. The church even ordained them as elders. Kari told me, "This church became my family and the members my biggest supporters. Our small group changed the trajectory of our lives and made us feel that we weren't just going to church—we were becoming a part of the church. Every day we are growing in our love for Jesus because some people are taking an interest in us and in our spiritual well-being."

ONE OF GOD'S GREATEST GIFTS

Community is one of God's greatest gifts.

> It is the gift of a rich and challenging life together. . . .
> Christian community is simply sharing a common life in Christ. It moves us beyond the self-interested isolation of private lives and beyond the superficial social contacts that pass for "Christian fellowship." The biblical ideal of community challenges us instead to commit ourselves to live together as the people of God.[1]

We have a perfect example of this kind of fellowship in the book of Acts:

> They devoted themselves to the apostles' teaching and to fellowship, to the breaking of bread and to prayer. Everyone was filled with awe at the many wonders and signs performed by the apostles. All the believers were together and had everything in common. They sold property and possessions to give to anyone who had need. Every day they continued to meet together in the temple courts. They broke bread in their homes and ate together with glad and sincere hearts, praising God and enjoying the favor of all the people. And the Lord added to their number daily those who were being saved. (Acts 2:42–47)

This was a praying and studying church, a worshiping and praising church, a giving and ministering church, a place where we'd want to belong, celebrate unity, and grow in maturity as we came closer to Christ.

We know all too well that maturity takes time. We know less well that it also takes [the support of] our sisters and brothers in Christ. It's a process that is revealed in the "each other" language of the New Testament: Love one another, forgive each other. . . . Teach and correct each other, encourage each other, pray for each other. . . . Serve one another and submit to one another out of reverence for Christ. This list just scratches the surface, but it is enough to remind us that we need the community of faith to grow up in Christ.[2]

The only prayer that Jesus taught us to pray begins, "*Our* Father," not "My Father." Jesus calls us into a living, active, worshiping community that regularly meets together. We partake in communion together. We sing together, pray together, confess together, grieve and heal and eventually die together. God gives us pastors. He gives us small groups. He gives us brothers and sisters in the faith. He gives us mature Christians to emulate and He gives us those far from the heart of God that we can share our faith with.

The church embodies a specific, personal way of life together in Christ. It strengthens us to live the life to which we are called; it conveys God's life and power to the world at large.[3]

THE BASIS OF FELLOWSHIP

"Salvation . . . is the basis of fellowship. When you became a believer, you entered the fellowship. . . . There is neither Jew, nor Greek, nor male, nor female, nor bond, nor free [Galatians 3:28]. Doesn't matter what gender you are, doesn't matter what race you are, doesn't matter what education you [have], what economic status you have. If you are in Christ, you are in the fellowship."[4]

John writes, "We proclaim to you what we have seen and heard, so that you also may have fellowship with us. And our fellowship is with the Father and with his Son, Jesus Christ" (1 John 1:3).

John says, we were there, we saw Him, we looked at Him, we touched Him with our hands, this living Word of Life. . . . We proclaim the gospel of eternal life, which was manifested to us. We proclaim it to you. Why do we proclaim the gospel of Christ? So that you may have fellowship with us, and our fellowship is with the Father and His Son, Jesus Christ. The proclamation of the gospel, then, is not an end in itself. The proclamation of the gospel is not to produce individual, isolated Christians. The preaching of the gospel is to produce a fellowship, a sharing, in-common life, purpose, power, ministry, testimony.[5]

A WAY TO SEE CHRIST IN OTHERS

"One of the most important ways the community helps us is by embodying Christ's continuing presence on earth."[6] Jesus said, "By this everyone will know that you are my disciples, if you love one another" (John 13:35). And Paul makes it clear that when we imitate his example we are also imitating Jesus (1 Corinthians 11:1). He wrote, "Consequently, you are no longer foreigners and strangers, but fellow citizens with God's people and also members of his household, built on the foundation of the apostles and prophets, with Christ Jesus himself as the chief cornerstone. In him the whole building is joined together and rises to become a holy temple in the Lord. And in him you too are being built together to become a dwelling in which God lives by his Spirit" (Ephesians 2:19–22).

"When my brothers and sisters love and accept me, I feel Christ's love, too. When I confess my sin and they forgive me, I know that God forgives me, too. When they pray for my brokenness, I know that they are sharing in the healing work of Jesus. . . . When we feel the crush of hostility and of our own failures, to have our Christian community surround us with compassion and encouragement lightens our loads, strengthens us, and gives us the courage to keep on trying."[7] "Bear one another's burdens, and so fulfill the law of Christ" (Galatians 6:2, ESV).

A SOURCE OF ACCOUNTABILITY AND GUIDANCE

The community is "a place where we teach each other and hold ourselves accountable to each other. When I hear what God is teaching others, it teaches me, too. When I submit to the guidance and scrutiny of my brothers and sisters, it forces me to grow and to be accountable."[8] Paul wrote, "Brothers and sisters, if someone is caught in a sin, you who live by the Spirit should restore that person gently. But watch yourselves, or you also may be tempted" (Galatians 6:1; see also Colossians 3:16).

"Such accountability doesn't need to have overtones of checking up and scolding. It works, instead, to encourage us and help us in our growth and commitments. We may ask for guidance about how to handle a difficult relationship [or how to have a meaningful family worship]. . . . The community gives us a place to air our growth and our struggles, our successes and failures," and it guides us "more fully in the ways of Christ."[9] We are urged to do all this in the love of Christ and to be "kind one to another, tenderhearted, forgiving one another, even as God for Christ's sake hath forgiven you" (Ephesians 4:32, KJV).

Our gathering together is for the purpose of celebrating our salvation in Jesus and to love, pray, and encourage one another in the Lord. We are to celebrate these two realities with great joy.

Our shared life with fellow believers makes life in general more complete and full of meaning and grace. By experiencing the love and acceptance that Jesus has shown to us, we will want to extend the same to other people.

A PLACE TO PRAY AND WORSHIP

"The community helps us grow, too, as it becomes a workshop for prayer and worship. . . . We are called as well to a life of worship and praise." (See Acts

2:42–47; see also Acts 4:32.) Yet our natural tendency to avoid intimacy leads us to be spectators instead of being actively involved. "Being spectators simply isn't enough. . . . We ourselves need to pray for each other. Each of us needs to be prayed for personally."[10] James admonished us to "pray for one another, that you may be healed" (James 5:16, ESV; see also Ephesians 6:18). Howard Macy writes:

> As we learn the ways of worship in the small community, we not only deepen our own lives but also enrich the life of public worship. . . . community is at its best when it becomes a workshop for prayer and worship.[11]

A PLACE TO SERVE

The Bible is full of statements urging us to care, love, and pray for one another. Paul admonished, "Serve one another humbly in love" (Galatians 5:13). I love the words of Paul to the Corinthians: "Have equal concern for each other" (1 Corinthians 12:25). And to the Romans, he wrote, "Be devoted to one another in love" (Romans 12:10).

> The community is also where we learn to strip away our self-interest in order to serve others. It is here that we learn to share what God has given us, whether it be goods or spiritual gifts. It is also here that we learn to be served, though we are sometimes prideful and reluctant like Peter, who balked at Jesus washing his feet (Jn. 13:2-10). Sometimes we are the washers and sometimes the washees, but in many ordinary ways we can learn what submission and service mean.
>
> One community I know gave time and money so a mother worn down by the demands of young children could take a spiritual retreat. Others have found practical ways to swap mowers and ladders and child care. . . . I have seen people abandon a special outing to bail out a friend's leaky basement. . . . Community means watching over one another for good, knowing that as we serve, all of us are growing stronger in Christ.[12]

A WITNESS TO THE WORLD

Christian communities, are a witness to God's presence in the world. Through service, acceptance and compassion, they show others what God is like. This kind of love led many to accept Jesus and become part of His love-filled community (Acts 2:42).

AMBASSADORS OF GOD'S LOVE

Christian communities "not only demonstrate God's love; they also mediate it. They carry 'the ministry of reconciliation' (2 Cor. 5:18) to those around them, bringing God's compassion and healing power into a broken world."[13]

Communities do this by being intentionally focused on spreading the good news of the hope and grace of Jesus Christ. "Each community with its particular mission is a guerrilla unit establishing a beachhead for God's peaceable Kingdom in a hostile world. And from those outposts God's love flows freely."[14]

COMMUNITY IN ACTION

In one of the churches I pastored, when the members learned that my family in Iraq was in dire need of money and medication because of the war, the believers got together and raised seventeen thousand dollars to send to my family. When I got the check from them to send to Iraq, at that moment I didn't feel that I just belonged to a church, I felt that I belonged to a group of believers who cared about me and loved me deeply. That is biblical fellowship. That is the dream church.

A CALL TO COMMUNITY

"God, from the beginning, never intended that we should go through the world 'alone.' We simply cannot experience fully the power and delight of life with God without also being drawn into life together with our sisters and brothers in Christ. Without experiencing such life together, we will not discover how wonderful the news about Jesus really is."[15] The reward of living in community is to experience life as God intended it to be lived.

---

1. Howard Macy, "Community: God's Design for Growth," Bible.org, May 29, 2011, https://bible.org/article/community-god%E2%80%99s-design-growth.
2. Macy, "Community: God's Design for Growth."
3. "Don't Make It Personal," *Northstar.Church* (blog), June 16, 2017, http://northstar.church/dont-make-it-personal/; emphasis added.
4. John MacArthur, "The Priority of Christian Fellowship," Grace to You, May 18, 2014, https://www.gty.org/library/sermons-library/44-12/The-Priority-of-Christian-Fellowship.
5. MacArthur, "The Priority of Christian Fellowship."
6. Macy, "Community: God's Design for Growth."
7. Macy, "Community: God's Design for Growth."
8. Macy, "Community: God's Design for Growth."
9. Macy, "Community: God's Design for Growth."
10. Macy, "Community: God's Design for Growth."
11. Macy, "Community: God's Design for Growth."
12. Macy, "Community: God's Design for Growth."
13. Macy, "Community: God's Design for Growth."
14. Macy, "Community: God's Design for Growth."
15. Macy, "Community: God's Design for Growth."

CHAPTER 17

CHRISTIAN FELLOWSHIP
Finding God in Community*

"For where two or three gather in my name, there am I with them."
—Matthew 18:20

During the final night of an evangelistic conference I took part in, the organizers discussed finding God in a faith community. We broke into small groups and were asked to reflect on the following question: When have you experienced a community of faith true to God's teachings and the story of Jesus? I was fortunate to be in a group with a Hindu who had been a sporadic attendee at our meetings. I was curious about how he would respond to the question, and I wasn't disappointed.

Let me rewind the story before I share what this man said. When he first attended the conference, several people made a special effort to connect with him. I sat down with him and talked about finding meaning in life. I invited him to join me for lunch later that week, and several days later, we went to a park to walk together. He had questions about the reasons for the relational pain from his past. We talked about the overarching narrative of the war between God and Satan and how this world is not fair, but it will be one day. He kept attending meetings when he could.

A couple of weeks later we went out for dinner. After our meal, we continued our discussion, picking up with evil and how God provides willpower and opportunities to make a choice for eternity, regardless of the brokenness we experience. We talked about how God doesn't allow any of us to face more than we can bear (1 Corinthians 10:13), but what we can bear varies as each of us is on a unique journey. At the end of our time together, I prayed with him, and he shared how that prayer and the idea of finding meaning and purpose in a relationship with God resonated deeply with him.

Thus, on the final night of the conference, when my Hindu brother was asked about experiencing God, he talked about us—our little faith community. He talked about how when he was with us, he felt such a spirit of peace and joy. He talked about how kind we were and how welcoming and loving we were. God used us, our

---

* Written with contribution from Jonny Moore, a pastor in Portland, Oregon.

imperfections and all, to reveal Himself to a Hindu man searching for meaning and wholeness. He found God in community.

In the twenty-first century, we are in danger of slipping into the trap of an individualistic Christianity. Our relationship with God is a private matter, but, as our Hindu brother discovered, our relationship with God is also a matter of community. We in the church are on the brink of missing this blessing. This chapter explores the biblical background for the God-community relationship and how the Christian community is God's conduit for revealing Himself to us through correction, healing, and encouragement. God longs for us to find Him, and one vehicle He has established to aid us in the quest is community.

BIBLICAL BACKGROUND

God exists in community. Before the angels, before the universe, perhaps before time itself, the Father, Son, and Spirit existed in continuous love.[1] Community is God's primal manifestation of existence. And when God created humankind, He intended for us to be able to relate to Him, so God created us male and female (Genesis 1:27)—equal counterparts but distinct in community.

The early church fathers believed that truly knowing something means being able to participate with that entity.[2] For example, rather than learning physics merely to recite formulas and laws, I learn physics in order to experience it, to glimpse the beauty of physics and of the universe that is revealed through physics. Understanding, then, requires ever deepening participation with reality through the lens of the subject. God's lens is one of community. When we participate actively in our human community, we develop the capacity to understand God in even the most basic ways. This scriptural picture of God and humanity reveals that our interaction with others is essential to conceptualizing God and ultimately experiencing and finding Him.

The Bible also demonstrates God's self-revelation through human community. The priesthood in the sanctuary system represented God and His work to the people (Leviticus 1:1–9; 10:10, 11; 16). When Naomi and Ruth returned to the faith community, God used Boaz as His representative to redeem them and saved them from a life of poverty. Hosea married a prostitute to become a living illustration of God's love for His people. In the New Testament, Paul called the church the body of Christ and instructed the church to live out its Holy Spirit–inaugurated responsibility to speak God's truth and reconcile the world to God (Romans 12:4–8; 1 Corinthians 12:4–31; 2 Corinthians 5:18, 19). Perhaps the best example of the community of faith revealing God to others is found in the book of Acts. The book starts with a description of an ideal community as the members encouraged, ate, healed, prayed, and lived together, gaining the favor of those around them (Acts 2:42–47). Throughout the Bible, individuals (and even whole tribes or communities) reveal

God to others. The history of the community of faith in the Old and New Testaments will be the motivating force behind the rest of this chapter.

FINDING GOD THROUGH COMMUNAL CORRECTION

One of the challenges that keeps us from finding God in community is our aversion to giving or receiving correction from one another: "I do my thing. You do yours." "It's not my place to correct them. The Holy Spirit will convict them if they're doing something wrong." The Holy Spirit will convict us, but we forget that the Holy Spirit often works through humanity to plant the seeds of conviction. Jethro corrected Moses (Exodus 18:13–27). Nathan corrected David (2 Samuel 12:1–15), which is emblematic of the role the Old Testament prophets took with erring rulers (e.g., Jonah, Jeremiah, and others). We're not advocating a culture of criticism, but when correction is given with the Spirit's leading, honest love, and a meaningful relationship, God speaks to reorient us to His way of life.

The paradigmatic teachings on correction in the New Testament come from Paul. He told Timothy that Scripture is useful for correcting others (2 Timothy 3:16, 17) and instructed the Ephesians to practice "speaking the truth in love" for the good of the community (Ephesians 4:15). Galatians exemplifies this correction. One church leader is confronted by another. Neither of them had rejected God or performed some heinous sin. Both were extremely influential (in fact, they are the main characters of the book of Acts). In Galatians 2:11–14, Paul recounts an altercation he had with Peter. Paul had been working in Antioch, and Peter came to visit. At first, Peter openly shared in table fellowship with everyone, but then some believers came from Jerusalem who were opposed to eating with the uncircumcised. Peter altered his behavior, influencing other members of the community as well, but Paul called him out. Peter was being hypocritical and was compromising the gospel, so he needed someone to set him straight. If this were the end of the story, we would not be able to arrive at a verdict about whether the confrontation was ultimately effective, but 2 Peter 3:15, 16, written years after Galatians, clarifies the nature of Peter's reaction to Paul. Peter calls Paul a "beloved brother" (KJV), and he says Paul's letters have wisdom from God in them. Sometimes, God corrects even the most sincerely converted believers through the voice of the faith community.

In the tenth year of his pastoral ministry, Clarence* was assigned to set up for camp meeting with one of his conference officials. As they worked, Clarence began to tell this official how much he appreciated his work. He gave the official some gushy compliments about how wonderful a job he was doing. But then, the conference official cut him off and said, "I don't feel like what you're saying is sincere. I feel like you have a hidden agenda behind what you are saying."

Clarence replied, "No, I don't have an ulterior motive."

The conference official retorted, "Maybe you don't, but what I would like for

---
* Names in this chapter have been changed.

you to do is pray over it, see if maybe what I'm saying is true, and then, if it is, you can address it."

At first, Clarence had a reaction of pain. His superior was thinking horrible things about him. He wanted to be good at his job and to be known for having a good character. Then his pain turned into anger. *How could he judge me like that? He doesn't know me well enough to talk to me that way.* Yet, as Clarence worked through this pain and anger, he did pray about it, and God convicted him that this official was in the right.

Clarence discovered that he did have an ulterior motive. He wanted the official to like him and appreciate what he did. Clarence was operating from an "I accept you, so you should accept me" perspective. This official's words of correction opened up an amazing stage of life for him. He was able to grow deeply with God and with others. He became conscious of how he manipulated people, surrendered it to God, and allowed God to transform him so he could stop living in such a dysfunctional way. He still compliments people, but now he has entirely different motives because this correction experience was life changing. One friend speaking the truth in love was God's method to reveal Himself to Clarence and alter the trajectory of his life.

FINDING GOD THROUGH COMMUNAL HEALING

A certain church had the practice of giving individuals time to share praises, thanksgiving, and requests after worship. Everything was going as usual, but then a middle-aged church member stood up. He seemed nervous. "I love God, and I want to be fully devoted to Him, but I have an ugly presence in my life that is keeping me from giving everything to Him. I have been addicted to pornography for years, and I want deliverance. I want to be right with God and honor Him in everything."

There was dead silence. No one knew what to say. Everyone knew what to do when someone shared a praise or talked about a grandmother who was dealing with illness, but in this case, the silence stretched on and felt like an eternity. Then the head elder came forward. He walked up to the man, put his arms around him, and said, "Jack, we love you. You are special to us, and we are going to pray for you."

He took a few more minutes to explain how God was the only one who could deliver him from his addiction and then pledged, "We won't just pray for you today. We are going to keep on praying for you. I am going to pray for you every day." Then he invited everyone to come forward and pray for Jack.

A month later Jack stood up at the end of a prayer meeting and announced, "Praise the Lord. For this last month, I have been free from my addiction. God does answer prayers. God delivered me."

Deliverance is a key function of God, and deliverance takes many forms. Sometimes God frees us of our habits, sometimes our situations, and sometimes our ways of thinking. Acts 12 gives a wonderful example of divine deliverance. King

Christian Fellowship: Finding God in Community

Herod imprisoned Peter because he saw how persecuting the church merited favor with the Jewish leaders. The believers, on the other hand, gathered together, earnestly seeking the favor of God in prayer (Acts 12:5). Late one night Peter, shackled between two guards, fell asleep, but an angel appeared to him and led him out of the prison. Peter went straight to a safe house where he found the believers still interceding for him.[3] God worked through them in a mighty act of deliverance. God's desire was manifested through, and because of, the community.

One additional point to remember regarding communal healing is that though deliverance is always supernatural, sometimes it feels less miraculous than depicted in the stories of Jack and Peter. God works through the faith community to communicate His grace and love as friends gather around a struggling individual and provide accountability, structure, and prayer.[4] Whether explicitly or implicitly miraculous, God strengthens those in need of healing and deliverance directly through those around them. People find God through healing in the community.

FINDING GOD THROUGH COMMUNAL ENCOURAGEMENT

Esther needed God. She contemplated an audacious act, going before the king unannounced to ask him to alter the royal edict condemning her people to death. That was a major problem. The previous queen had been stripped of her title for dishonoring the king. For going before the king unannounced, Esther could have been killed. How did she deal with this high-stakes situation? Esther sought God in the context of community. To bolster her courage, she instructed Mordecai to gather as many Jews as possible and fast for her for three days, and she did the same with her entourage (Esther 4:16, 17). After this intense gathering, Esther had the strength to stand up for the cause of God and His people in exile. Community is the conduit God used to encourage Esther. He does the same thing today.

A church leader named William was very discouraged about some issues in his life and felt that life was unfair. He felt overwhelmed by his work and lacked motivation to completely invest in it. His unresolved issues kept him from seeing a way out. He was living in a negative world.

One day, in the small Bible fellowship group he belonged to, he had the courage to share his discouragement and doubts about what God could do in his life. The group members surrounded him, shared encouraging scripture promises, and prayed for him. One of them assured him that in spite of all his problems, God was still in control and was making all things work for good in William's life. Another friend claimed the promises of Isaiah 43:1–3:

> But now, this is what the LORD says . . .
> "Do not fear, for I have redeemed you;
>   I have summoned you by name; you are mine.
> When you pass through the waters,

> I will be with you;
> and when you pass through the rivers,
> > they will not sweep over you.
> When you walk through the fire,
> > you will not be burned;
> > the flames will not set you ablaze.
> For I am the LORD your God,
> > the Holy One of Israel, your Savior."

This friend told William that God had a purpose in mind for him. It did not matter what the problems or the circumstances were—God was with him. All this encouragement brought tremendous joy to William's heart. He went to the meeting feeling discouraged, but he left filled with hope and determination, like Esther, to do what God called him to do. He found God in his small group. He found God in the encouragement of community.

God's encouragement through the community is important for every follower

---

PRACTICAL STEPS TO HELP YOUR CHURCH FIND GOD IN COMMUNITY

Pray earnestly and daily for the perspective to see God through the people around you.
Also pray that God will give this perspective to your church. Then take time regularly to recognize how God has answered these prayers. As you embrace this practice, you will begin to model this way of life to your faith community.

Share with other members about finding God in community.
As you go through the teaching process, unpack the tremendous spiritual value of actively engaging with others and help other members share their stories of finding God in one another with the rest of the church.

Develop safe and authentic small groups and Sabbath School classes that do more than talk about a lesson.
Explain to your church members how safety, authenticity, and acceptance in small groups enable people to experience and extend grace.[5]

Model conflict resolution and forgiveness as the modes of dealing with interpersonal difficulties.
Some of the greatest barriers to finding God in those around us come from the conflicts we have with them. By mediating and training members in conflict resolution and forgiveness, attitudes will begin to change, and the walls will come down.[6]

Remember time is a key ingredient in God's recipe for growth.
One of Jesus' primary word pictures for working with people is that of plants in the field that grow

of Jesus. Sometimes in ministry, we become so used to being the ones with the answers that we never open ourselves up like William. We need to receive sometimes. Before the Crucifixion, Jesus took three disciples to encourage and pray with Him. Instead, they fell asleep. Matthew 26:40, 41 depicts a Jesus who needed comfort from others in His darkest hours when God's love and presence seemed far off. If Jesus longed for and sought out others, shouldn't we seek them out as well?

CONCLUSION

Dietrich Bonhoeffer, in his book *Life Together*, wrote about rich Christian fellowship, which he lost during the imprisonment leading up to his death.

> The physical presence of other Christians is a source of incomparable joy and strength to the believer. . . .
>
> . . . The prisoner, the sick person, the Christian in exile sees in the companionship of a fellow Christian a physical sign of the gracious presence of the triune God. . . . How inexhaustible are the riches that open up for those who by God's

---

over long stretches of time (Mark 4:26–29). As you implement these steps, instead of rushing, allow for change and transformation in God's time.

Celebrate milestones.
Help foster fellowship by celebrating birthdays, anniversaries, and other special events in people's lives. This helps the group members feel valuable and appreciated.

Plan a retreat together.
Arrange for a weekend when the members of the group can be together. The time spent in fellowship on an overnight trip is equivalent to many weeks of group meetings. I took my church on two retreats every year—one in the summer and one in the winter. People said that these were some of the best times they had spent as a community. They built strong relationships and bonded the church.

Host a night of fun.
Instead of the usual study time, surprise the group with a night full of games and fun. Such a change of pace is both healthy and refreshing for the group.

Take on a cause.
This can be a ministry project or mission trip that the group can do together (or the group can sponsor). Some of the best friendships I have developed started on mission trips.

Make sure that the essentials are taken care of.
Essentials of community life include the study of God's Word, prayer, worship, mission or ministry work, and social activities at least once a month (Acts 2:42–47).

will are privileged to live in the daily fellowship of life with other Christians![7]

He added, "Let him thank God on his knees and declare: It is grace, nothing but grace, that we are allowed to live in community with Christian brethren."[8] This is God working in community.

God has so much more for us than isolationist spirituality. Finding God is more than solitary experiences: what you do in your closet, at your desk, or on your knees by your bed. God has given us fellowship so we can understand who He is and what love is. He brings us back to the way of life by giving our brothers and sisters words of correction for us. He delivers us from bondage through the prayers and support of our community. He encourages us through the words and actions of others. May we open our hearts and minds and find God in our community.

---

1. Here are a few biblical texts supporting this point: Isaiah 57:15 contends that God inhabits eternity. Genesis 1 shows that God was active before Creation. James 1:17 and Hebrews 13:8 point out that God does not change. First John 4:8 reveals that God is love. Texts such as Matthew 3:16, 17; Matthew 28:19; and 2 Corinthians 13:14 attest to the presence of Three Members in the Godhead. Ellen G. White also speaks to the nature of the Trinity:

> The Father is all the fulness of the Godhead bodily. . . .
> The Son is all the fulness of the Godhead manifested. . . .
> The Comforter that Christ promised . . . is the Spirit in all the fulness of the Godhead, making manifest the power of divine grace to all who receive and believe in Christ as a personal Saviour. There are three living persons of the heavenly trio. (Ellen G. White, *Testimonies for the Church Containing Messages of Warning and Instruction to Seventh-day Adventists*, Series B, no. 7 [Sanitarium, CA: self-pub., 1906], 62, 63.)

2. Jürgen Moltmann, *Jürgen Moltmann: Collected Readings*, ed. Margaret Kohl (Minneapolis, MN: Fortress Press, 2014), 73.

3. Although the content is not specified explicitly by the biblical text, Ellen G. White clarifies that these prayers were requests for help and deliverance because of Peter's importance to the church at that time. See Ellen G. White, *The Acts of the Apostles* (Mountain View, CA: Pacific Press®, 1911), 145.

4. Henry Cloud and John Townsend, *How People Grow: What the Bible Reveals About Personal Growth* (Grand Rapids, MI: Zondervan, 2001), 121–133.

5. We recommend *How People Grow* by Henry Cloud and John Townsend (Grand Rapids, MI: Zondervan, 2001) and *Experiencing God* by Henry Blackaby and Richard Blackaby (Nashville, TN: B&H, 2008) to foster small-group discussions that go below the surface.

6. We recommend *The Peacemaker* by Ken Sande (Grand Rapids, MI: Baker Books, 2004); *The Peacemaking Pastor* by Alfred Poirier (Grand Rapids, MI: Baker Books, 2006); and *Redeeming Church Conflicts* by Tara Klena Barthel and David V. Edling (Grand Rapids, MI: Baker Books, 2012) as great books on conflict resolution. *Cleansing the Sanctuary of the Heart*, 2nd ed., by David Sedlacek and Beverly Sedlacek (Berrien Springs, MI: Restful Heart, 2014) has an excellent section on the forgiveness process, and *Love, Acceptance, and Forgiveness*, rev. and updated ed., by Jerry Cook and Stanley C. Baldwin (Grand Rapids, MI: Bethany House, 2009) is another excellent work on forgiveness.

7. Dietrich Bonhoeffer, *Life Together*, trans. John W. Doberstein (New York: Harper and Brothers, 1954), 19, 20.

8. Bonhoeffer, *Life Together*, 20.

PART 7

Journey to the
Heart of God
Through Fasting

CHAPTER 18

FASTING
Gaining by Denying*

"When you fast, put oil on your head and wash your face, so that it will not be obvious to others that you are fasting, but only to your Father, who is unseen; and your Father, who sees what is done in secret, will reward you."
—Matthew 6:17, 18

Fasting, the spiritual discipline of disconnecting from food, social media, sports, television, and/or other distractions, is mentioned numerous times in both the Old and New Testaments.[1] The practice continued with the early Christians.[2] Reformers such as Martin Luther, John Calvin, and John Wesley encouraged regular fasting.[3] Adventist pioneers, including James and Ellen White, also advocated fasting.[4]

Yet we do not hear much about the spiritual discipline of fasting today, unless it is in the context of times of distress or desire for revival.

Some may shy away from fasting due to misuses of the discipline or in an attempt to distance themselves from the legalistic view of ritual fasting as proof of piety. Others do not feel the need to take part in what they consider antiquated customs or maneuverings for God's grace. Fasting does not fit into our Western desire to compartmentalize the sacred and the secular.

But there is a profound connection between prayer and fasting. Our prayers connect us with God intimately, whereas fasting disconnects us from the world and ultimately connects us more deeply with our Creator, bringing great joy and spiritual renewal. For a heightened spiritual experience, we must both pray and fast. The aim of this chapter is to present a biblical view of fasting and demonstrate how and why it should be a part of every believer's individual and corporate Christian experience.

THE BIBLICAL MEANING OF *FASTING*
The Old Testament uses four main words to denote fasting. The most common of these are צוֹם (*tsowm*), used twenty-six times, and its cognate צוּם (*tsuwm*), used

---
* This chapter was cowritten with Kristy Hodson.

twenty-one times.⁵ Each time these words are used, it is in the context of temporarily denying oneself food. Fasts described with these words are usually declared by humans to beseech God's favor (Ezra 8:21), show repentance (Jonah 3:5), or to serve as a sign of mourning (2 Samuel 1:12).

The Hebrew word נָזַר (*nazar*), translated in Zechariah 7:3 as "fast" (NIV), "abstain" (ESV), or "separating" (KJV), is only used ten times in the Bible. It carries with it the sense of permanent or long-term separation and consecration of oneself for the sake of holiness. This term is most notably used (five out of the ten times) in respect to the vows of the Nazirites (Numbers 6:2–6, 12).

The word עָנָה (`*anah*), meaning "to afflict or humble," is sometimes used in the context of denying oneself through fasting. Two prominent examples of this use are the fast of the Day of Atonement in Leviticus 23:27–32 and David's intercessory prayer and fasting in Psalm 35:13.⁶

Based on its use in the Old Testament, fasting was a temporary denial of food and humbling of oneself before God to show great sorrow or to seek God's favor.

In the New Testament, there are three Greek words, all from the same root, used for fasting: νηστεύω (*nēsteuō*) used twenty-one times, νηστεία (*nēsteia*) used eight times, and νῆστις (*nēstis*) used twice.⁷ These can be literally translated as "not eating," yet the context tells us that these words are used to refer to a ritual or religious practice.⁸ For many during New Testament times, fasting had become a ritual to show piety or habit rather than a way to draw closer to God (Luke 18:9–14). There was no joy in their fasting. This is evidenced by the chastisement Jesus gave those who intentionally brought attention to their fasting (Matthew 6:16–18).

Jesus and the first-century church promoted fasting with a purpose. For Jesus, fasting was an intimate personal experience with God, done individually or collectively, to build strength in spiritual warfare (Matthew 4:2; Mark 9:29). The early church continued fasting in this manner and also fasted when committing church leaders to the Lord (Acts 14:23).

WHAT FASTING IS

In the Bible, fasting was denying oneself food and drink to focus on a period of spiritual growth (Matthew 17:21; Acts 9:9),⁹ prayer (Daniel 9:3), consecration (Acts 13:3; 14:23), deliverance (Esther 4:16; Psalm 109:24), corporate festivals (Leviticus 23:26–32), resolution of conflict (Judges 20:26), repentance (Deuteronomy 9:18; Jonah 3:5), mourning (2 Samuel 1:12; 1 Chronicles 10:12), supplication (Joel 1:14; 2 Samuel 12:16), or seeking God's will (Acts 13:2).

Fasting was not merely an individual practice; it was also done on a corporate scale by the whole nation or faith community. National days of fasting other than the Day of Atonement, which was a fast declared by God for the nation, were rare for the preexilic Israelites. Days of fasting were called as part of mourning a death as was done by Israel after the death of King Saul (1 Chronicles 10:11, 12) or in times of great crisis, famine, or invasion (Joel 1:14; 2 Chronicles 20:3). National fast days later increased to commemorate the destruction of the temple and the events leading to the Exile.[10] However, individual fasts remained more common than corporate fasts in both the Old and New Testaments.

Today, fasting can be expanded to include a partial fast of specific foods, such as dairy, sugar, meat, highly processed food, or fast food. It can also mean going without social media, shopping, sleep, sports, sex, or any other activity that may distract one from fully focusing on God.

One pastor refers to fasting as "blessed subtraction," noting that the aim is to give up something—not necessarily a bad something—for the purpose of drawing closer to God.[11] When fasting, I (Kristy) not only deny myself something but also add something else. For example, by "fasting" from my usual wake-up time, I will get up one hour early and use that hour for extended quiet time and deeper devotionals. When the cravings for certain food items are felt, that becomes a trigger to pray for God's blessing and guidance or to thank Him. There is a rejuvenation that accompanies these times of fasting.

Fasting without focusing on God is merely a diet. But when we fast, we notice the fake, destructive things that we are attached to. Therefore, the purpose of fasting is to enhance our relationship with God and go deeper in our prayer life. Jesus, the Bread of Life and Gift of heaven, is sufficient to satisfy our needs and leads to eternal life (John 6:32–48). Psalm 63:1–5 demonstrates that seeking after God wholeheartedly and praising Him will lead to a satisfaction that no food can bring:

> You, God, are my God,
>   earnestly I seek you;
> I thirst for you,
>   my whole being longs for you,
> in a dry and parched land
>   where there is no water. . . .
> I will be fully satisfied as with the richest of foods;
>   with singing lips my mouth will praise you (verses 1, 5)

Ellen White encourages believers to fast, seeing abstinence from food as a way in which to focus on spiritual growth: "Men need to think less about what they shall eat and drink, of temporal food, and much more in regard to the food from heaven, that will give tone and vitality to the whole religious experience."[12] This is the motivation when my (Joseph's) wife, Denise, observes regular fasting. For her, scheduled fasting is about asking God for nothing more than a deeper connection to Him. The hunger she finds for God and the closeness to Him that she feels while fasting carries her through long after her fast has ended. Everyone can temporarily give up something in order to draw closer to God. By choosing to go against our human desires, we are allowing space for personal and spiritual growth. "Fasting helps to discipline the self-indulgent and slothful will which is so reluctant to serve the Lord, and it helps to humiliate and chasten the flesh."[13] Fasting takes our attention away from ourselves and redirects it to heaven.

WHAT FASTING IS NOT

Fasting, as a spiritual discipline, has at times been misunderstood or used in ways contrary to the will to God. In order to understand what fasting is, it is prudent to also look at what fasting is not.

Coercion. Fasting is not about twisting God's arm. It is not some kind of spiritual hunger strike that compels God to do our bidding. God explains this in Isaiah 58:

> "Why have we fasted," they say,
>   "and you have not seen it?
> Why have we humbled ourselves,
>   and you have not noticed?"
> Yet on the day of your fasting, you do as you please
>   and exploit all your workers.
> Your fasting ends in quarreling and strife,
>   and in striking each other with wicked fists.
> You cannot fast as you do today
>   and expect your voice to be heard on high. (verses 3, 4)

Any pious intent the Israelites had was overshadowed by their lack of justice and compassion due to the evilness in their hearts (see also Zechariah 7:4–13). Their acts of fasting were not practiced in conjunction with the humbling of their hearts. Instead, their intentions were to force God into an action that the people did not merit. "They fasted merely to gain favor with God and to secure His approval of their evil deeds, as if abstention from food was of more importance in God's sight than abstention from iniquity!"[14]

Attitude is everything when it comes to fasting. In Acts 23:12–15, there was a group of more than forty Jews that resolved to fast until they were successful in their conspiracy to kill Paul. They did not desire God's will but their own selfish agenda. Fasting is supposed to change us, not God.

Penance. God's forgiveness of our sins comes with no requirement except confession and repentance (1 John 1:9). There was a time in church history, however, when fasting was "linked with a legalistic theology and the concept of meritorious works."[15] This nonbiblical idea used fasting as a way to prove to God that one is worthy of forgiveness and to punish oneself. This false view of fasting has carried through to some corners of contemporary Christianity. There are those who undertake fasting as a way to punish the body for sinning or to force it into compliance. Fasting as penance is not the same as the biblical concept of fasting for repentance (Jonah 3:5–9).[16] Repentance is the sign of a contrite heart and the desire to turn from sin, while penance is a self-inflicted punishment with the purpose of gaining God's favor. Penance focuses on one's selfish past; repentance focuses on one's God-filled future.

We shouldn't deprive ourselves of food to punish ourselves and gain favor with God. We already have God's favor through Jesus. "And all are justified freely by his grace through the redemption that came by Christ Jesus" (Romans 3:24; see also Romans 5:1).

THE PURPOSE AND BENEFITS OF FASTING

Fasting is a discipline that is both physical and spiritual; building our faith muscles so that we can withstand the bigger contests that come our way. Fasting is more than just a spiritual training in self-control. Throughout Christian history, people have shared their positive spiritual experiences with fasting and its role in maintaining a balanced life.[17] One primary biblical reason to fast is to develop a closer walk with God and acknowledge our need for Him. We see this in the fast of the people of Nineveh, proclaiming their repentance (Jonah 3). By taking our eyes off the things of this world, we can focus better on Christ. An awareness of our physical needs reminds us of our spiritual needs. Jesus shared in Matthew 4:4 that "man shall not live on bread alone, but on every word that comes from the mouth of God." Fasting reminds us that we can get by without most things for a time, but we cannot get by without God.

Fasting was an expected discipline in both the Old and New Testaments. Moses fasted for at least two recorded forty-day periods (Exodus 24:18; 34:28; Deuteronomy 10:10). Jesus fasted for forty days (Matthew 4:2) and reminded His followers to fast: "*when* you fast," not "*if* you fast" (Matthew 6:16; emphasis added). David fasted for seven days (2 Samuel 12:16–18). Mordecai, Esther, and her maidens fasted for three days (Esther 4:16), and the whole nation of Israel fasted for the Day of Atonement (Leviticus 23:26–32). Following are some biblical examples of why people fasted:[18]

- Fasting combined with prayer is a means that can be used to seek and find a more joyful, intimate relationship with God. " 'Even now,' declares the Lord, 'return to me with all your heart, with fasting and weeping and mourning.' Rend your heart and not your garments. Return to the Lord your God, for he is gracious and compassionate, slow to anger and abounding in love, and he relents from sending calamity" (Joel 2:12, 13).
- Fasting in the Bible is used as a way to humble oneself before God (1 Samuel 7:6; Ezra 8:21). King David said, "I . . . humbled myself through fasting" (Psalm 35:13).

- Fasting allows the Holy Spirit to work in you, showing you the "true spiritual condition [of your heart], resulting in brokenness, repentance and a transformed life"[19] (1 Kings 21:27).
- Fasting transforms your prayer life into a more meaningful and personal worship experience (Luke 2:37, 38; Colossians 3:17).
- Fasting can give you courage to do what is right in times of distress. Esther fasted and asked those around her to fast as she prepared to visit the king without being called. Such a visit could have cost her life; instead, it saved her people (Esther 4:16).
- Fasting and ministry go hand and hand in the Bible. Jesus fasted at the start of His earthly ministry (Luke 4:1, 2). Paul fasted immediately after his Damascus Road encounter (Acts 9:9). Elijah fasted to once again hear the voice of God (1 Kings 19:8). Prayer and fasting were part of the laying on of hands before sending out missionaries and appointing elders in the early church (Acts 13:3; 14:23). Prophets often fasted on behalf of their people (Daniel 9:1–19). For example, Ezra "ate no food and drank no water, because he continued to mourn over the unfaithfulness of the exiles" (Ezra 10:6).

Fasting and prayer are strongly linked together in the Bible (Luke 2:37; 5:33).[20] When you fast, you will find yourself being humbled. You will discover more time to pray and seek God's face. As He leads you to recognize and repent of unconfessed sin, you will experience special blessings from God.

FROM FASTING TO FEASTING

The Bible presents fasting as something that is good, profitable, and beneficial. Fasting is not about a lack of food or depriving the body but rather a refocusing away from this world and feasting on the things of God. "Fasting is an exceptional measure, designed to channel and express our desire for God and our holy discontent in a fallen world. It is for those not satisfied with the status quo. For those who want more of God's grace. For those who feel truly desperate for God."[21] Fasting is an acknowledgment of our commitment to enhance our relationship with Him. It helps us gain a new perspective and a renewed reliance on God.

---

1. This chapter was originally published in a slightly different form in S. Joseph Kidder and Kristy L. Hodson, "Gaining by Denying: The Benefit of Christian Fasting—Part 1 of 2," *Ministry* 88, no. 7 (July 2016): 6–9.

2. In chapter 8 of the second-generation Christian work known as the Didache, believers are told to fast on Wednesdays and Fridays. *The Didache, or Teaching of the Twelve Apostles*, trans. Charles H. Hoole (London: David Nutt, 1894), 80, https://archive.org/details/didacheorteachin00hool/page/80.

3. Martin Luther, *Treatise on Good Works*, in *Works of Martin Luther*, vol. 1, ed. Adolph Spaeth, and Henry Eyster Jacobs (Philadelphia: A. J. Holman, 1915), 243–286; John Calvin, *Institutes of*

the Christian Religion, vol. 2, bk. 4, trans. Henry Beveridge (Edinburgh: T&T Clark, 1863), chap. 12; John Wesley, "Upon Our Lord's Sermon on the Mount: Discourse Seven," in *The Sermons of John Wesley*, Wesley Center Online, accessed February 11, 2019, http://wesley.nnu.edu/john-wesley/the-sermons-of-john-wesley-1872-edition/sermon-27-upon-our-lords-sermon-on-the-mount-discourse-seven.

4. To read about Ellen White's views and experiences with fasting, see chapter 10 of *Counsels on Diet and Foods*.

5. Word counts are taken from the Blue Letter Bible's Hebrew lexicon. *Strong's Concordance*, s.v. "H6685," accessed February 11, 2019, https://www.blueletterbible.org/lang/lexicon/lexicon.cfm?strongs=H6685&t=KJV; *Strong's Concordance*, s.v. "H6684," accessed February 11, 2019, https://www.blueletterbible.org/lang/lexicon/lexicon.cfm?strongs=H6684&t=KJV.

6. Word counts are taken from the Blue Letter Bible's Hebrew lexicon. *Strong's Concordance*, s.v. "H5144," accessed February 11, 2019, https://www.blueletterbible.org/lang/lexicon/lexicon.cfm?Strongs=H5144&t=KJV; *Strong's Concordance*, s.v. "H6031," accessed February 11, 2019, https://www.blueletterbible.org/lang/lexicon/lexicon.cfm?t=kjv&strongs=h6031.

7. Word counts are taken from the Blue Letter Bible's Greek lexicon. *Strong's Concordance*, s.v. "G3522," accessed February 11, 2019, https://www.blueletterbible.org/lang/lexicon/lexicon.cfm?Strongs=G3522&t=KJV; *Strong's Concordance*, s.v. "G3521," accessed February 11, 2019, https://www.blueletterbible.org/lang/lexicon/lexicon.cfm?Strongs=G3521&t=KJV; *Strong's Concordance*, s.v. "G3523," accessed February 11, 2019, https://www.blueletterbible.org/lang/lexicon/lexicon.cfm?Strongs=G3523&t=KJV.

8. Friedrich S. Rothenberg, "Fast," in *The New International Dictionary of New Testament Theology*, vol. 1, ed. Colin Brown (Grand Rapids, MI: Regency Reference Library, 1975), 611.

9. Some manuscripts, such as those used in the KJV and NKJV, note that Cornelius fasted in Acts 10:30 for this same purpose.

10. The fasts of the fifth and seventh months, as kept during the seventy years of exile (Zechariah 7:5), were two such fasts. John J. Collins, *Joel, Obadiah, Haggai, Zechariah, Malachi*, vol. 17, New Collegeville Bible Commentary, ed. Daniel Durken (Collegeville, MN: Liturgical Press, 2012), 94.

11. Wesley D. Tracy, E. Dee Freeborn, Janine Tartaglia-Metcalf, and Morris A. Weigelt, *The Upward Call: Spiritual Formation and the Holy Life* (Kansas City, MO: Beacon Hill Press of Kansas City, 1994), 95.

12. Ellen G. White, *Counsels on Diet and Foods* (Washington, DC: Review and Herald®, 1938), 90.

13. Dietrich Bonhoeffer, *The Cost of Discipleship* (New York: Touchstone, 1995), 169.

14. "Isaiah," in *The Seventh-day Adventist Bible Commentary*, vol. 4, revised ed., ed. Francis D. Nichol (Hagerstown, MD: Review and Herald®, 1976), 306.

15. R. D. Linder, "Fast, Fasting," in *Evangelical Dictionary of Theology*, 2nd ed., ed. W. A. Elwell (Grand Rapids, MI: Baker Academic, 2001), 438.

16. Biblical repentance has its roots in the concept of turning away from sin and turning toward God. Fritz Laubach, "μεταμέλομαι," in *The New International Dictionary of New Testament Theology*, vol. 1, ed. Colin Brown (Grand Rapids, MI: Regency Reference Library, 1975), 611.

17. Richard J. Foster, *Celebration of Discipline: The Path to Spiritual Growth*, 25th anniversary ed. (San Francisco: HarperSanFrancisco, 1998), 56.

18. This list is partially inspired by Bill Bright, "Why You Should Fast," Cru, accessed February 11, 2019, http://www.cru.org/train-and-grow/spiritual-growth/fasting/personal-guide-to-fasting.2.html.

19. Bright, "Why You Should Fast."

20. Jacques B. Doukhan, *Secrets of Daniel: Wisdom and Dreams of a Jewish Prince in Exile* (Hagerstown, MD: Review and Herald®, 2000), 94.

21. David Mathis, "Sharpen Your Affections With Fasting," Desiring God, June 4, 2014, http://www.desiringgod.org/articles/sharpen-your-affections-with-fasting.

CHAPTER 19

FASTING

Working Up an Appetite for God*

"Even now," declares the Lord, *"return to me with all your heart, with fasting and weeping and mourning." Rend your heart and not your garments. Return to the* Lord *your God, for he is gracious and compassionate, slow to anger and abounding in love, and he relents from sending calamity.*
—Joel 2:12, 13

In the previous chapter, we discussed the biblical meaning and benefits of the Christian discipline of fasting.[1] We shared how fasting can bring great depth to one's personal relationship with God when it is done in conjunction with feasting on Jesus. In this chapter, we invite you to share in the joys of fasting as we discuss when and how to undertake a personal or corporate fast.

ATTITUDE WHILE FASTING

Fasting is to be done in a spirit of humility and with a joyful attitude. Throughout the Bible, God rebuked the Israelites for their misplaced views on fasting. Rather than being a way in which to humble themselves before their great Creator, "it came to be regarded as pious achievement."[2] To correct this view of fasting as an outward show of piety, Jesus taught, "When you fast, do not look somber as the hypocrites do, for they disfigure their faces to show others they are fasting. Truly I tell you, they have received their reward in full. But when you fast, put oil on your head and wash your face, so that it will not be obvious to others that you are fasting, but only to your Father, who is unseen; and your Father, who sees what is done in secret, will reward you" (Matthew 6:16–18).

The customary weekly days of fasting, Monday and Thursday, coincided with the busy market days. It was not uncommon to see people deliberately modifying their appearance in order to play up their piety for the crowds. They did not partake in the usual grooming habits and even used cosmetics to give the impression of paleness; their attempts to exaggerate humility were in fact pride and pretentiousness.[3]

---
* This chapter was cowritten with Kristy Hodson.

Furthermore, Ellen White adds that fasting is not a way to appear more spiritual than others: "Fasting or prayer that is actuated by a self-justifying spirit is an abomination in the sight of God."[4] Just as with any spiritual custom or discipline, it is not the action itself that brings one righteousness. Only the opening of the heart and the surrendering of the will to God will bring forth a saving relationship with Christ.

Our attitude when fasting is representative of our relationship with God. "External religious observances are useless if the relationship with God has been lost. . . . God takes no notice of piety that does not issue out of a listening and obedient heart."[5] A friend recently shared that she felt her relationship to music was blocking her relationship with Christ. As a result, she began fasting from music and patiently waited for six months to hear from God on when to end this fast. When she felt the urge to listen to music, she instead began to praise God. The focus was not on what was given up but on the joy she gained in a rejuvenated connection to God.

When the goal of fasting is to deepen one's relationship with God, it must be undertaken with seriousness and sincerity. Great joy can be found in humbly approaching the King of kings. It is this joy and expectation of connection with the Holy Spirit that should permeate your fasting experience.

WHEN TO FAST

The question may arise regarding when people should fast. Following is a list of several instances from the Bible when God's people chose to fast. They can help us determine when situations in our lives might benefit from prayer combined with fasting.

- *Fasting can be an integral part of one's spiritual journey.* Bill Hull refers to this type of fasting as one that "intensely nourish[es]. . . [the] soul."[6] We see this in the life of Jesus when the Spirit led Him into the wilderness to prepare Him for ministry (Matthew 4:1, 2; Luke 4:1, 2). Paul also fasted after experiencing Christ in vision and seeing his need for personal revival (Acts 9:9). Both Jesus and Paul spent the rest of their lives bringing revival to others. One college student described her prayer and fasting as a way in which to speed up her Christian growth. She said that it "tenderizes my heart toward the Lord. My spirit becomes all the more sensitive to his promptings, his voice, his touch."[7]
- *Fasting can be part of allowing the Holy Spirit to work in us to overcome sin (Matthew 4:4).* This is God's desire for fasting, as shown in Isaiah 58:6: "Is not this the kind of fasting I have chosen: to loose the chains of injustice and untie the cords of the yoke, to set the oppressed free and break every yoke?" Fasting can show us the things that we have ig-

Fasting: Working Up an Appetite for God

nored in our lives. "Without our usual comforts . . . , we turn to God with more honesty and intensity. There we connect with the richness of God, who truly meets our needs."[8] We see our need to repent of sins, which only He can free us from.

- *Fasting is often undertaken before making important decisions or major life events.* This was the case when Esther decided to risk her life to go before the king (Esther 4:16). Fasting can also be done by the church as a whole when looking for a new pastor, deciding to undertake a building or renovation project, or starting a church plant. For individuals, fasting can be a part of the decision-making process when looking for a new job, considering a possible marriage, or making a major move.

- *Fasting can help in facing or overcoming personal challenges and problems.* When David was falsely criticized or accused, he sought to humble himself and pray for vindication rather than retaliate (Psalms 35:13; 69:10; 109:24). As a pastor, there were times in which I (Joseph) felt as if I were being criticized. I would pray and fast, asking God to open my eyes to any legitimate criticism and to vindicate me against any falsehoods. This brought me much peace and allowed me to stay focused on the mission of reaching people for Christ.

- *Fasting and prayer can signify our sorrow and regret.* Through fasting, Ezra showed his deep sorrow over the unfaithfulness of God's people and his desire for the community to repent and experience spiritual renewal (Ezra 10:6). Criticism is a common response when we feel slighted or at odds with those around us. James warns against the damage this can cause (James 3:6–10). Instead, spend time in prayer and fasting not only for those who have fallen away from God or who hold a differing viewpoint but also for you to have a more Christlike attitude in order to show love and mercy to those you interact with.

- *Fasting can be a part of intercessory prayer.* Esther asked that all of the Jews in Susa fast for her as she faced the danger of going before the king (Esther 4:16). Additionally, we see instances of leaders, such as Nehemiah, fasting and seeking forgiveness on behalf of their people (Nehemiah 1:4–11). One pastoral couple felt the need to include fasting along with their prayers for their adult daughter to return to God and the church. They noticed that their attitude changed to be more accepting and loving of their daughter. It was this change in her parents that stirred a desire in the daughter's heart to once again look to God.

- *Fasting was a part of the selection process for early church leaders and also signaled the start of their public ministry, as evidenced in the ordination of Barnabas and Saul and the appointing of elders (Acts 13:2, 3; 14:23).* A modern example can be seen in my experience with a church I

(Joseph) pastored. We intentionally spent a great deal of time in prayer and fasting when selecting a nominating committee and again when the nominating committee was working on their selections for church leadership. Our congregation grew into a healthy and lively church family through the prompting of God regarding our leaders.

- *Fasting was used when God's people were under threat of persecution.* The plot by Haman to eradicate the Jews led to communal fasting (Esther 4:3). Today, this type of fasting is commonly seen when groups fast for the release of Christians falsely imprisoned for their faith or when the Christian community is threatened by persecution.
- *Fasting was seen as the appropriate response to impending calamity.* When war was unexpectedly waged against Judah, the people came together to seek help from God. "Alarmed, Jehoshaphat resolved to inquire of the LORD, and he proclaimed a fast for all Judah" (2 Chronicles 20:3).

By examining the preceding list, we can conclude that it is biblical for people to fast when they are desperate for God to act. Fasting can bring a note of urgency to our prayers, though it does not guarantee a favorable answer. It "express[es] legitimate hope in the mercy of God."[9] Today, we would do well to fast for rescue from a bad situation or habit, healing or salvation of a loved one, direction in life, or other requests that are close to our hearts. The struggle and discomfort felt during fasting mirrors our emotional and spiritual aches.[10]

We are coming to our Father and telling Him (and ourselves) how important He is to us. "Christian fasting, at its root, is the hunger of a homesickness for God. . . . Christian fasting is not only the spontaneous effect of a superior satisfaction in God; it is also a chosen weapon against every force in the world that would take that satisfaction away."[11] Those who combine prayer with fasting are showing God that they are earnest in their pleas. Fasting has become "an outward

HOW TO PREPARE FOR FASTING

Because attitude is a key element in fasting, there should be intentional preparation before undertaking a spiritually motivated fast:
- Examine your motives (Isaiah 58:3–7).
- Surrender your life fully to Jesus Christ as your Lord and Savior (Romans 12:1, 2).
- Ask God to reveal your sins to you (Psalm 19:12).
- Confess your sins (1 John 1:9).
- Seek forgiveness from those you have offended (Mark 11:25; Luke 17:3, 4).
- Make restitution as the Holy Spirit leads (Matthew 5:23–26).
- Ask God to fill you with His Holy Spirit (Ephesians 5:18; 1 John 5:14, 15).

> **WHAT TO DO WHILE FASTING**
> - Fill the space created by fasting with prayer (Ephesians 6:18).
> - Meditate on the Word of God (Psalm 1:1, 2; Colossians 3:16).
> - Consider the attributes of God: love, wisdom, compassion, sovereignty (Psalms 48:9, 10; 103:1–13).
> - Expect God to bless you and reveal Himself to you (Hebrews 11:6).
> - Do not underestimate spiritual opposition (Galatians 5:16, 17).
> - Refuse to yield to your worldly nature (Romans 12:1, 2).
> - Exhibit an attitude of joy (Zechariah 8:19; Matthew 6:17, 18).

expression of the person's inner total commitment and reliance on God's preserving and rescuing power."[12]

HOW LONG TO FAST

Once the decision to fast has been made, the question becomes how long to fast. Biblical examples of extreme forty-day fasts (such as Moses' in Exodus 34:28, Elijah's in 1 Kings 19:8, and Jesus' in Luke 4:2) were divinely commissioned and irregular. A normal early Christian fast would only be undertaken during daylight hours.[13] The corporate fast in Judges 20:26 is an example of a fast that lasted until evening.

Esther proclaimed a full fast for three days (Esther 4:16). We are not told how long Daniel's fast was in Daniel 9:3, but we are told he undertook a three-week partial fast (Daniel 10:2, 3). The duration and extent of your fast often will be dictated by what you are fasting from and what you are fasting for.[14] Some people may fast on an annual basis, while others opt for a single day of fasting each week.

As noted earlier, single-day fasts on a regular basis were part of the religious rituals of the Jewish and early Christian experience. Today, a full fast of no food or water usually will last only a day, a juice fast may last for three days, and partial and/or nonfood fasts tend to last from one week to one month or more. Keep in mind that a fast is a temporary giving up of something and not a permanent lifestyle change, such as moving to a plant-based diet or giving up gluten.

REVIVAL AND FASTING

First Samuel provides an example for us in terms of fasting and revival. The Israelites knew that they were in need of a spiritual reconversion and turned to God with repentance and fasting. Mere words were not enough—they fasted to show their sincerity.[15] "When they had assembled at Mizpah, they drew water and poured it out before the Lord. On that day they fasted and there they confessed, 'We have sinned against the Lord' " (1 Samuel 7:6).

The early Adventist pioneers also fasted for revival. When speaking to a group in Colorado, Ellen White noted, "It is your privilege to receive more of the Spirit of God, as you engage in fasting and earnest prayer. You need to accept the promises and assurances of God and walk out on them in faith. You need to learn how to present the truths of the Word to those around you in all their binding force and in all their encouragement, that the unconverted may feel the influence of the Spirit of God upon heart and mind and character."[16]

One such example is given of prayer and fasting taking place before evangelistic meetings, which resulted in the baptism of six people and the forming of a new congregation. Isaac Sanborn, in a report to the *Advent Review and Sabbath Herald*, wrote the following:

> For some time previous to my meetings here, the brethren observed every other Sabbath as a day of fasting and prayer, for a revival of God's work in their own hearts, and for the conversion of their neighbors. Their prayers were most signally answered during our meetings. Six were baptized, and a church of twenty-two members was organized. Bro. Wm. H. Slown was ordained elder, under whose faithful watchcare we trust the Lord will build up and strengthen the little band. We had at the close of our meetings a great blessing in attending the ordinances. We also found that much prejudice had been removed from the minds of some, who we trust will soon find their place among the remnant.[17]

For early Adventists, fasting brought about an increased sensitivity to God's leading and the desire to share God's love with sinners. Author Lynne M. Baab puts it this way: "Fasting reflects the fact that the world is not as it should be, that we are called to pray fervently for the needs of this broken world. When we fast, we engage with the pain of the world. . . . Fasting is a step into the heart of God, who grieves for the pain of the people he created and loves."[18]

When I (Joseph) was pastoring a small church of about forty, I became intentional about praying and fasting for the church to grow. My wife and I committed every Monday for prayer and fasting, and I began to teach the members about fasting. During this extended period, spanning eight and a half years, we saw the church grow from forty members in attendance to five hundred. We built into the church calendar days of prayer and fasting for the entire congregation. The church would also have additional days of prayer and fasting leading up to our evangelistic meetings, climaxing with prayer sessions on Friday, often accompanied by a Communion service.[19] These things set the tone for the event by refocusing the church on our mission to humbly spread the gospel to hurting people in our community.

WORKING UP AN APPETITE FOR GOD

When you fast, you will find yourself being humbled (Isaiah 58:3) and will discover more time to pray and seek God's face. "Fasting can bring breakthroughs in the spiritual realm that will never happen in any other way."[20] An increased awareness of the greatness of God and His love often accompanies the fasting experience. Your worship is heightened, and your relationship with Christ is more intimate and vital. Bill Bright shares that by fasting "the Word of God has become even more alive to me. My prayers are more meaningful and effective. Fasting has enabled me to experience an increased joy of the Lord and the power of His resurrection in a new way."[21] When you commit to come before the Lord in fasting, you and those around you will experience special blessings from God.

---

1. This chapter was originally published in a slightly different form in S. Joseph Kidder and Kristy L. Hodson, "Gaining by Denying: An Invitation to the Discipline of Fasting—Part 2 of 2," *Ministry* 88, no. 9 (September 2016): 17–19.

2. Friedrich S. Rothenberg, "Fast," in *The New International Dictionary of New Testament Theology*, vol. 1, ed. Colin Brown (Grand Rapids, MI: Regency Reference Library, 1975), 612.

3. William Barclay, *The Gospel of Matthew*, vol. 1, Daily Study Bible (Philadelphia: Westminster Press, 1975), 235.

4. Ellen G. White, *The Desire of Ages* (Mountain View, CA: Pacific Press®, 1898), 280.

5. Elizabeth Achtemeier, *Nahum–Malachi*, Interpretation: A Bible Commentary for Teaching and Preaching, ed. James Luther Mays (Louisville, KY: Westminster John Knox Press, 2012), 135.

6. Bill Hull, *The Complete Book of Discipleship*, Navigators Reference Library (Colorado Springs, CO: NavPress, 2006), 197.

7. Lynne M. Baab, *Fasting: Spiritual Freedom Beyond Our Appetites* (Downers Grove, IL: InterVarsity Press, 2006), 42.

8. Jan Johnson, *Simplicity and Fasting*, Spiritual Disciplines Bible Studies (Downers Grove, IL: InterVarsity Press, 2003), 33.

9. John J. Collins, *Joel, Obadiah, Haggai, Zechariah, Malachi*, vol. 17, New Collegeville Bible Commentary, ed. Daniel Durken (Collegeville, MN: Liturgical Press, 2012), 21. A biblical example of this is David fasting for seven days for the healing of his and Bathsheba's firstborn child, but the child still died (2 Samuel 12:13–22).

10. Rothenberg, "Fast," 612.

11. John Piper, *A Hunger for God: Desiring God Through Fasting and Prayer* (Wheaton, IL: Crossway, 1997), 14.

12. Ángel Manuel Rodríguez, "Go Fast," *Adventist Review*, September 13, 2001, https://www.adventistreview.org/archives/2001-1537/story3.html.

13. R. D. Linder, "Fast, Fasting," in *Evangelical Dictionary of Theology*, 2nd ed., ed. W. A. Elwell (Grand Rapids, MI: Baker Academic, 2001), 438.

14. An in-depth discussion on the various types of food-based fasts, how they affect the body, and how to end an extended fast can be found in Baab, *Fasting*, 90–101.

15. Walter C. Kaiser Jr., *Quest for Renewal* (Chicago: Moody Press, 1986), 59.

16. Ellen G. White, as quoted in W. C. White, "Mrs. White's Visit to Boulder, Colorado," *Advent Review and Sabbath Herald*, January 13, 1910, 9.

17. Isaac Sanborn, "Report From Bro. Sanborn," *Advent Review and Sabbath Herald*, April 10, 1866, 149.

18. Baab, *Fasting*, 138, 139.

19. I personally found that Fridays, rather than Sabbaths, worked best for church-wide fasting. This would prevent the congregation from seeing the Sabbath as a day of want instead of experiencing the joy of God's special day.

20. Richard J. Foster, *Celebration of Discipline: The Path to Spiritual Growth*, 25th anniversary ed. (San Francisco: HarperSanFrancisco, 1998), 60.

21. Bill Bright, "Calling America to Revival," in *Fasting Can Change Your Life*, eds. Jerry Falwell and Elmer Towns (Ventura, CA: Regal, 1998), 52, 53, http://pobmt.org/ckfinder/userfiles/files/Fasting Can Change Your Life - ETowns.pdf.

PART 8

Journey to the Heart of God Through Giving

CHAPTER 20

GIVING

Blessed to Be a Blessing

"In everything I did, I showed you that by this kind of hard work we must help the weak, remembering the words the Lord Jesus himself said: 'It is more blessed to give than to receive.'"

—Acts 20:35

The focus of Christian giving is loving and worshiping God. We often equate offering with money, but Scripture gives a broader perspective. It is about giving our lives to God: "Therefore, I urge you, brothers and sisters, in view of God's mercy, to offer your bodies as a living sacrifice, holy and pleasing to God—this is your true and proper worship" (Romans 12:1). It is about giving our talents to God and others: "Each of you should use whatever gift you have received to serve others, as faithful stewards of God's grace in its various forms" (1 Peter 4:10). It is also about giving our praise to the Lord:

> Sing to the Lord, all the earth;
>   proclaim his salvation day after day.
> Declare his glory among the nations,
>   his marvelous deeds among all peoples.
> For great is the Lord and most worthy of praise;
>   he is to be feared above all gods. (1 Chronicles 16:23–25)

It is important to note that the worship of God began with offering. Throughout the history of Israel, starting with Cain and Abel (Genesis 4), God's people erected altars and made offerings upon them to the true God.[1] Whether it was during the lives of the great patriarchs, or in the wilderness, or at the temple in Jerusalem, to worship God was to bring an offering to Him. The psalmist gave the invitation clearly, "Ascribe to the Lord the glory due his name; bring an offering and come into his courts" (Psalm 96:8). This is perhaps the simplest statement in Scripture as to what the offering of worship to God involves. Offering our worship is not about what we get from God but what we give to Him. Offering is worship. If there is anything that we need to understand today, it is this.

The great majority of the offerings of the Old Testament were sacrifices. Since Jesus Christ offered Himself as the perfect Sacrifice for our sins, there is no longer any need for blood sacrifices. All this is included in His offering of Himself for sinners. Nothing can ever be added to that sacrifice; this sacrifice is sufficient for our salvation. However, it is clear that Christians are to continue to sacrifice to the Lord as a part of their worship.

What are the spiritual sacrifices that the Bible tells us believers are to offer God? Let us look in Hebrews 13:15, 16: "Through Jesus, therefore, let us continually offer to God a sacrifice of praise—the fruit of lips that openly profess his name. And do not forget to do good and to share with others, for with such sacrifices God is pleased."

WE ARE TO OFFER THE LORD OUR PRAISES

First, the writer of the epistle to the Hebrews tells us, "Let us offer the sacrifice of praise to God continually, that is, the fruit of our lips giving thanks to his name" (verse 15, KJV). This does not mean that the mere singing of songs or the recitation of prayers with our lips in our worship constitutes acceptable sacrifices or offerings. The "fruit of the lips" must be the response of the heart to the incomprehensible grace of God in Jesus Christ. As we sing and praise God, let us remember that our songs are to be sung to the Lord, to His glory, and to His honor, even though they also serve to edify and admonish other believers as well as ourselves. "Let the message of Christ dwell among you richly as you teach and admonish one another with all wisdom through psalms, hymns, and songs from the Spirit, singing to God with gratitude in your hearts" (Colossians 3:16). This is our spiritual sacrifice.

WE ARE TO OFFER THE LORD OUR GOOD WORK

A second spiritual offering that Christians are urged to present to the Lord is good works. "And do not forget to do good and to share with others, for with such sacrifices God is pleased" (Hebrews 13:16). Not all the good deeds we humans do are acceptable to God. People who presume to offer God their own good works instead of placing their full trust and confidence in the sacrifice of Christ are offering contempt to God. The apostle Paul spoke of the sad condition of the Jews, who, "since they did not know the righteousness of God and sought to establish their own, . . . did not submit to God's righteousness" (Romans 10:3). He warned such individuals that "the wrath of God has come upon them at last" (1 Thessalonians 2:16).

However, the true believers were reminded by the same apostle that they were to "be careful to devote themselves to doing what is good" (Titus 3:8). These are the works that are a spiritual sacrifice. What do they include? Any deed done because of the love of God and the desire to honor Him is a spiritual sacrifice acceptable to God.

The first priority of God's people is to build His kingdom, serve Him, pursue His purpose, glorify His name, and honor Him in everything they do. They do these things by offering Him their good works. The focus of all faithful Christians is the Master. The goal of all faithful Christians is to bring glory to the Master. This is done through acts of mercy, loving without boundaries, and giving without limits.

Often I hear people say, "But I do not have a talent with which to serve the Lord. I can't sing. I can't preach or witness. And I don't have money to give." It's not the gift we have, but how we allow God to use it for His glory. As believers in Jesus Christ, we need to offer ourselves, in our entirety, to Him.

WE ARE TO OFFER THE LORD OUR POSSESSIONS

The third spiritual offering mentioned in Hebrews is sharing (Hebrews 13:16). Whenever believers, in sheer thanksgiving to God, share their material substance with those who are in need or with those who are engaged in the ministry of the Word, or when they cheerfully place a generous check in the offering plate to support the work of God and His church, they are making an acceptable offering to the Lord. This comes out of the recognition that Christ has paid for our redemption (see verses 11, 12).

Ellen White sees the connection between our redemption by the blood of Jesus Christ and our offering to Him:

> Christ has purchased us by the price of His own blood. He has paid the purchase money for our redemption, and if we will lay hold upon the treasure, it is ours by the free gift of God.
>
> "How much owest thou unto my Lord?" Luke 16:5. It is impossible to tell. All that we have is from God. He lays His hand upon our possessions, saying: "I am the rightful owner of the whole universe; these are My goods. Consecrate to Me the tithes and offerings. As you bring these specified goods as a token of your loyalty and your submission to My sovereignty, My blessing shall increase your substance, and you will have abundance."[2]

Giving and redemption go hand in hand. The genuine offering of our possessions and money to God is our response in worship to Him. The presentation of our offering should be a sincere act of worship. It should be clearly evident that this is a response of the entire heart to the saving goodness of God.

There are 31,102 verses in the King James Version of the Bible. Out of these verses, about 500 of them are on faith and 500 are on prayer. But there are more than 2,000 verses on money and possessions. That amounts to 6.43 percent of all the verses in the Bible. Sixteen of Jesus' thirty-eight parables are on the subject of money, and one out of ten verses in the Gospels (288 in all) deal directly with the topic of money.[3] Why the emphasis on money? Because how we relate to money is a good indication of the location of our hearts (Matthew 6:21).

"Jesus Christ said more about money than about any other single thing because, when it comes to a man's real nature, money is of first importance. Money is an exact index to a man's true character. All through Scripture there is an intimate correlation between the development of a man's character and how he handles his money."[4]

It's not how much money we have, but our attachment to it. The widow in the Bible did not have much, but she gave her two mites willingly. "As Jesus looked up, he saw the rich putting their gifts into the temple treasury. He also saw a poor widow put in two very small copper coins. 'Truly I tell you,' he said, 'this poor widow has put in more than all the others. All these people gave their gifts out of their wealth; but she out of her poverty put in all she had to live on'" (Luke 21:1–4). It was this amazing generosity on the part of the poor widow that won the Lord's praise and has touched the hearts of so many generations since.

A REFLECTION ON TRUE GIVING

An excellent model of true giving that involves the offering of our praise, good works, possessions, and lives is demonstrated in the experience of the Magi. Giving is something these Magi came a long way to do. Their giving was a demonstration of their worship. Offering is always an indication of our true worship.

We learn in Matthew 2:16 that Jesus may have been two years old by the time the wise men showed up. They must have considered the worship of Jesus a high priority when they spent two years of their lives to come see the newborn King and worship Him.

Their worship was accompanied by gift giving. It is worth noting that these gifts were substantial gifts—gold, frankincense, and myrrh. In addition to the honor and value of these gifts, they were chosen for their special symbolism regarding Jesus Himself. The gold represented Jesus' kingship, frankincense was a symbol of His priestly role, and myrrh prefigured Jesus' death and embalming.[5] For them, Jesus was King, Priest, and Savior. In our offerings to Jesus, we also acknowledge Him as our King, Priest, and Savior.

We give of our praise, good works, and possessions as stewards to support others and the church, but there is also a much higher reason for giving. We give to acknowledge Jesus as our Lord and Savior and our special connection with Him.

---

1. This chapter was originally published in a slightly different form in S. Joseph Kidder, "Offering and Worship: The Trust Factor of Our Worship," in *Majesty: Experiencing Authentic Worship* (Hagerstown, MD: Review and Herald®, 2009).

2. Ellen G. White, *Testimonies for the Church*, vol. 9 (Nampa, ID: Pacific Press®, 2002), 245.

3. Howard L. Dayton Jr., *Leadership* 2, no. 2, quoted in "Statistic: Jesus' Teachings on Money," *Preaching Today*, accessed February 12, 2019, http://www.preachingtoday.com/illustrations/1996/december/410.html.

4. Richard Halverson, quoted in Randy Alcorn, *Money, Possessions, and Eternity*, rev. and updated ed. (Carol Stream, IL: Tyndale House, 2003), 3.

5. Biblical Archaeology Society Staff, "Why Did the Magi Bring Gold, Frankincense and Myrrh?" Bible History Daily, last updated December 21, 2018, https://www.biblicalarchaeology.org/daily/people-cultures-in-the-bible/jesus-historical-jesus/why-did-the-magi-bring-gold-frankincense-and-myrrh/.

CHAPTER 21

GIVING

Let Go and Trust God

The people rejoiced at the willing response of their leaders, for they had given freely and wholeheartedly to the LORD.
—1 Chronicles 29:9

Are you a risk-taker or a security-seeker? The idea of taking a risk can excite and strike fear into our hearts at the same time." "Some people just love taking risks. They like the rush of adrenaline and the feeling of escaping the ordinary. But most of us are not risk-takers. Most of us are security-seekers committed to a lifestyle of playing it safe. . . . From being over-insured to eating low-fat diets, most of us want to minimize the risks." We love to watch others do daring stunts, as long we don't have to leave our couches. "We want a life that is free from pressure and uncertainty."[1]

Learning to take proper risks with our money may be one of the hardest but most important lessons that comfort-conscious Christians need to learn. It's a lesson that carries with it the potential for astonishing growth and spiritual excitement, if we dare. So let's look at what the Bible has to say about giving, tithing, and offering: "Follow God's example, therefore, as dearly loved children and walk in the way of love, just as Christ loved us and gave himself up for us as a fragrant offering and sacrifice to God" (Ephesians 5:1, 2).

GOD WILL SUPPLY ALL MY NEEDS

When I went to the seminary for my graduate studies, my wife and I were very poor as we paid the full tuition and had undergraduate loans. Of the three years we were there, we went out to eat once because my mother-in-law sent us a check to do so for our anniversary. Despite living in poverty, we decided to put God first and honor Him by being faithful in our tithe and offerings.

At the end of one month during my third year at the seminary, after paying many bills, there was no money left, except that for tithe and offering. We struggled with the thought of using the money to buy food, but we decided to give it as tithe.

We trusted in God and prayed about it. A few days later we opened the mail, and there was a check for two hundred dollars from a friend as a gift for our wedding. The irony was that our wedding happened two and a half years earlier. He wrote in the letter, "I was thinking about you today, and I remembered I did not attend your wedding. I am very sorry. I was on a business trip, but I wanted to send you a gift." The date on the envelope matched the day we had been praying.

We decided to honor God and take the risk, and He was always faithful in taking care of our needs. He used a variety of ways to care for us, but that time, God made an impression on our friend's heart precisely when we needed help most. "And my God will meet all your needs according to the riches of his glory in Christ Jesus" (Philippians 4:19).

WHAT ELLEN WHITE SAYS ABOUT OFFERING

Ellen White reminds us that everything we have—our "money, houses, and land"—all belong to God:

> God is testing every soul that claims to believe in Him. All are entrusted with talents. The Lord has given men His goods upon which to trade. He has made them His stewards, and has placed in their possession money, houses, and lands. All these are to be regarded as the Lord's goods and used to advance His work, to build up His kingdom in the world. In trading with the Lord's goods, we are to seek Him for wisdom, that we may not use His sacred trust to glorify ourselves or to indulge selfish impulses. The amount entrusted varies, but those who have the smallest gifts must not feel that because their talent of means is small, they can do nothing with it.
>
> Every Christian is a steward of God, entrusted with His goods. Remember the words: "Moreover it is required in stewards, that a man be found faithful." 1 Corinthians 4:2.[2]

TITHES AND OFFERINGS ARE SIGNS OF OUR ALLEGIANCE TO GOD

A read through the Bible shows that tithing was a common practice.[3] It was a sign of lordship and allegiance. Abraham demonstrated his worship in returning his tithe to God (Genesis 14:17–20). This simple yet significant act of worship was a public acknowledgment of God's sovereign claim and ownership as well as His lordship. Love and gratitude are expressed in a tangible way through our tithe and offerings. When Abraham gave out of the abundance God provided for him, God blessed him with fullness of life, prosperity, strength, and hope (Hebrews 7:1–4).

TITHES AND OFFERINGS ARE ASSOCIATED WITH GOD'S BLESSING

The Bible instructs us to give out of a joyful heart. "Each of you should give what you have decided in your heart to give, not reluctantly or under compulsion, for

God loves a cheerful giver" (2 Corinthians 9:7). When we give gladly, willingly, and cheerfully, we demonstrate an unselfish attitude. This attitude comes out of our appreciation for what God has done for us by giving us new life and hope through Jesus Christ. God loves a cheerful giver.

Giving is a result of our obedience to God and our wholehearted trust in Him. It is selfless on our part and shows our willingness to share what we possess. " 'Jesus Christ must be Lord of all or not Lord at all'—including, of course, our purse or wallet."[4]

Some people hold their money tight: no matter what the need is, or the appeal in church, nothing comes out of them. Others need to be persuaded to be generous. Therefore, the more skillful the one who asks for the offering, or the more guilt woven into the appeal, the more money that person can get out of them. Still others give to others as God has given to them. They have experienced God's blessing, acceptance, and love, and they overflow with generosity, love, giving, and sweetness. When we give in that kind of spirit, we are indeed worshiping God.

TITHES AND OFFERINGS ARE CLEAR INDICATORS OF OUR PRIORITIES

In Matthew, Jesus said, "Do not lay up for yourselves treasures on earth, where moth and rust destroy and where thieves break in and steal, but lay up for yourselves treasures in heaven, where neither moth nor rust destroys and where thieves do not break in and steal. For where your treasure is, there your heart will be also" (Matthew 6:19–21, ESV). What is our focus? Do we focus on earthly possessions or heavenly possessions?

Jesus is not against savings accounts. He is against our preoccupation with money and material things. Greed can cause us to be so distracted with secular pursuits that we forget why we are here. The more we give to God of our money and service, the more we show we are focused on God and service to people.

On a cold Sabbath morning in October, my pastor stood up in front of the whole congregation and said, "The church boiler died, and we need to buy a new one. The new boiler will cost about seventy-five thousand dollars. We need to raise this money right away if we want to continue to worship in our building." I live in Michigan, and the boiler is a must-have during the winter. I thought to myself, *This is a worthwhile cause, and we need to contribute to it.* The first figure that came to my mind was fifty dollars. Then I decided to be generous and take it all the way up to one hundred dollars. My wife turned to me and asked me how much we were going to give. Very proudly, I said to her, "One hundred dollars." She said to me, "Shame on you. It costs us more than one hundred dollars when we take our whole family out to dinner. You need to repent." She was right. I wanted to give but not to let it affect my pocketbook. I can live without one hundred dollars. Jesus is inviting us to give generously and lovingly (2 Corinthians 9:6–8).

Billy Graham once wrote, "Tell me what you think about money, and I will tell you what you think about God, for these two are closely related. A man's heart is closer to his wallet than anything else."[5] Many have attributed the following words to Martin Luther: "There are three conversions a person needs to experience: The conversion of the head, the conversion of the heart, and the conversion of the pocketbook."[6]

TITHES AND OFFERINGS ARE INDICATORS OF OUR TRUST IN GOD

Money is important to us. Giving it demonstrates a level of trust and obedience to God. The psalmist declares, "Offer the sacrifices of the righteous and trust in the LORD" (Psalm 4:5).

One day a member of a church I pastored confided in me about his trouble with the concept of tithing and giving. He revealed his doubts to me by saying, "Pastor, I just don't see how I can give ten percent of my income to the church when I can't even keep on top of my bills."

I said to him, "If I promise to make up the difference in your bills if you should fall short, do you think you could try tithing for just one month?"

After a moment of thinking about it, he responded, "Sure, if you promise to make up any shortage, I guess I could try tithing for one month."

"Now, what do you think of that?" I asked. "You say you'd be willing to put your trust in a mere man like yourself, who possesses little materially, but you couldn't trust your heavenly Father, who owns the whole universe!"

On the next Sabbath, this man gave his tithe and has been doing so faithfully ever since. Within two years of paying that tithe, he was able to pay off all of his debt, and the Lord blessed his small business to the point he was able to expand it to two or three times what it was originally. When we trust God and give Him everything, God will bless us (Malachi 3:10).

WE ARE TO OFFER THE LORD OUR LIVES

Finally, all true Christians are called to offer their lives continually to the Lord and to live pure and holy lives before Him. "I beseech you therefore, brethren, by the mercies of God, that ye present your bodies a living sacrifice, holy, acceptable unto God, which is your reasonable service" (Romans 12:1, KJV). In offering our bodies as living sacrifices, we are united with Jesus Christ "who through the eternal Spirit offered himself unblemished to God" (Hebrews 9:14). Included in such an offering is the willingness to do God's will no matter what the cost, to love others with wholesome Christian love, and to seek to demonstrate in all aspects of life the reality of the living Christ dwelling within. No sacrifice that we can offer to God can be a substitute for self-sacrifice and self-offering.

The purpose of life is not worldly success or accumulation of wealth. The purpose of life is to glorify God. We were created to know and worship Him. Paul says, "So whether you eat or drink or whatever you do, do it all for the glory of

God" (1 Corinthians 10:31). What does this insight mean for those of us who desire to be true worshipers of the living and true God? It means we have to make offering a continual part of our lives—a moment-by-moment gift to God. When we give the Lord our lives, we give everything to Him with contentment, joy, and excitement.

A graduate student told me a personal story once. She said that after graduating from a state university, she went to teach elementary school for the first time in a church school. The education superintendent came to observe her classroom one day and told her that since she did not have her denominational teaching certificate and was a first-year teacher, she was the lowest-paid teacher in the entire conference. Though she had not known this, she was perfectly content when she found out. She even said with a smile, "This is the most money I have ever made. I have everything I could ask for. God has always provided for me. I am happy with what I have."

The education superintendent still felt bad. When this teacher finally got denominationally certified, the superintendent requested the conference treasurer give her financial credit for the months after she became certified instead of waiting until the next fiscal year when the contracts were renewed. She did not ask for nor push for this bonus, but she was grateful nonetheless. In her story, she showed me an example of what Paul meant when he said, "I know what it is to be in need, and I know what it is to have plenty. I have learned the secret of being content in any and every situation, whether well fed or hungry, whether living in plenty or in want" (Philippians 4:12).

In spite of being the lowest-paid teacher, she found a place in her heart to give anonymously to a friend's college account so that the friend could register for classes. She also sponsored a child from another country each month and faithfully gave her tithe and offering to the church. She found joy in giving her life and possessions to the Lord.

A PERSONAL APPEAL

In 1815, the Duke of Wellington defeated Napoleon in the Battle of Waterloo. One of the duke's biographers claimed to have an advantage over all the other previous biographers. His advantage was that he had found an old account ledger that showed how the duke had spent his money. That, says the biographer, was a far better clue to what the duke thought was really important than reading his letters or his speeches.

Can you imagine if someone wrote your biography on the basis of your checkbook, your income-tax return, your work, or your time? What might it say about you? What about your loyalties, focus, and whom you serve? What is more important to you: trusting God or your possessions?

1. Robert Russell, "Take the Risk," *Preaching Today*, January 2009, https://www.preachingtoday.com/sermons/sermons/2009/january/taketherisk.html.

2. Ellen G. White, *Testimonies for the Church*, vol. 9 (Nampa, ID: Pacific Press®, 2002), 245, 246.

3. Portions of this chapter were originally published in a slightly different form in S. Joseph Kidder, "Offering and Worship: The Trust Factor of Our Worship," in *Majesty: Experiencing Authentic Worship* (Hagerstown, MD: Review and Herald®, 2009).

4. Charlie Riggs, *Learning to Walk With God* (Minneapolis, MN: World Wide Publications, 1990), 155.

5. Billy Graham, "Guard Against Greed," Billy Graham Evangelistic Association, accessed February 13, 2019, https://billygraham.org/devotion/where-is-your-treasure-2/.

6. Greg Laurie, "Money and Motives," Crosswalk.com, September 4, 2008, https://www.crosswalk.com/faith/spiritual-life/money-and-motives-11581312.html.

PART 9

Journey to the
Heart of God
Through Touching Lives

CHAPTER 22

DIVINE APPOINTMENTS
Making Yourself Available to Be Used by God

Let the morning bring me word of your unfailing love, for I have put my trust in you. Show me the way I should go, for to you I entrust my life.
—Psalm 143:8

I believe that God has appointments for each of us, which, when taken seriously, will lead us to another level of blessings. These appointments originate with the Lord Himself. It is His desire to meet His people on His terms and on His grounds of approach. These are His arrangements. In keeping His appointments, the believer will come to experience more of the blessings of God.

AN APPOINTMENT AT THIRTY-FIVE THOUSAND FEET

I was flying back from Fiji, sitting in an aisle seat in a row where there were four seats.[1] The seat next to me was the only empty seat on the plane. A girl came to tell me she was sitting in the back of the plane with a university group that went to Fiji to do medical work. She said that she needed to break away from her group for some time by herself, so she was going to request to change her seat to the empty seat next to me.

I had been praying that no one would sit next to me for the eleven-hour trip, but God had other plans. The girl came back, and because it was late at night, we both went to sleep. About four hours later, the flight attendants woke us for breakfast before we arrived in Los Angeles. I introduced myself to her and asked her what she was doing in Fiji. She asked me what I did there. I told her I went to speak to pastors and church members on one of the islands.

At that moment, she became sad. She told me that a few years earlier she had given her heart to Jesus and lived a Christian life. Those couple of years were the best years of her life. She had felt joy, purpose, and excitement. She enjoyed her church, the music, and the sermons. Then she went to college, and the atmosphere pulled her away from her relationship with Christ.

This gave me the opportunity to talk to her about the Lord. For the next three hours, I encouraged the young woman to reconnect with Jesus, to restore her first love for Him. I shared with her scriptures and tips and ideas for how to reconnect with God. I also shared with her my own personal testimony. Then I asked if I could pray for her. She said, "Please, please pray for me. I need it. I want that experience back in my life." So I prayed for her. When I opened my eyes at the end, she was crying. She gave me a hug and said, "This was a divine appointment. There are three hundred and forty seats on the plane, and the only empty seat was next to you. God was leading me to sit over here. I am going to do the stuff you shared with me. God, for a purpose, brought us together."

I realized through this encounter and others that "God is working through us, and He is sending us out to share His love. Our words are powerful, but our actions are too, no matter how seemingly small or insignificant. Look for opportunities and moments in your life when God is using you, a divinely appointed son or daughter, to be a great source of hope, comfort and love."[2]

WHAT IS A DIVINE APPOINTMENT?

A divine appointment is a meeting with another person that has been specifically and unmistakably ordered by God. The Holy Spirit arranges these meetings because there is something the other person needs from God that you can offer. You are one conversation away from God bestowing His favor on that person as you act as God's channel of blessing.

Jesus taught His disciples to pray for God's will to be done. Often, His will requires a special meeting with someone you have never met. Praying for God's will to be done opens divine appointments, conversations, and blessings. These types of meetings are filled with God's favor, which will bless all of the people involved and change the course of their lives.

> Have you ever had a coincidence, which was so special that it seemed like God was in it? . . . God is sovereign; He is all knowing and all-powerful.
>
> Sometimes God wants to bless us and other people. . . . The possibilities of divine appointments are endless! If we are willing to be led by the Holy Spirit, great things are possible.
>
> Throughout the Bible there are many examples of divine appointments. Time after time God leads the faithful to cross another person's path and great things happen![3]

THE BIBLICAL BACKGROUND

Scripture says, "The steps of a good man are ordered by the Lord" (Psalm 37:23, KJV). The first truth of the text is that God orders, arranges, and establishes the details of His children's lives, including some unexpected divine appointments. "After decades of walking . . . with God, I can tell you that seeing God set up these 'appointments' is a thrill that is beyond comparison."[4]

"How often do we experience delays, changes of plans, and redirections and treat them as intrusions? It could be that God is detouring us so we can do something different or new for Him. Consider Paul's trip to Philippi in Acts 16. He had gone to Macedonia because of a God-directed vision (vv. 9-10). How could he know that he would end up in prison there? But even that trip to jail was God-led, because He used Paul to bring salvation to a jailer and his family (vv. 25-34)."[5]

Many such appointments are recorded in Scripture. The story of Esther and the story of Philip and the eunuch are beautiful illustrations of the appointments that God makes for Christians who walk in the Spirit.

THE STORY OF ESTHER

The book of Esther records the faithfulness of Esther and her divine appointment to become a queen in order to help save her people. The book also tells of the wickedness of Haman, the second-highest official in the Persian kingdom of King Ahasuerus, the world's most powerful leader at that time (Esther 1:1).

"Haman . . . wanted to annihilate the Jewish race. His anger was particularly fuelled" by a Jewish relative of Esther, Mordecai, who refused to honor him by bowing to him. "After a deceptive plot, Haman received permission from Ahasuerus to murder God's people (3:7-15)."

The king was married to Esther, a Jew, but her heritage was unknown to him. Esther asked her people to fast with her for three days. Then she risked her life by going to the court unsummoned to tell her husband, the king, that Haman wanted to kill her and her people. The king was so angry that he ordered Haman to be hanged on the gallows that he had made for Mordecai (Esther 5–7).

Esther revealed that Mordecai was a relative, and the king promoted him to Haman's position. Mordecai reversed the old law that said the Jews should be killed on a certain day and instead decreed that "the Jews should protect themselves and defeat their enemies on that day."[6]

Esther was an orphan that became a queen. She was in the right place at the right time as queen. "For if you remain silent at this time, relief and deliverance for the Jews will arise from another place, but you and your father's family will perish. And who knows but that you have come to your royal position for such a time as this?" (Esther 4:14). She overcame her fears and told the king of her people's problems, which saved a whole nation. It was her divine appointment.

THE STORY OF PHILIP

While Philip was preaching in Samaria, an angel sent him on a trip to Gaza. On the road, he came beside a traveler who was reading the book of Isaiah. Led by the Holy Spirit, Philip offered to help him understand scripture. This allowed him to share the gospel with the Ethiopian with life saving results.

Philip could have ministered only to the vast crowds in the cities, but God sent him to the desert for a divine appointment with a single man. We must always seek God's leading and let Him determine where we're best suited to serve Him.

Ellen White talked frequently about God guiding His followers to the people who need to know the gospel. For example, she once wrote, "An angel guided Philip to the one who was seeking for light and who was ready to receive the gospel, and today angels will guide the footsteps of those workers who will allow the Holy Spirit to sanctify their tongues and refine and ennoble their hearts. The angel sent to Philip could himself have done the work for the Ethiopian, but this is not God's way of working. It is His plan that men are to work for their fellow men."[7]

It is a wonderful thing to walk in the Spirit as He makes appointments for us in miraculous ways so that we, as Spirit-filled Christians, can cross the paths of those who need help and salvation.

HOW TO SET YOURSELF UP FOR DIVINE APPOINTMENTS

Victoria West Henady explains how we can act out our divine appointments:

> Each of us has a divine purpose . . . [for] our lives, and when we walk out that purpose each day we find ourselves walking in divine appointment, carrying the Holy Spirit with us.
>
> You may find yourself waiting on a word from God without realizing that by living your everyday life you are not only walking out His purpose for your life, but you are also influencing those around you. As believers, if we open our eyes and ears to those around us, whether it be . . . close friends or just a passing stranger, we can recognize how God brings our paths to cross with the paths of others, all in His perfect timing.[8]

Following are three specific things to help us capture divine opportunities.

1. PRAY FOR DIVINE APPOINTMENTS

How does a Christian have the Holy Spirit make such appointments for him or her? The answer is one word: *pray*. Every morning when I get up, I kneel beside my bed and pray to the Holy Spirit to give me a divine appointment. I go on to do this several times a day.

In the Bible, two men, who had no connection with each other, had been praying, and God miraculously put them together. Cornelius, a God-fearing Gentile who had a heart for the poor, was praying one day when an angel told him, "Your prayers and gifts to the poor have come up as a memorial offering before God. Now send men to Joppa to bring back a man named Simon who is called Peter. He is staying with Simon the tanner, whose house is by the sea" (Acts 10:4–6).

Meanwhile, Peter had a vision about a sheet filled with clean and unclean animals. "While Peter was still thinking about the vision, the Spirit said to him, 'Simon, three men are looking for you. So get up and go downstairs. Do not hesitate to go with them, for I have sent them' " (verses 19, 20).

Peter went to Cornelius's house. Through the vision of the sheet and the invitation initiated by God to meet Cornelius the Gentile, Peter realized God accepted the Gentiles. "Then Peter began to speak: 'I now realize how true it is that God does not show favoritism but accepts from every nation the one who fears him and does what is right' " (verses 34, 35). This led to Peter baptizing Cornelius and his family.

Two praying men were led to an unexpected divine appointment that changed their lives and those of the Jewish and Gentile nations.

Annoying or anointed appointment? Jane, a pastor's wife, felt the need to study the Bible and share her faith with somebody. She started to pray about this. She prayed for several months with no answer. One day Jane went to Walmart to buy a pot of flowers. As she knelt down to look at one of the pots, she heard a voice from behind her say, "This kind of flower does not survive. It needs a lot of attention. I bought one a couple of weeks ago, and it died on me, and I am good with flowers." Jane looked back and said, "Thank you." But the woman kept talking and giving her advice about the flowers.

Jane felt annoyed by the woman's persistence. Finally, Jane picked one of the flowerpots and put it in her cart. As she started walking away, the woman followed her and kept talking. Jane really felt annoyed and bothered by this woman's relentless conversation. Jane tried to give polite answers, but she had no desire to converse with her.

This went on for about thirty minutes. Finally, it dawned on Jane that maybe God had sent this woman to her to study the Bible with. So she started to talk with the woman and ask personal questions about her life. She discovered that this woman's father had died recently and his death had left a hole in her heart. She was grieving. Jane shared comforting words and testified of her faith in Jesus, our Comforter.

They exchanged phone numbers and email addresses and began talking regularly. After meeting at cafés a few times, Jane eventually invited the woman to come to her house for tea. When the woman showed up at Jane's house, Jane was startled to discover that she had brought her husband and children with her too. Quickly, Jane sent her husband to the store to buy some food to cook a meal for this family.

Jane's husband connected with the woman's husband, and the children from both families played together. This was the beginning of a friendship between the two families. The woman and her family began coming over every week.

One day the woman and her family asked the Adventist family what they believed. This started a Bible study between the two families. The family began going to the Seventh-day Adventist Church, and eventually, the whole family was baptized.

Sometimes, when we are in a hurry and easily annoyed, we miss something

God has for us. Jane did not understand what God was doing until she took the opportunity to minister to this woman, which led to a wonderful result. "God can use inconveniences in our lives if we look at them as divine appointments."[9]

2. OPEN YOUR EYES AND EARS TO DIVINE APPOINTMENTS

The Bible states in 2 Timothy 4:2 that we are to "preach the word; be prepared in season and out of season." Also, in 1 Peter 3:15, the Bible says, "But in your hearts revere Christ as Lord. Always be prepared to give an answer to everyone who asks you to give the reason for the hope that you have. But do this with gentleness and respect." We should always be ready. We should always be looking for opportunities, and if we are willing to be His vessels, God will use us.

I believe this is a great lesson for all of us. If we all start looking for those divine appointments, we will find them. If we all start being *available* to the Lord, we will see things happen that we would have never expected. If we were to multiply these divine appointments by the many people in the body of Christ, what a change would take place in the world we live in!

Upgraded for a divine appointment. Once, when I was flying from Chicago to San Antonio, the plane was oversold in coach, so I was upgraded to first class. The seat next to me was still empty. A few minutes later I saw the gate agent come inside the plane. She told the flight attendant that the man who was supposed to sit next to me was on a delayed flight, so they were going to move someone from the back of the plane next to me.

At that time, I was frantically working on a presentation. Then the pilot came on and said, "We have to be deiced. It is going to take half an hour, but don't worry, we will still get you there on time." Two minutes later, I felt a compelling urge to talk to the man who had been moved to the seat next to me. I resisted the urge at first, but I heard the voice of God telling me to talk to this man. I did not know what to say to him, so I came up with an obvious observation: "Isn't it interesting that we will be delayed half an hour with deicing but will still make it to our destination on time?" He ignored my comment and asked if I lived in San Antonio. I said, "No, I live in Michigan. I am going to some Adventist churches to present on the topics of church growth and spiritual growth." He asked if I was Seventh-day Adventist. I said, "Yes, I am a Seventh-day Adventist pastor."

He started asking a series of questions, beginning with, "What do you believe about Christ?" I said to him, "For my church and me personally, Christ is everything. He is our Savior, our Lord, the One who has paid our debt, so we may live with Him for eternity. We are an imperfect people who are in love with a perfect God who sent His Son to die on the cross for us. He gives us hope, meaning, and purpose."

At that point, he asked, "Tell me, what do you believe about the Sabbath, and why?" After I explained to him what we believe about the Sabbath, he asked about the eight texts in the New Testament that lend themselves to the belief that the disciples kept Sunday and not Saturday as the Sabbath. I went through each text and explained the context and the conclusion that the disciples and the church in the New Testament kept Saturday as the Sabbath and not Sunday.

He then asked, "What do you believe about what happens to us after we die?" So I explained to him our biblical understanding of the state of the dead. As soon as I finished, he fired back with another question, "Do you believe that hell is forever or a short duration of time?" Then he asked me what we believe about the sanctuary.

This went on all the way from our departure in Chicago to when we parted ways in San Antonio, almost three hours later. He asked question after question about what we believe as Adventists. Finally, he told me, "My neighbor was an Adventist and shared with me some of that stuff. My neighbor moved out of the area, and I have been struggling and thinking about some of these things ever since."

As we parted ways, the young man said, "This was a divine appointment. God brought us together from two different sides of the plane so you could explain many things to me. You gave me a lot of food for thought, and I need to think about what I should believe."

Like the conductor of a symphony, God orchestrated circumstances to accomplish His purpose. He brought me together with this man so that I could answer his questions. This was a divine appointment.

3. ACT ON THE OPPORTUNITY FOR A DIVINE APPOINTMENT

The story of the Samaritan woman is another example of a divine appointment (John 4:5–42). Jesus met the woman at Sychar's well and seized the opportunity to minister to her. The result was that she and the whole village believed in Him, and it changed all of their lives.

It's obvious that Jesus felt compelled to speak to her. We know that this was truly a divine appointment because of the results.

> I believe that this story is recorded in scripture for us to realize that God desires divine appointments in our lives.
>   He wants us to realize that they happen in the regular course of events, but we need to be prepared. They will be the most satisfying experiences that you will ever have.[10]

We need to recognize that God wants us to act on these things by yielding to the Holy Spirit's power.

An appointment for hope. A few years ago I went to speak to the pastors of a conference. I arrived in the afternoon, and the executive secretary of that conference met me at the airport. He said to me, "The meeting starts at seven in the evening. I will take you out to dinner at five, before we drive to the meeting place, but between two and five, we have plenty of time. I know you are into prayer. There is something I have been wanting to experiment with for a long time—I would like to knock on doors and get at least ten people to respond to us as to whether they would like prayer or not."

We knocked on doors until we got our ten. We asked them if we could pray, and they all said yes with various degrees of enthusiasm. The last one was a young woman. When we asked her if we could pray for her, she broke down and started to weep. She said to us, "I just lost my baby son to sudden infant death syndrome."

We ended up spending two hours with this woman, comforting her, trying to give her hope, and sharing with her that God loved her and cared for her in spite of all of this sorrow. She told us that she grew up in a small community, and somehow she had drifted away from church but not God. She then told us she did not have any support system. Her parents lived far away, and her husband worked many hours. She did not have a lot of friends because she was new to the area. She said to us, "The pain today was so strong, I prayed the whole day that God would send someone to comfort me. God sent you both here today to do that. It was a divine appointment."

We left her house at 6:00 P.M., missing dinner, but it was well worth it. We couldn't miss the opportunity. My friend and I are not counselors, and we are definitely not grief counselors, but what this woman needed was someone to listen to her. So we offered her the ministry of presence, and through our presence and prayers, we offered her the presence of Jesus. God cared about this woman without any support system, so He sent two strangers to comfort her. Divine appointments demonstrate how much God cares about His people.

DIVINE OPPORTUNITIES

"God is not interested in our ability but our availability. Are you willing to be used by God to advance His Kingdom or to help another brother or sister?"[11]

> **BIBLE VERSES ABOUT DIVINE APPOINTMENTS**
> - **Psalm 32:8:** "I will instruct you and teach you in the way you should go; I will counsel you with my loving eye on you."
> - **Ephesians 2:10:** "For we are God's handiwork, created in Christ Jesus to do good works, which God prepared in advance for us to do."
> - **2 Corinthians 5:7:** "We live by faith, not by sight."
> - **Psalm 143:8:** "Let the morning bring me word of your unfailing love, for I have put my trust in you. Show me the way I should go, for to you I entrust my life."
> - **Colossians 3:2:** "Set your minds on things above, not on earthly things."
> - **Philippians 2:3, 4:** "Do nothing out of selfish ambition or vain conceit. Rather, in humility value others above yourselves, not looking to your own interests but each of you to the interests of the others.."
> - **Habakkuk 2:3:** "For the revelation awaits an appointed time; it speaks of the end and will not prove false. Though it linger, wait for it; it will certainly come and will not delay."

If we have been baptized in the Holy Spirit, then we can be open to His leading. "He may give us a word of knowledge, a word of wisdom or He may let us discern God's will in a specific situation. . . . If we are God's sheep, then we should learn to hear the Shepherd's voice (John 10)."[12]

The Lord will make it natural and easy for us to be engaged in conversation with other people. We will have opportunities for many divine appointments. These may be to give comfort, encouragement, or a Bible study or just being present. They will vary, but God will always use us to be blessings to others. Act on these divine appointments, and we will bring a blessing to someone and we will be blessed as well.

"We are walking with God's love on us and the Holy Spirit in us."[13] I encourage you to ask God to help you recognize His hand moving in your everyday situations. Tell God you are available to be used by Him in this way. As you seek His face with a pure heart, and as you ask Him to use you, He will give you many opportunities.

---

1. This chapter was originally published in a slightly different form in S. Joseph Kidder, "Divine Appointments," *Ministry*, August 2018, 14–17.
2. Victoria West Henady, "How to Set Yourself Up for Divine Appointments," Charisma, May 25, 2016, https://www.charismamag.com/spirit/evangelism-missions/560-evangelism/26460-how-to-set-yourself-up-for-divine-appointments.
3. Paul Backholer, "Divine Appointments," ByFaith, August 9, 2004, https://www.byfaith.co.uk/pauldivineappointments.htm.
4. Dennis Rainey, "Divine Appointments," FamilyLife, accessed February 25, 2019, https://www.familylife.com/articles/topics/faith/essentials-faith/reaching-out/divine-appointments/.
5. Dave Branon, "Divine Appointments," Our Daily Bread, October 26, 2011, https://odb.org/2011/10/26/divine-appointments/.
6. Backholer, "Divine Appointments."
7. Ellen G. White, *The Acts of the Apostles* (Nampa, ID: Pacific Press®, 2002), 109.
8. Henady, "How to Set Yourself Up."
9. Branon, "Divine Appointments."
10. David Cawston, "Divine Appointments," SermonSearch, accessed February 25, 2019, https://www.sermonsearch.com/sermon-outlines/14192/divine-appointments/.
11. Backholer, "Divine Appointments."
12. Backholer, "Divine Appointments."
13. Henady, "How to Set Yourself Up."

CHAPTER 23

SERVING

Surrender Everything to Jesus

Taking the five loaves and the two fish and looking up to heaven, he gave thanks and broke the loaves. Then he gave them to the disciples, and the disciples gave them to the people. They all ate and were satisfied, and the disciples picked up twelve basketfuls of broken pieces that were left over.
—Matthew 14:19, 20

Jesus' hands are the most amazing and powerful hands.

"Two fish and 5 loaves of bread in my hands is a couple of fish sandwiches. Two fish and 5 loaves of bread in God's hands will feed thousands. It depends whose hands . . . [they're] in."

Jesus' hands transformed everything he touched. A blind man once lived in a black vortex, but touched by Jesus' hands color and movement flooded his life. A leper's body was diseased and rotting, he was covered with shame and no one would come near him out of fear—that is until Jesus touched the untouchable and his body was made whole and his relationships were restored. A widow's son died, and his death meant excruciating loss to her in every way. But as they carried the young man's body on a stretcher, . . . Jesus' hands held him and he smiled at his mother as life pulsed through his body. The funeral procession stopped and a dance began.[1]

What would happen if you surrendered everything into the hands of Jesus?

FEEDING THE FIVE THOUSAND

All four Gospel writers record the miracle of the loaves and fish. It must have been a very important event. One day Jesus took His disciples and withdrew to a deserted place to be alone. He wanted some time to rest, to take a deep breath, and to think and pray. However, people discovered where He was and followed Him. These people followed Jesus with outstretched hands and pleading voices rising out of a sea of sorrow, sickness, pain, and need. Everyone wanted something from Him, and He gave to everyone who came. In Mark's account, it says that Jesus was moved with compassion when He looked on the people, "because they were like sheep without a shepherd" (Mark 6:34). Jesus spent the whole day teaching, healing, and ministering to the crowd (verses 32–34; see also Matthew 14:13, 14).

"If it were most of us, we would have . . . [felt] irritation, but he had compassion. He put his needs aside and ministered to the needs of those around him. What he wanted did not come before what everyone else wanted. He was not self-centered, but centered on the needs of those he loved."[2]

Later in the afternoon, His disciples came to Him and urged Him to send the hungry crowd away so that they could buy food in the surrounding villages. His answer was, "You give them something to eat" (Mark 6:37). They replied that they did not have enough food to feed the crowd and that it would take two hundred denarii to buy enough food. (At that time, a denarius was a day's wages for the average worker. Philip said that even if the disciples worked for more than half a year, there would not be enough for everyone to have a bite.) But Peter said that there was a little boy with five loaves of barley bread and two fish and wondered how they could possibly make a difference to such a crowd (John 6:7–9).

The disciples were saying that even if they worked for more than half a year,

"We couldn't satisfy all these people. We couldn't even give them all a taste. It's impossible!"

. . . Jesus said, *"Feed them!"* The disciple[s] answered and said, *"We can't! We don't have the resources. This [is] a problem that cannot be solved!"* These men considered their problem and they summed it up as insurmountable![3]

Jesus knew the entire crowd was hungry. The disciples also knew that the crowd was hungry and came up with three options to solve the problem:

1. Send the people away; get rid of the problem (Mark 6:35, 36; Matthew 14:15).
2. Raise money, but that would take a minimum of half a year (John 6:7).
3. They had a little food—five loaves of bread and two fish—but that would never be enough for such a large crowd (John 6:9).[4]

The disciples lived in a small world of limited possibilities, but Jesus lived in a world of unlimited possibilities. The disciples tried to convince Jesus that the problem they had of feeding the crowd by themselves was impossible to solve. They didn't have food and couldn't earn money fast enough to do it. Peter finally found one young boy who was willing to help. He had a small lunch of five loaves of barley bread and two fish and was willing to give it away to help others (John 6:9).

Jesus had the people sit down and prepare to receive a miracle. He asked the disciples to seat them in groups of hundreds and fifties and wait on Him (Mark 6:39, 40). Then He looked up to heaven and offered a simple prayer of blessing. As He did so, He took the two fish and five little loaves and started breaking them. As He broke them, they were miraculously multiplied. By doing this, He fed thousands and thousands of people who were in the middle of a wilderness. There was plenty left over—twelve baskets, one for each doubting disciple. "Every need was met, possibly 20,000+ people were fed. . . . Jesus took the little and turned it into a lot! . . . Place your little in the Lord's hand and He will multiply it."[5]

"We have nothing to give people without Jesus. We have nothing to say, nothing to give, nothing to offer. What we do have is something to offer to Jesus. We take the little bit that we have . . . and give it to him. . . . He takes our pitiful little offering and turns it into something that can not only satisfy the needs of other people, but an abundance beyond that. A little in my hands becomes a lot in Jesus' hands."[6] As we surrender everything to Him, in His hands, it will be multiplied.

There are two lessons to be learned from this story. Let's examine them.

1. God is the Lord who multiplies our limited resources. The disciples realized they had very limited resources, and the crowd had many needs. They knew they had nothing to offer. This miracle pictures

> a scene that is absolutely impossible in the eyes of man, but to God, it is merely an opportunity to display His awesome power. It is an opportunity for Him to showcase His ability to overcome any and all situations, without exception! . . .
>
> . . . God is able to use the little things[:] . . . a stick to part a Red Sea; a stone and sling to remove a giant; . . . [a] starving widow to speak to Elijah; manna to . . . [feed] 2 million people. . . . Your ability, or resources may be small, but God is still God and He can use anything! . . . Often, He will use the resources you already possess and multiply them in marvelous ways![7]

"There is no question that we serve a God Who specializes in the spectacular; Who majors in the miraculous and Who operates in omnipotence. But, I would also point out that He is also *Lord Of The Little*! He is a God Who moves in big ways, but He is also a God Who is able to take the small, insignificant things of this world and use them for His glory."[8]

Remember that the disciples lived in a small world of limited possibilities, but Jesus lived in a boundless world of unlimited possibilities.

If you can ever learn to bring your little to Jesus and let Him have it, He can use it in a great way for His glory!

- Bring your little faith to Him and watch Him move your mountains.

- Bring your little testimony and watch Him save souls.
- Bring your little praise and watch Him get glory. . . .
- Bring your little talents and abilities and watch Him use you.
- Bring your little gifts and watch Him multiply them for His glory.
- Bring your little self and watch Him use you.[9]

And we can bring Jesus even more!

- Bring your little ministry and watch Him empower it.
- Bring your little church and watch Him grow it.

2. God is the Lord who overcomes our little faith. Jesus' command to feed the people was immediately met with an expression of absolute unbelief by the disciples, along with many excuses for why it could not be done. But then Jesus performed the miracle and fed a crowd of possibly twenty thousand people.

It seems that the disciples found it difficult to believe that Jesus could do the impossible. In Matthew 15, right after the miracle of feeding the five thousand men, Jesus encounters another hungry crowd—this time of four thousand men. The disciples again seem perplexed about what to do, for they say, "Where could we get enough bread in this remote place to feed such a crowd?" (Matthew 15:33). They just saw Jesus feed a crowd of possibly twenty thousand people, yet they doubted He could feed this crowd that was smaller in number.

It didn't matter that they had already seen Jesus turn water into wine; heal lepers; cast out legions of demons; calm violent storms; heal people with incurable diseases; and raise the dead. It didn't matter that He had proven Himself to them more times than they could probably remember. All that mattered at the moment was the obstacle they saw before their eyes. They looked at the need and they said, "*We can't, and we don't believe that You can either!*" That's little faith! . . .

. . . It doesn't take great faith to get big answers from the hand of the Lord. Consider the following truths.[10]

- "Truly I tell you, if you have faith as small as a mustard seed, you can say to this mountain, 'Move from here to there,' and it will move. Nothing will be impossible for you" (Matthew 17:20).
- "Everything is possible for one who believes" (Mark 9:23).
- "Truly I tell you, if you have faith and do not doubt, not only can you do what was done to the fig tree, but also you can say to this mountain, 'Go, throw yourself into the sea,' and it will be done. If you believe, you will receive whatever you ask for in prayer" (Matthew 21:21, 22).

- "But when you ask, you must believe and not doubt, because the one who doubts is like a wave of the sea, blown and tossed by the wind. That person should not expect to receive anything from the Lord" (James 1:6, 7).

God will honor little faith! . . . But, He can't do much with unbelief. . . .
When we act like the disciples and look at the problem instead of the Problem Solver, we can expect nothing but failure. However, when we believe God, even for the impossible, we will see Him do the incredible time after time. . . . *Jesus is the Lord of the little, even little faith!*[11]

Jesus specializes in using our little faith and the little things we have available and multiplying them. When we surrender what we have to Him, He will amaze us with what He can do with them.

Jesus took the little things that the boy offered—five loaves of bread and two fish—and He was able to feed thousands of people. He took someone whose name, age, address, and parents were unknown and used him to perform a miracle that made it into the Bible in all four Gospels. God used this little one to bless everyone else. "Bring your little and place it in His hands today. He will take it and use it in ways you could never imagine."[12]

HANDING MY CHURCH OVER TO JESUS

I went through a multiplication experience as I surrendered one of the churches I pastored to Jesus and watched Him do something unbelievable.

On a Sunday afternoon, I got a telephone call from my conference president. He said to me, "Pastor Joe, I am going to be in your area Wednesday afternoon. Can I take you out to dinner?"

I replied, "As long as you pay, I'll go out to dinner anytime you invite me!"

On Wednesday afternoon, we went out to dinner. I knew there was more to this meeting than just a casual visit. After we ate our supper, he said to me, "We are really hurting for money. We are at the point where we have to lay off three full-time pastors in order to balance the budget. But the pastor of the district next to you is leaving the conference. So we thought about giving you one of his churches and his other church to another pastor. In this case, we only have to lay off two people."

I said, "No problem; we would love to have another church added to our district. Tell me more about this church."

He said, "A group of German immigrants came to this valley, and they built a marvelous church, Community Services center, school, and auditorium to reach the community. The membership grew to about one hundred and twenty."

I noticed that everything he was saying was in the past. So I asked him, "So what about today?"

He said, "I have to be honest with you and tell you that, because of internal fighting, this church has dwindled down to thirteen people."

I said, "That's fine. Tell me, do they do any evangelism? Do they have any baptisms?"

He replied, "There has not been any form of evangelism in this church for twenty-six years. The last baptism they had was twenty years ago."

I said, "I do not want this church."

He said, "It is yours. It is our gift to you." The whole thing was a done deal.

On my first Sabbath there, I took my family, and I noticed there were only nine people, not thirteen. In fact, I never saw thirteen people. I only saw nine. But if you added me, my wife, and my two children, it brought the total to thirteen. They must have been a people of hope.

At my first board meeting, I went armed with ten ideas to revive the church. I started with a simple thing that I thought nobody would argue with: "Why don't we have a bulletin here so we can know what is going on?" The head elder stood up (he was in the habit of standing whenever he talked). He said, "We do not need a bulletin. We already know everything that needs to be known." Then he went on to lecture about how bulletins would damage the environment. As he went on and on, I lost interest and never went over any of my other items.

At my second board meeting, I proposed that we have potluck once a month. The head elder stood up. My heart fell as he said to me, "Pastor, that is the worst idea that I have ever heard in my life."

I asked, "Why? It's a good thing to eat together."

The head elder replied, "Pastor, here in this church, we hate one another. If we eat together, we will kill one another." Then he went on to give me a detailed history of all the conflicts they had experienced in the church. I again left very discouraged.

I went back again the third month with more ideas to revive this church. I proposed that we would have Sabbath School for the children and that we would go out into the community and invite the children to come to Sabbath School. The head elder stood up, and my heart despaired. *What is he going to say?*

He said, "That is not a bad idea."

I was shocked. I was dumbfounded. I couldn't believe it. Then he added, "As long as you will be in it." He viewed me as a terrible pastor, and he wanted to take the Sabbath School time as the opportunity to teach me how to become a better pastor. I didn't think it was a good idea. I didn't have the time for it. I already had three churches that I was taking care of.

It was about nine o'clock when I left the board meeting. I was very discouraged again. So I called a friend of mine and told him about my situation. He answered, "You need to do two things: First, surrender the church to Jesus. It's not your church. It's God's church. You are trying too hard. You need to let God do His work. You need to trust in Him." Then he reminded me of the story of the boy who gave his lunch to the disciples and how in the hands of Jesus it was multiplied. He said, "Second, we need to surrender this church to Jesus. Pray the prayer of John Knox."

I said, "I don't know the prayer of John Knox."

My friend explained, "He prayed that God would give him Scotland or that he would die."

I shot back, "I am not praying this prayer. I don't want to die. It is not worth it for me."

"Just pray. You are not going to die."

We both prayed and surrendered that church to Jesus.

The church was in a valley, so I started to walk on the hills around the valley where the city was. I claimed that valley for Jesus. Then I started to challenge the congregation to do the same thing.

One individual caught the vision—Edna, the youngest woman in the church at eighty-one years old.

On one Sabbath, I preached a sermon that encouraged intercessory prayer. Edna started to pray, but one of the things she struggled with was who to pray for. So she pleaded with God to reveal who she was to pray for. The Lord directed her to her neighbor—a twenty-five-year-old woman named Michelle who was in the habit of breaking many of the Ten Commandments every day. She slept with a different man every night. She was an alcoholic, a smoker, and was frequently high on drugs.

When Edna started to pray for her neighbor, God gave her His love for that woman. Prior to that, Edna had been judgmental, but after praying, she began to see her as a child of God. She actually started to visit her neighbor in her home, and Edna invited her to come visit her. They spent hours with each other, discussing the meaning of life and other topics. Edna became her mentor.

A few months later, I went to the church board. I said, "I would like to have an evangelistic meeting."

The head elder stood up and said, "For as long as I am here, we are not going to do anything like that. I am putting my foot down." Then he said, "We did this twenty-six years ago, and it did not work."

"Look, I will make a deal with you," I replied. "If you allow me to hold this evangelistic meeting, and if it does not work, I will not ask you to do anything after that."

"Are you willing to put this in writing?" he asked.

So I signed a document that stated if the evangelistic meeting didn't work, I would never ask the church for anything after this.

I knew that the stakes were very high. If this evangelistic meeting did not work, we were done in the church. I called the conference and asked for additional money for advertisement, and they agreed to give it to me. I called all my friends and people at the church to pray and fast on behalf of the evangelistic meetings.

The evangelistic meetings were to start on a Friday night. On Tuesday of that same week, Michelle went deer hunting with her mother. She drank, became disoriented, and shot her mother in the arm, mistaking her for a deer. Her mother survived, but the experience shook Michelle up. For comfort, she went to Edna's home. Edna did a marvelous job of ministering to her. She even had Michelle stay in her home. On Friday night, Edna brought Michelle to the evangelistic meeting.

At five on Friday night, I went to the church, put together my sermon slides, and went to a side room to pray. I prayed for almost two hours. At seven o'clock, I came out to preach, and my heart sank. In spite of all the heavy advertising we had done, no one showed up, except my faithful nine and Michelle.

At that moment, I became angry with God. I felt He had let me down, that we could not do anything in this church anymore. I knew who Michelle was, and I had no hope that anything would happen with her. Then I opened my mouth to preach about the Second Coming, and nothing came out. This went on for two or three minutes and created a very awkward time for me and the congregation.

Finally, I heard the voice of God in my heart saying, *"Don't preach about the Second Coming tonight. Preach about My love."* For forty-five minutes, I went from story to story from the Bible and personal experience to tell Michelle about the love of God. I told her that Jesus valued her life by the value of His life. And that if she was the only person on planet Earth, He still would have died for her. That is how much He loved her. I told her that He wanted her to be with Him and that He had a wonderful life for her as I quoted Jeremiah 29:11: "I know the plans I have for you, . . . plans to give you hope and a future."

Then I gave an altar call, and Edna dragged Michelle to the front. I offered a blessing and the people left, except for the three of us. We sat in the front, and I told Michelle that God wanted to forgive all of her sins; that she could have a new life in Him; and that no matter what she did, it was all nailed to the cross. I told her that God was really not interested in her past because He had a wonderful future for her. Then I started talking to her about the wonderful new life in Jesus and that when we accept Jesus, we become new people. He will fill our lives with meaning and significance.

Around two in the morning, Michelle said, "I do not have to sleep with a different guy every night. Jesus loves me. I do not have to do drugs to feel good about myself. Jesus loves me."

I looked at her as all three of us were crying and said, "Would you like to give your heart to Jesus?" She said yes. We prayed together, and Michelle gave her heart to Jesus.

Then I went to one of the pews and took a Bible, opened it to the first chapter of John, and said to Michelle, "This Bible is our gift to you. I would like you to go home and read the first chapter and come back this evening."

At 5:00 P.M. that day, I went back to the church and prayed for two hours. Then

I came out at seven to preach. On Friday night, there were nine people plus Michelle. On Saturday night, there were my faithful nine, plus Michelle, and fifty-four more people. Michelle had read John 1, and the Word of God got a hold of her heart, so she read chapter 2. She became immersed in knowing more, so she read chapter 3 and read about the love of God. She read chapter 4, including the story of the woman at the well. The story made such an impact on her, she said, "If this woman could bring her village to Jesus, I can bring all of my friends and relatives to hear about Jesus." She spent Sabbath inviting all of her friends and relatives to come and hear about Jesus. Fifty-four of them showed up. The evangelistic meeting lasted five weeks, and on the last night, Michelle and eleven of her family members were baptized in a church that had not had any baptisms for twenty years.

The Lord took two unlikely women—an eighty-one-year-old woman who grew up in the church and never rebelled and a twenty-five-year-old woman who grew up on the streets—and through their ministries and prayers brought a wonderful revival to that church.

The first Sabbath I was there, there were nine people, plus myself and my family. Four and a half years later, we gave this church to another pastor. On my last Sabbath, there were nine people, plus my family, plus Michelle, and 179 other people that God brought to that church. We gave our little prayers to Jesus, and He turned them into a wonderful revival for a dying church. In the process, He brought salvation to 180 people.

What happened to my head elder? God changed his heart. At the end of the evangelistic meetings, he came to me and said, "Pastor, can we do this again next year?"

God specializes in changing hearts. If you will surrender everything to Him in prayer, even the little things, He will use you in ways you never imagined.

---

1. Rodney Buchanan, "Loaves and Fish," SermonCentral, August 1, 2011, https://www.sermoncentral.com/sermons/loaves-and-fish-rodney-buchanan-sermon-on-trust-159214?page=1&wc=800.
2. Buchanan, "Loaves and Fish."
3. Alan Carr, "The Lord of the Little," Sermon Notebook, accessed February 26, 2019, https://www.sermonnotebook.org/mark/Mark 30 - Mark 6_35-44.htm; emphasis in the original.
4. Carr, "The Lord of the Little."
5. Alan Carr, "When a Little Becomes a Lot," Sermon Notebook, accessed February 26, 2019, https://www.sermonnotebook.org/new testament/John 6_1-13.htm.
6. Buchanan, "Loaves and Fish."
7. Carr, "When a Little Becomes a Lot."
8. Carr, "The Lord of the Little"; emphasis in the original.
9. Carr, "The Lord of the Little."
10. Carr, "The Lord of the Little"; emphasis in the original.
11. Carr, "The Lord of the Little"; emphasis in the original.
12. Carr, "The Lord of the Little."

APPENDIX 1

BIBLE STUDY JOURNAL

Date: _____

Text: _____

The first step to studying the Bible is to ask God to send the Holy Spirit to teach you through His Word so that your heart's needs are fulfilled and you are prepared to serve Him.

Second, choose a passage of Scripture for today's study, and write the text on the line above.

Third, read the passage several times.

Fourth, answer the following questions.

What new insight do I gain from the passage? In what new way is the text affecting me today?
_____
_____
_____
_____

What is the passage saying about God's character? (Think about His power, His love, and other qualities.)
_____
_____
_____
_____

Is there an example for me to follow?
_____
_____
_____
_____

Bible Study Journal

Is there a sin for me to avoid?

Is there a command for me to follow?

Is there a promise for me to claim?

Is there a difficulty for me to explore?

What does this passage teach about God the Father, Jesus Christ, and/or the Holy Spirit?

What is the main truth in this passage for my life?

What in this passage contributes to Christian doctrine?

What other passages of Scripture shed light on this one?
_____
_____
_____
_____

Is there something here I should pray about today?
_____
_____
_____
_____

What text from the passage would I like to memorize?
_____
_____
_____
_____

What do I think is God's special word that He is speaking to me today?
_____
_____
_____
_____

Finally, close with prayer, asking God to give you power to obey His commands and follow His will. Claim His promises to help. Carry this paper with you throughout the day to remind yourself what God has taught you.

PRAYER CONCERNS
Write out your prayer requests, praises, and questions to God in the space below.

___

PERSONAL DIARY
This is a spiritual interpretation of what happened to you during the previous day. Where did you see God's presence and guidance in your life?

___

APPENDIX 2

REASONS FOR UNANSWERED PRAYER

This is a partial list of why some of our prayers are not answered. This list is especially focused on what we can do in order to live lives that honor God.

But God has His wisdom, His sovereignty, and His reasons for not answering some of our prayers in the way we wish He would. At the end, when we have the ability to look back at our lives, we will see that God always did the best for us.

Following are six reasons, along with pertinent Bible verses and Ellen White quotations, why God may not answer our prayers in the way we would like.

1. NOT SEEKING GOD WITH OUR WHOLE HEART

"You will seek me and find me when you seek me with all your heart." (Jeremiah 29:13)

Why is it that so many prayers are never answered? Says David: "I cried unto Him with my mouth, and He was extolled with my tongue. If I regard iniquity in my heart, the Lord will not hear me." By another prophet the Lord gives us the promise: "Ye shall seek Me, and find Me, when ye shall search for Me with all your heart." Again, he speaks of some who "have not cried unto Me with their heart." Such petitions are prayers of form, lip service only, which the Lord does not accept.[1]

2. CHERISHED SIN

If I had cherished sin in my heart, the Lord would not have listened. (Psalm 66:18)

Let none deceive themselves with the belief that God will pardon and bless them while they are trampling upon one of His requirements. The willful commission of a known sin silences the witnessing voice of the Spirit, and separates the soul from God.[2]

3. DISHONESTY WITH GOD

"Will a mere mortal rob God? Yet you rob me.

"But you ask, 'How are we robbing you?'

"In tithes and offerings. You are under a curse—your whole nation—because you are robbing me. Bring the whole tithe into the storehouse, that there may be food in my house. Test me in this," says the Lord Almighty, "and see if I will not throw open the floodgates of heaven and pour out so much blessing that there will not be room enough to store it." (Malachi 3:8–10)

There is another matter too often neglected by those who seek the Lord in prayer. Have you been honest with God? By the prophet Malachi the Lord declares, "Even from the days of your fathers ye are gone away from Mine ordinances, and have not kept them. Return unto Me, and I will return unto you, saith the Lord of hosts. But ye said, Wherein shall we return? Will a man rob God? Yet ye have robbed Me. But ye say, Wherein have we robbed Thee? In tithes and offerings.". . .

. . . If we withhold from Him that which is His own, how can we claim His blessing? . . . It may be that here is the secret of unanswered prayer.[3]

4. ASKING UNWISELY OR SELFISHLY

When you ask, you do not receive, because you ask with wrong motives, that you may spend what you get on your pleasures. (James 4:3)

We are so erring and short-sighted that we sometimes ask for things that would not be a blessing to us, and our heavenly Father in love answers our prayers by giving us that which will be for our highest good—that which we ourselves would desire if with vision divinely enlightened we could see all things as they really are.[4]

5. DIFFERENCES WITH BRETHREN NOT MADE RIGHT

Whoever claims to love God yet hates a brother or sister is a liar. For whoever does not love their brother and sister, whom they have seen, cannot love God, whom they have not seen. And he has given us this command: Anyone who loves God must also love their brother and sister. (1 John 4:20, 21)

One of Christ's last commands to His disciples was "Love one another as I have loved you.". . . Do we obey this command, or are we indulging sharp, unchristlike traits of character? If we have in any way grieved or wounded others, it is our duty to confess our fault and seek for reconciliation. This is an essential preparation that we may come before God in faith, to ask His blessing.[5]

6. LETTING GO OF THE ARM OF THE LORD TOO SOON

But when you ask, you must believe and not doubt, because the one who doubts is like a wave of the sea, blown and tossed by the wind. (James 1:6)

I asked the angel why there was no more faith and power in Israel. He said, "Ye let go of the arm of the Lord too soon. Press your petitions to the throne, and hold on by strong faith. The promises are sure. Believe ye receive the things ye ask for, and ye shall have them." I was then pointed to Elijah. He was subject to like passions as we are, and he prayed earnestly. His faith endured the trial. Seven times he prayed before the Lord, and at last the cloud was seen. I saw that we had doubted the sure promises, and wounded the Saviour by our lack of faith.[6]

---

1. Ellen G. White, *Testimonies for the Church*, vol. 4 (Mountain View, CA: Pacific Press®, 1881), 533, 534.
2. Ellen G. White, *Messages to Young People* (Washington, DC: Review and Herald®, 1930), 114.
3. Ellen G. White, *Christ's Object Lessons* (Battle Creek, MI: Review and Herald®, 1900), 144.
4. Ellen G. White, *Steps to Christ* (Mountain View, CA: Pacific Press®, 1892), 96.
5. White, *Christ's Object Lessons*, 144.
6. Ellen G. White, *Early Writings* (Battle Creek, MI: Review and Herald®, 1882), 73.